MW01142007

HOLDING THE HAND OF DARKNESS

by

Arthur Hood

Llumina Press

ISBN: 1-932303-50-2
1-932303-51-0

Printed in the United States of America

DEDICATION

◆◆◆◆◆◆◆◆◆◆◆◆◆◆◆◆◆◆◆◆◆

This book is for Carolyn. She not only tolerated the strange demands of a profession that kept me away from home for long months at a time, but put up with me, and encouraged me while I wrote this book.

My sister, Judith Hammond, spent many long hours editing my drafts and suggesting improvements. Without her help and patience I could not have completed this task.

I also owe thanks to my son Bob. He was both tenacious and tireless in researching detail. He also suggested the title.

INTRODUCTION

◆ ◆

My story is about aviation. Unfortunately, war is the background of the story. It begins the month that Sputnik, the first satellite, was launched by Russia, and continues through the Vietnam War. It is about a time in the history of aviation when airplanes grew more sophisticated, politics more sinister, and warfare more insane. The aviators were the sons and younger brothers of those men who had come home after 1945 and were sent back to war, just short of five years later, in Korea. Now, they had done their share. These new aviators were their replacements.

By the end of World War II, many young boys in America had airplanes on their minds. The local airport was a favorite place to spend a Saturday afternoon. My friends and I would walk to the ferry slip and ride the ferry to East Boston. We would spend the day wandering around Logan Airport. It was there that I first saw a B-36. This enormous airplane lifted from the ground, shaking our twelve-year-old bodies with the sound of its passage. Somehow, I had to become an aviator. No matter that the war was won and there were no more heroic deeds to perform.

We were of the generation of children that grew up during World War II. We remember the gloom of defeat early in the war, and the oil and wreckage on the beaches of the East Coast. We remember the hysterical threat of imminent air raids that sent us home from school, and the shoes, meat, sugar, and fuel that were severely rationed or not at all available. We were eager to take our turn and entered the Cold War filled with faith in our country and reverence for our leaders.

While we earned our wings in Air Force trainers, Curtis LeMay's Strategic Air Command was rising to its awesome peak of power. The avalanche of technology, triggered by war, continued to gain momentum. Jet-powered aircraft of all types were becoming common. Bombers now could fly from America to any target in the world and the nuclear-tipped ballistic missile threatened all mankind.

In October 1962, in a confrontation with Russia over their positioning of ballistic missiles in Cuba, the theory of "deterrence by might" was tested before the world. The outcome is history. What might have been is speculation.

The Cold War dragged on and finally, in a fog of inadequate foreign policy, we blundered into the Vietnam Conflict. We were prepared and able to win that conflict, but were denied this by the conditional and uncertain policies of our leaders. These uncertain policies are best summed up by President Johnson's statement, "This is a limited war with limited objectives." Perhaps this tentative approach to waging this war stemmed from the government's uncertainty concerning our reasons for being there. It dragged on longer than any war fought by our country, and planted the seeds of distrust in our government in the minds of the American people.

There are times when a government is confronted with implacable evil, or its citizens murdered by others, and that government is forced to lead a nation into war. When there is no reasonable alternative to war, the objective must be to win and to do so quickly, as brevity is an essential mercy in war. Our leaders had learned nothing from the past; they hid their activities from Americans behind the veil of national security, in both the Cold War and the Vietnam Conflict. They used the trust, innocence, and bravery of a generation of young men to further their position of power. Anything that might be politically embarrassing was "classified." Many of the military records of that era remain classified to this day.

Little boys played on the airfields of the fifties. They grew up to fly the airplanes of the sixties and seventies. Some were captured and then denied by their country; many of them died. We began our careers with youthful patriotism and ended them with tired cynicism. I have written of a small bit of that history from the point of view of the airmen who lived it, and I have tried to remain true to the attitudes and political opinions of those airmen.

I asked a young man at his high school graduation what he had been taught of World War II. He confessed to having heard of it, but knew nothing of the issues or nations involved. He knew nothing of the Korean War or Vietnam Conflict, his excuse being that "they don't teach history anymore." Such ignorance of our past will lead us into these wars again.

Arthur Hood
Arizona, 2001

ONE

◆◆◆◆◆◆◆

When Duty whispers low, "Thou must."
The youth replies, "I can."
-Emerson

In October of 1957, America's belief in its technological superiority was toppled by Russia's Sputnik. Not since the Japanese Zero had swept the Brewster Buffalo (our supposed up-to-date fighter plane of 1941) from the skies of the Pacific had the need to play catch-up been so manifest. Americans listened in disbelief as the little basketball-sized satellite beeped its insolent way overhead, announcing that the outcome of the Cold War would be decided on the field of scientific achievement.

As the hot days of summer were slowly surrendering to the more comfortable temperatures of fall, Sputnik was not on my mind. I stared down at the Virginia countryside from the Lockheed Constellation that carried me south towards San Antonio. From my seat, I could see the two great propellers on the right side. The sun glinted from the spinning discs that they made. The muted roar of those engines provided a soporific background as I daydreamed. It was just possible that in the not too distant future I would fly an airplane like this. Two days ago I had stood in the Air Force recruiting office in Boston and had sworn to do all the things that the officer swearing me in required. I had been handed an airline ticket and some indecipherable orders and told to be at Logan Airport two days hence. Two days seemed much too long to sit at home and wait. I would have gone directly to the airport had it been possible.

Late the past summer, I returned from a six month long trip in the engine room of an oceangoing tanker. Restless and bored after the confinement of a ship's engine room at sea, I drove aimlessly about. Absent-mindedly, I fiddled with the tuning knob of my car radio. An Air Force radio commercial, accompanied by the roar of zooming airplane engines and suitable martial music, promised a career as an Air Force Aviator. After such a long trip on a merchant ship wandering the waterfronts of the world, it seemed that a newly engaged man needed a more respectable occupation, and Carolyn, my fiancé, deserved it. The fact that I earned approximately four times that of a Second Lieutenant on flying status did not occur to me. Neither did it occur to me, at that time, that no one was shooting at merchant seamen. Since the age of fifteen, I had spent as much time as possible on anything that would float and had picked up a passable knowledge of navigation. This had emboldened me to think that I had a chance to win a spot as a Navigator Cadet. It sounded like just the adventure for me, and the decision was very easy to rationalize. The local recruiting office was delighted to have a "live one" walk in the door. Flattery was laid on as thick as a winter coat.

"You'll fly in the newest jets. A young fellow as smart as you will make general easy," he gushed.

This guy was a real salesman and not at all inhibited in the use of flattery, but then that is why he was a recruiting Sergeant. A flurry of forms followed. He was most helpful in guiding me through them.

"Now, there are a few exams that you will have to take. Just a routine physical and some aptitude tests," he casually informed me.

"OK," I answered, eager to get on with it. "Let's get started."

"Well actually, we don't give the tests here. You have to go to Otis Air Force Base down on Cape Cod. But we'll give you a bus ticket." He added the last hurriedly, fearing that his catch might be slipping away.

"That's fine," I said, being agreeable. I could spend a day on The Cape without too much trouble.

In a flash he produced a voucher for a round trip bus ticket dated the first of the coming week. "Better pack a bag," he said. "The tests take at least three days."

Several weeks later, a letter arrived from Flying Training Air Force. With the trepidation that goes with such events, I went down into the basement workshop to open the letter in private. I was sure that it would be a polite note saying something about better luck next time. It was notification that I had been accepted for pilot training in Aviation Cadet Class 59E. I was certain that the word pilot was a clerical error and it was supposed to be navigator; however, I saw no reason to call this to anyone's attention. During the weeks that followed, my daydreams were filled with all of the great feats of aviation that my imagination could conjure up. At twenty-one years of age, there was nothing in my future except heroic deeds. There were no thoughts of incredible boredom, fear, or death.

The muted roar of the four engines faded. With a rumble, the landing gear extended and the airplane banked towards another airport. At each stop, more young men got on the airplane, and from the conversation, it seemed that most were en-route to San Antonio and the Air Force. In the way of all young men off on their way to adventure, the talk was loud and boastful. I listened but kept my own counsel. Eventually, the Constellation arrived at San Antonio and we assembled on the pavement next to the airplane.

A blue Air Force bus and a staff car waited for us. A tall, immaculately attired Sergeant, complete with clipboard and papers that rattled in the breeze, addressed us and asked that Mr. Hood and Mr. Long step aside. The others were directed to the bus; we were invited to the staff car. With a glance at each other and glowing with our status as cadets, we sat in the back of the staff car and enjoyed the ride to Lackland Air Force Base. Charles Long introduced himself. He was from Stoughton, Massachusetts and had been on the airplane all the way from Boston. Neither of us had been aware of the other on the flight and we both wondered at the preferential treatment that we seemed to be getting. The trip from the airport on the north side of San Antonio to Lackland Air Force base took a little over half an hour. The driver, a young airman, chattered away and grinned as if he were suppressing some imminent practical joke. He talked of the various attractions that San Antonio had to offer.

"You cadets will have plenty of time to get to town. You know...see the sights, chase wimmin, all that good stuff. Those local girls really go for the cadets. Yuh gotta be careful though; they all wanna marry officers."

From where I sat in the right rear seat, I could see that he had almost choked to death on that little bit of tourist information. Our illusion about our importance died as soon as we stepped out of the car and entered the Aviation Cadet Tiger program. The Aviation Cadet part of the title was official, the Tiger part was added by the cadets themselves, in the way of school boys who boast that their father administers more fearsome beatings for indiscretions than any other father. And we were very proud of that.

Even though I had heard stories and seen movies about various cadet programs, the change from the independence of a merchant seaman to an underclass cadet was an enormous jolt. A cadet about the size of a southern conference linebacker approached me. His uniform looked as if it would crack if he moved too much and his shoulder boards were covered with white bands. I had no idea what rank they indicated, but I supposed that he was some kind of a big shot. Thinking that a friendly approach was best in a strange situation, I stepped forward and stuck out my hand and introduced myself. The effect was stunning. His face turned red, his eyes bulged, and his neck—already the size of my thigh—swelled out over his collar as a vein began to throb in his forehead. Startled, I thought that he might have suffered a major vascular event.

With his nose very nearly touching mine, he launched into a tirade.

"You don't even talk to me without permission! When you do have permission, you will call me by my nickname—Sir! You are a preflight, underclass cadet, mister, and that is lower than whale shit!" He continued on with his imitation of a Marine drill sergeant, which he must have seen in an old war movie. He hadn't a lot of practice at this, as he quickly ran out of colorful insults and was beginning to bluster. This he covered by ordering me onto the ground to perform some push-ups. I could feel my cheeks and the back of my neck flush. My instinct was to settle this on the spot. When signing on a merchant ship with a bully on board, such matters are best resolved before sailing. A tiny warning bell tinkled in the back of my mind and I remembered my father's chuckle the day before I left.

"You won't make it. Your temper and the fact that you are too much of a smart-ass will get you thrown out," he had taunted me in a gentle but serious manner.

I didn't know the rules yet. All about me, other new arrivals were being greeted with similar courtesy. It seemed wise to dummy up until I found out what the form was. As the confusion of the first several days coalesced into regimented order, I learned that the cadets managed the day-to-day operation of the program themselves. Those noisy folks that greeted us were cadets from class 59D, just six weeks longer in the service than we were.

We saw very little of staff other than our upperclass cadets and classroom instructors. Young males are very malleable. The seeming mindlessness of the day-to-day cadet activities took wise advantage of this. The class system developed an "us against them" mind-set and we rapidly learned to work together for simple survival. The promise of getting a chance to fly real airplanes was a huge carrot, and no matter what inner misgivings any one of us might have had, not even torture could have torn an admission from us that we might fail. In a very short time, these wise old veterans of our upperclass changed us from an unorganized group of civilians into regimented squadrons of look-a-likes. Civilian clothes were packed and stored. Uniforms and personal supplies were issued, hair was cut and we were marched to the Base Exchange and advised on items that we would be wise to purchase. Of course, shoeshine materials were at the top of the list. I expected that, but the strange wire and spring device that would keep a shirt collar from sticking out and an elastic contraption that attached the shirt tail to the top of the socks to keep one's shirt tucked in were items that I had never dreamed of. Judging by the apparent waist sizes of the upperclass cadets, I half expected to be instructed to buy some sort of a corset. I soon learned that a corset was one item that I had no need to worry about. Excess insulation about the waist vanished quickly with an hour of vigorous calisthenics every morning, a practice that would last through the entire cadet program. All of these purchases were made from a seventy-five-dollar advance on our pay. We could not be required to buy these items, but not one of us declined the council of our wise and experienced upperclass cadets.

Several rules of the game emerged immediately. Although hazing was limited only by the imagination of the upperclass cadets, physical contact was prohibited. Even making a minor adjustment to an underclass cadet's uniform was preceded by, "Permission to touch, mister?" The underclass cadet, vibrating at an exaggerated position of attention, would respond, "Permission granted, Sir." An upperclass cadet could demand an outrageous exercise penalty for some infraction of military custom, but he had to be prepared to perform the punishment himself, side by side with the miscreant, should the underclass cadet request it. The availability of this request eliminated the physical abuse that so easily arises in hazing environments. The permission to request "company" was quickly noted and frequently led to contests of physical endurance. There was no such relief for the psychological pressure, which was intense and unremitting.

There never seemed to be time enough to get everything done. To a lay observer, the petty rituals and continuous harassment would have seemed mindless and silly. The constant corrections and the requirement to keep track of endless and trivial detail kept us in a constant state of alert tension. To us, flying an airplane was the end and this unpleasantness was just the hoop that needed to be jumped through to get to those airplanes. Much in the manner of a child who has been promised a toy for good behavior, we did our best to comply. Toys were not the reward in our case. In our future there certainly were airplanes, but they would not be flown for pleasure. We would fly those airplanes under terrible conditions and many of us would die or suffer great torture. Flying Training Air Force was responsible for all aviation training and they knew this. They were doing their best to give us some chance of survival. The cadets, protected by youth's indomitable belief in their own immortality, gave not a thought to such grim possibilities. These thoughts did not trouble us as we struggled through our first day.

Late in the afternoon of that first day, we were marched to the base theater. All of us were a bit bewildered by hours of frantic activity. Even the upperclass cadets did not march quite as tall and their uniforms were not near as crisp as they had been when they first greeted us. The uniforms that had been issued to us consisted of several sets of olive drab fatigues and a pair of brogans. It was hard to feel very military in those ill-fitting clothes and clumsy shoes. We would not get our full uniform issue for two weeks. The Air Force anticipated sending a number of us to the enlisted ranks before then, and saw no reason to waste money on a full cadet issue. In the meantime, we would become experts at shining brogans—not an easy task, as any person who has had military training can attest. Our formation was ragged and several upperclassmen circled us like sheepdogs, while another marched beside us counting cadence. It seemed to take forever before we reached our destination. The late afternoon sun was in our eyes and the dust raised by those ahead of us was in our nostrils.

We hadn't been seated more than a minute or two when a cadet at the back of the room roared, "Room, tenhut!" Straight out of a scene from Twelve O'clock High, a Captain and several cadet officers stomped their way to the front with grim determination. The Captain stepped to the podium, sucked in his stomach, conscious of the contrast between his own well-nourished figure and the whip-like appearance of the cadet officers with him, and invited us to be seated. After welcoming us to the Aviation Cadet Program and telling us what wonderfully smart people we were to have survived the obstacles used to thin out the many applicants, he immediately spoiled our first twinges of confidence by telling us that between forty and sixty percent of us would be "eliminated" prior to graduation. There were many sidewise glances as we all took a quick peek at the person next to us who would not graduate. To achieve this distant goal, we would spend three months of preflight training at Lackland, six months of primary flight training in propeller-driven aircraft, and six months of jet or multi-engine training. Our time at Lackland would be devoted to academics and military training.

It was abundantly clear that many of us would be eliminated from the cadet program before any of us would get close to an airplane. By now our Captain, long gone soft in his desk job, was growing red in the face from the effort of holding in his stomach. It was with obvious relief that he turned the briefing over to the cadet staff and took a seat. A cadet officer took his place at the podium. He was slender and about five feet, eight inches tall. His uniform was straight off a recruiting poster and his shoulder boards were covered with the stripes of his cadet rank. It did not occur to us that his drawn face was the price of that rank. He carried all of the duties of any cadet, in addition to the duties of his position.

"I am Cadet Colonel Calder, your Cadet Commander. In the books that were issued to you this morning, there is one titled *Officer Training Manual for Aviation Cadets*. It contains the information necessary for you to complete the military requirements of this program. You are responsible for all of the information contained in that book. There are a number of items called "Required Cadet Knowledge" that you must commit to memory. The first is the Military Code of Conduct. There are six articles to this code. These six articles have the force of law and are directive in nature. The second is the Aviation Cadet Honor Code. This is to be your way of life for as long as you wear the uniform, and hopefully, the rest of your life. Practice it and it will serve you well. Fail in it and you will be tried by the Honor Court, and if found guilty, you will be eliminated from the cadet program. You will be instructed by your upperclass in the remaining Cadet Knowledge that must be memorized."

The room was silent. The "if found guilty" sounded more like "when found guilty." Calder stared at us, seeming to hold eye contact with each of us. He had made his point, at least with me. He began again,

"You may not leave the cadet area unless directed on some specific errand, such as a dental appointment. While proceeding about the cadet area you will march, squaring all corners in a military manner and reciting Cadet Knowledge in a loud clear voice."

You have got to be kidding, I thought.

"Any upperclassmen may stop you at any time and require you to recite any part of the required Cadet Knowledge. As you leave the room today, you will be issued what looks like a small pad of notepaper. These are called gig slips. You will carry three on your person at all times and keep three in the holder on the wall outside of your room. If an upperclassman asks for a gig slip, you will present one to him in a military manner. Do not ask why."

He demonstrated this by standing at attention, staring straight ahead, and in a single motion, slapping his left breast pocket and removing a gig slip. This he presented straight out at arm's length.

"Should that senior cadet ask why you failed in some duty," he continued, "you will reply that you have no excuse. I will remind you of article four of the Aviation Cadet Honor Code: 'An Aviation cadet will not quibble, use evasive statements or technicalities in order to shield guilt or defeat the ends of justice.' A violation of this article or any other will see you out of the program by the time retreat is sounded that day. Any infraction that you have been written up for on a gig slip will be posted on the punishment roster on Friday afternoon. You will find that roster on the bulletin board in your squadron day room. If you earn more than three demerits in any one week, then you will march them off on the tour ramp at the rate of two hours for each demerit over three."

He then followed with a seemingly endless list of restrictions that all seemed to lead to immediate elimination. These proscriptions covered every contingency of normal living and were followed by an outline of our training, both military and academic. The military training seemed made up of scrubbing floors with a toothbrush and scraping wax off of stairs with a razor blade. For good measure, inspections and parades were thrown in on the weekends. To break the monotony, there would be adventures on the obstacle course and the firing range. Failure to perform any activity in less than a maximum magnificent manner would result in the usual dismissal. The academic outline seemed less defined, although numerous examinations were promised, all to be graded on the Bell curve, which guaranteed a certain number of failures. Phone calls were limited to one a week and there was no mention of time off to go to San Antonio.

This was beginning to look like something less than the casual playboy life that the recruiting sergeant in Boston had described. Long voyages on oceangoing tankers didn't seem quite so tedious now, but I couldn't back out. Besides, if I could hang on long enough, I might actually get to fly an airplane.

In the next several days, we memorized the required cadet knowledge. In fact, it was seared into our minds. It took me several years to realize that the political leaders that held us to these ideals kept much more relaxed standards for themselves and looked upon our naiveté with perceptible condescension. We were just entering the third decade of our lives. American Bandstand was the rage of our civilian contemporaries and the Edsel was beginning its journey to oblivion. Fidel and Raul, along with Che Guevara and nine others had evaded Batista's troops and made it to the safety of the Sierra Maestra Mountains in Cuba's southeast. They would overthrow Batista and take over Cuba before we graduated, an event that would change the rest of our lives. In our minds, our country was always in the right and all of the brothers were valiant. We marched back to our barracks, each carrying a determination that failure was not an option.

The next several days proved the intent to eliminate as many of us as possible. A repeat of our flight physical picked off several. In the first week, five cadets were eliminated. The program was fifteen months long. At that rate of attrition, in a little over six months there would be no one left. According to our recruiting contract, if a cadet washed out any time within the first six months, he would have to complete a two-year obligation as an enlisted man. Any time after the first six months, he would be returned to civilian life and his military obligation considered met.

A feeling of dread prevailed in all of us. I could not imagine having to return home and admit failure to my parents. The thought of having to tell my father that his predication was correct provided enormous incentive. It was his challenge that enabled me to "put a lid on it" when anger started to take over. What I thought would be fun had turned into a grim contest of determination. This did not leave me until I finally graduated and paid the ceremonial dollar for that first salute.

In spite of these grim thoughts, it was impossible to completely suppress the high spirits of healthy young men of this age. Even though the upperclass did everything possible to appear remote and severe, hilarity, fueled by tension, erupted frequently. On occasion, when an upperclass cadet stopped an underclassman and "braced him" in the position of rigid attention, one or the other would show the faintest trace of a grin. This was known as blithering. The more senior cadet, in an effort to preserve the dignity of his rank, would roar, "Are you blithering mister?" even if he was the one grinning. If the junior cadet lost any more of his composure, it was usually good for a couple of hours on the tour ramp marching off punishment tours.

The next step in this pursuit of levity was the employment of silly games. This required the underclass cadets to perform ridiculous activities in a most military manner. At the noon meal one day, silly games were on. During meals, the underclass sat five to a side at the tables while an upperclass cadet sat at each end. The junior cadets were required to eat at a rigid position of attention while sitting on the edge of their seat. The fork was required to describe square corners and straight lines on its journey from the plate to his mouth, all the while the seniors at each end of the table harassed the underclass demanding recitations of Cadet Knowledge or requiring the performance of some inane game. Rapid weight loss followed and reassured me on the corset concern. One day, Upperclass Cadet Bower was inspired to institute a most outrageous game.

"Misters," he announced, "the roadrunner is about to depart from my position and proceed about the table in a clockwise direction at a speed of one hundred knots. You must provide him with unobstructed passage." His tactical wisdom was delivered with all of the gravity of a briefing for a bombing mission over Europe in 1943.

The plan required that each of us in turn would have to lift our plate in order to allow the imaginary creature safe passage and further reduce the time allotted to eat our meal. I was very hungry. The smell of the food teased as I sat at a ridiculous position of attention on the very edge of my chair. I was not in the mood for this, and the idea of that damned roadrunner seemed idiotic.

Bower shouted, "Go!" and with a sound like a drum roll, plates were lifted and thumped back down as the creature supposedly sped past. "He is speeding up. Speed is now one hundred and fifty knots."

Bits of food flew into the air as cadets tried to accommodate the speeding roadrunner. One more step up in speed and there would be a shower of food. Bower was enjoying this a little too much. I was beginning to lose it. As the damned, scrawny, imaginary bird came roaring down the straightaway towards me, I picked up my fork and stabbed the sucker to death, pinning him solidly to the tabletop. The silence was shattering. My classmates stared. Someone snickered and that was the end of any dignity at that meal. None of us got any more to eat; I had to bury the imaginary creature in my mashed potatoes with suitable military honors and spent the next Saturday afternoon marching on the tour ramp.

The tour ramp is a simple and effective way to apply pressure by depriving the cadet of valuable time. Each hour walking off punishment tours is an hour not available for other time-consuming activities. The tour ramp is simply an out of the way paved area. Each punishment tour is one hour long and consists of fifty-five minutes of marching in a square, single file, and squaring each corner as if on parade, and followed by a five-minute rest period. The miscreant must wear a class A or dress uniform, white gloves, and pass inspection prior to beginning his punishment tours. The senior cadet walking tours is the tour ramp commander and he is responsible for maintaining suitable order and timing the breaks. Walking punishment tours can often be the beginning of the end. A cadet may accumulate time on the tour ramp because he is unable to keep up with the fierce pace, thus collecting demerits. He falls further behind because of the time lost walking off punishment tours; and the pressure is increased. I walked off my final tours the night before I graduated from cadets. A cadet is not allowed to graduate with tour ramp hours outstanding. In my first introduction to the tour ramp, I was convinced that, in this case, it was worth it. I chuckled to myself wondering what the civilian secretary must have thought when she typed up the weekly punishment roster with my name and punishment: "Cadet A. Hood, gross military disorder, murdered Air Force roadrunner at the dinner table."

Saturday actually began after dinner Friday afternoon with the preparation of the always-spotless barracks and grounds for inspection in the morning. The grounds were maintained manually. That is, we crawled around on our hands and knees and picked the grass by hand. In this pursuit, I discovered a fascinating creature called a trap-door spider. During the course of pursuing my grass picking duty, I disturbed one of these creatures. The large, hairy spider popped open his trapdoor in the ground, stared at me with a malevolent eye, and slammed shut his door. I had never heard of such a creature and continued my duty with great caution. It was one in many lessons about expecting the unexpected.

When we completed our outdoor duties, our attention turned to the interior of our barracks. Stripped to gym shorts, we scrubbed, scraped, and polished everything. This had to be completed prior to taps. The final step was to take our showers and then clean the shower rooms and latrines. Once this was done, the showers and toilets were shut down except for a single toilet to be cleaned first thing in the morning. Paper towels were laid on the floor to make stepping spots. These would be snatched up and hidden away just before inspection in the morning. They had to be hidden because nothing could be in the trashcans. When reveille sounded it was a mad scramble to get into our uniforms, march to mess hall for breakfast, and return to our barracks before the inspecting officer arrived. When this august person, usually a 2nd Lieutenant, entered the barracks, someone would scream, "Barracks, tenhut!" as if we weren't already there, and then the fun would begin. His majesty, accompanied by the senior cadet staff, would inspect each individual and each room. Until we learned the tricks of the trade and how to beat an inspection, we were snowed under by demerits.

Shortly after the inspection was completed, an announcement was made to fall out for parade. In very short order, we learned the time-honored routine of military parade and most cadets marched very well. I had a rolling, bouncing gait that drove my upperclass to distraction as they frantically tried to teach us formation marching. It seemed that no matter where they tried to hide me in the formation, my head could be scene bobbing up and down like a sea buoy in a field of heads that were all steady. I also noticed that the rest of the squadron had trouble keeping in step with me. I had never experienced a problem moving about, even on a small ship in the wildest of seas, but this marching in formation was a frustrating skill for me to learn. Finally in desperation, I was made guidon bearer. This is the individual who marches ahead of the formation and behind the officers in a parade and carries the unit flag or guidon. The reasoning was that I would attract less attention if I were at some distance from the rest of the smoothly marching formation.

In six weeks time, our upperclass completed their preflight training and dispersed to the various primary flying schools scattered over the southern third of the country. Class 59 Foxtrot had arrived. We were now the exalted upperclass. This was a status that we had lusted for during the six endless weeks that we had suffered under the instruction of those soulless bastards of 59 Delta. Life did not improve. It got worse. Not only did we continue to struggle to avoid the ax, but also we had to look after the cadets coming up the pipeline behind us. The vast store of military knowledge that we had assimilated in the past six weeks very urgently needed to be transmitted to our underclass. To us it seemed that 59 Foxtrot was made up entirely of retarded range cattle. It seemed that we not only were responsible for our own failings, but theirs as well. I could now see some of the unkind remarks regarding our intelligence, which had been made by the harried cadets of our upperclass, in a little different light. A new enemy surfaced. The Tactical or TAC Officer had always been around, but just didn't have much to do with the underclass cadets. His reason for being was to keep the heat on the upperclass cadets. It had been our belief that, upon our elevation to upperclass status, we would be at the top of the food chain. We were wrong. The TAC Officer was top predator. Unencumbered by the duties of a cadet, he was able to devote a great deal of time and energy to his responsibilities.

A stray dog wandered into the cadet area and was promptly adopted. Keeping a pet was a heinous crime, probably punishable by death. Hiding the dog from the TAC officers was a challenge that we could not resist, and the effort crossed the class lines completely. Some fool taught the dog to bite TAC officers and the little dog made that his reason for being. He would lay in wait behind some shrub, and when a TAC officer came by, he would bushwhack him and run into the nearest cadet barracks. There were frequent searches in an effort to remove this ferocious beast, but when the search party came into the barracks, the dog was hustled out of one of the fire doors and handed through a window of the next barracks. He seemed to enjoy his precarious existence and took his biting duties very seriously. He was handed off to the underclass whenever a class left. Over a year later, I heard through the grapevine that he had not been captured and was still carrying out his duties.

By now most of us had figured out that the three months of preflight had little to do with flying airplanes. This part of the program was nothing more than a sieve to filter out those whom the Air Force deemed incapable of becoming good pilots in the allotted training time. What the deciding factors were we did not learn. The ax seemed without prejudice. Paranoia reigned and we dug in and held on the best we could. Eventually, the three months passed and the greatly thinned ranks of Cadet Class 59 Echo received orders to the various primary flying schools. My assignment was to Hondo Air Base in Hondo, Texas. I had never heard of Hondo, but was so relieved to have those orders in my hands that I would not have minded if it were located in the Sahara Desert. Ranches surrounded Hondo and it would have made a fine movie set for an old western. Local wildlife consisted of tarantulas, jackrabbits, and rattlesnakes. The nickname of this base was "Hondo by the Sea," but who cared. It was a flying school with real airplanes and that was what we had endured for.

TWO

◆◆◆◆◆◆◆

After the three months of preflight training at Lackland Air Force Base, we were all prepared for more of the same treatment that we had become accustomed to, but the military pressure was diminished somewhat and replaced with the pressure to perform in an airplane. We had to learn to fly airplanes, and learn quickly. It was made plain to us that there would be few second chances and many would be left behind.

Hondo Air Base lies about twenty miles west of San Antonio. It was a quiet, little Texas town and, aside from a few bars and a movie theater, offered little in the way of entertainment for young men in their early twenties. The climate, countryside, and isolation made it an ideal location for a flying school.

Civilian contractors operated the Air Force primary flying schools. The instructors, both flight and academic, were civilians, and so were the flight line maintenance staff. There was a minimal military staff that provided quality control in the form of check pilots and military presence. We still had inspections and parades and there certainly was a tour ramp marked out on a portion of unused paved road. The flight line was covered with long rows of T-34s and T-28s. All of the airplanes had international orange cowlings and gray bodies, with large Air Force roundels and the letters USAF painted on the topside of the right wing and the underside of the left wing. The flight line or parking ramp was a huge concrete area that formed the shape of the letter L. The larger T-28s took up the long side of the ramp while the T-34s occupied the short side. The control tower was built of timbers with an enclosed cab at the top and was an obvious veteran of the Second World War, as were the other buildings. During the day, a colored flag was displayed from the cab of the tower, green when flying was unrestricted, orange when only dual flight was permitted and red when flight operations were suspended. Texas Aviation Industries did an excellent job of running the place, especially the mess hall. After our three months of preflight training, we thought that we had arrived in an aviation dream world.

The barracks also were vintage WW2, but were partitioned into rooms, with two cadets to a room. The attic space was open and air circulated freely. The barracks were spotless and the cadet area clean and groomed, and we would keep them that way. There also was a base swimming pool for our use. It usually was very busy on hot afternoons when the day's lessons were over. This was a major improvement over our near captive status at Lackland. Our time would be divided equally between academics and flying. The academics consisted of topics germane to aviation, such as navigation, Morse code, aeronautics—all much more interesting than the theoretical nonsense that had been the academic program in preflight. But the airplanes were the good part. We couldn't wait to get at them.

Eventually the several days of orientation passed. We had been given an idea of what was expected of us and finally were marched to the flight line. The flight room was a large rectangular room with two rows of tables, each with room for four people, running the length of it. There we met the dispatcher, Travese Metheny. His job was to assign us the particular airplane we were to fly, and when we operated from our auxiliary field some thirty miles away, he would drive the students and instructors there in an asthmatic, blue Air Force bus. He divided us into threes from an alphabetical roster and assigned us to tables. Each table had a card with the instructor's name on it. Mr. Anderson was the name on the card at my table. There were three of us assigned to the table, but I had not met the other two cadets at Lackland, as they had lived in different barracks. Don Hawley introduced himself and shook hands. I did not know it at the time, but I would share the same instructor with this slender Texan from Fort Worth for the remainder of our time as cadets. He had just a few months over seven years left to live. Pete Graff, an affable and relaxed Californian filled out the threesome. Shortly after we had settled at our tables, the instructors came in, dressed in uniforms of gray slacks and short sleeved white shirts with the TAI wings over the left breast pocket.

Mr. Anderson seemed tall to me, but he wasn't over five foot ten. Perhaps it was his husky build or the fact that he was a pilot of some experience that made him an awesome creature in our eyes. His voice was soft and his manner courteous, almost to the point of shyness. In just a very few days, I would find out that his quiet demeanor didn't hold in the air when he was instructing. He wasted little time on social niceties but herded us out to the flight line and introduced us to the T-34. This little training airplane made by Beech Aircraft was adapted from their excellent Bonanza design. As we walked around the airplane I ran my hand over the smooth aluminum skin. It smelled of gasoline and hot metal. We climbed up on the wings and slid open the greenhouse type canopy. The interior was all business and painted olive drab. The two seats were in tandem, effectively forming two cockpits, and were designed for seat-pack parachutes. Mr. Anderson went over every item in the cockpit as we clutched our brand new, blue covered checklists.

"Learn this by heart," he said. "Before you solo you must pass a blindfold cockpit check. You will sit in the seat blindfolded and I will call out various items. You will have to reach out and touch whatever I have named on the first try. So when you are waiting your turn to fly, don't waste time. Have Mr. Metheny give you the tail number of an airplane that's not scheduled to fly, get together with another cadet, climb in it, and teach each other the cockpit. Also, you must always have your checklist with you whenever you are on the flight line. Do not refer to it, memorize it. Know it by heart. Be able to recite it in your sleep. Each flying session, I will ask each of you a different emergency procedure. If you cannot recite it, you will have failed your lesson for the day. That's a pink slip. Three of those and you are out. There's not any time to spare and some of you may not make it as far as the first solo."

We glanced at each other, each thinking that it must be the other person he was referring to. It seemed that every time things were looking up, someone threw cold water on us. Most people can be taught to fly given enough time. In military flying, training time is so valuable that flight training must be accomplished in the minimum amount of time. With little more than two dozen hours of flight training, we would be expected to fly an airplane of greater performance than early WW2 fighters. The primary purpose of this little Beechcraft was to identify those students who would require more than this minimum amount of flying time before the budget of Flying Training Air Force was strained. Thus, elimination from cadets continued with a vengeance. Don and Pete soloed well within the maximum time allowed. The assistant flight leader, Mr. Stanga, soloed me at the auxiliary field after, what I suspected was, a do or die flight.

There would be a year more of cadet flying training and six months of advanced flying training before any of us would be on the duty roster of an operational unit. The thinning out process would continue through all of that time. Like a bunch of tax cheats dreading the notice from the IRS, we were constantly looking over our shoulders, but this was mitigated by the joy of flying. Once we had qualified to fly solo, at least half of our flying time was spent alone in the airplane. The contrast between flying solo and the restricted life of a cadet was intoxicating.

After little more than twenty hours of flying time, those who survived the T-34 moved on to the next airplane. The T-28 seemed an enormous airplane. It had a radial engine given to belching flame and explosions if over-primed during starting, and a cockpit big enough to play tennis in. We couldn't wait to fly this beast without the supervision of an instructor on board. Given that a twenty-one-year-old should not be trusted with a powerful automobile, there was bound to be a good deal of hell raising when we were turned loose with an airplane such as the T-28. I had heard rumors that all of the livestock for fifty miles around Hondo were routinely fed tranquilizers.

That day came for me late in a morning flying session. Mr. Anderson had been working me hard in the traffic pattern. With every awkward landing his anger rose, finally reaching towering proportions. It seemed that I could not perform even the simplest maneuver correctly. He heaped abuse and scorn on every attempt, sometimes even before I had begun the required maneuver. I didn't realize that I had to learn to perform my flying tasks under the worst possible distractions. Round and round the traffic pattern we went, each landing brought scalding criticism and contempt. I was in despair, certain that I would be drummed out the gate, with my shoulder boards torn off, before the sun set.

On the next downwind leg he said, "I have the airplane" and snatched control from me.

I sank down into my seat in a lump of self-pity. Without a word, he made one of his usual "are we on the ground yet?" landings and turned off the runway at the first taxiway. The canopy slid open, and with a look of grim determination, he climbed out on the wing. I was certain that he was going to drag me out of the airplane and beat the tar out of me before kicking me out of cadets, but he tied his seat belt and shoulder harness so that they could not tangle in the controls.

He leaned over from his position on the wing and said, "Make two touch and goes and a full stop landing. Pick me up here before you taxi in and we'll call it a day. If you break this airplane, I will rip your face off."

With those soothing words of encouragement, he jumped down from the wing and walked off of the taxiway to a position on the grass where he could watch. Years later, I found out what it feels like to turn a student loose with an airplane for the first time, but at this time I gave not a thought to his anguish. Without him in the airplane, my safety net was gone. I was scared but I truly wanted to do this. Hondo Tower cleared me for take-off from the taxiway intersection. The airplane sped down the runway and lifted into the air. I don't know why I was surprised, as that is exactly what it was supposed to do. The wheels retracted when I raised the gear handle and everything behaved as if Mr. Anderson were sitting behind me, silently waiting for me to make a mistake. Somehow, I made my three trips around the pattern. I am sure that Mr. Anderson suffered agonies watching me wallow down final approach and awkwardly touch down without his being able to do anything about it, but the T-28, true to it's fine lineage, did most of the work for me. In truth, one would have to try very hard to get hurt in this fine machine. With a huge sigh of relief, I turned off of the runway after that third landing and taxied back to the parking ramp quite satisfied with myself.

As soon as I shut the engine down, maintenance people swarmed over the airplane getting it ready for the afternoon flying session. I had a feeling that I had overlooked something. Mr. Anderson! I had left him out on the far side of the airfield! The ticking of the cooling engine sounded very ominous. I could not restart the engine and taxi out for him. Both sides of the cowling were unlatched and hinged up.

Mechanics were checking hydraulic and oil levels. There was nothing for it; I went back to the flight room to await my fate. I didn't even have the good sense to tell Traverse Metheny, who would have taken a radio equipped car out onto the field and picked him up.

At our table, Don and Pete were waiting impatiently to be dismissed. We could not leave until our instructor dismissed us, but our instructor was on safari far out in the wilderness of a Texas flying field.

"Shit, Art, you are dead." Don said after I confessed to what I done. "Where do you want me to send your personal effects?"

Pete made the sign of the cross and put his hands together in prayer. I was sure that this was the end. When Mr. Anderson finally arrived, his flight suit was soaked with sweat, his shoes were covered with dirt and mud, and his face was quite red. I looked at him much as a turkey looks at a man with an ax in November. His composure was amazing. He greeted us in his usual soft "on the ground" voice, then handed me the parachute that he had carried on his journey.

Smiling he said, "Put this on, Mr. Hood." He then pointed out the window to the airfield and said, "Now double time the perimeter."

I had always thought that airfields were flat. This is not so, at least in Texas. Hondo was criss-crossed with ditches that seemed like canyons. There were all kinds of weeds and stickers and an occasional rattlesnake. It took me all of lunch time and most of the afternoon to circumnavigate this wasteland. The airfield is well over a mile square. Of course, I missed all of my afternoon classes. Don told the instructors that I was under punishment, but that did not amuse them as they duly noted my absence for the punishment roster. There simply were no acceptable excuses. While returning to the barracks after my journey, an upperclass cadet posted me for "uniform in mass disorder." I had to admit that Mr. Anderson had looked like a real snappy dresser compared to my appearance. This would cost me a lot of hours on the tour ramp walking off punishment tours, but I was still in the program and I had soloed the T-28. My logbook recorded a grand total of thirty-five hours.

The North American T-28 is a wonderful airplane. The unusual amount of dihedral makes it very stable and its enormous flaps allow the beginner to make slow and gentle landings. Its rugged construction allows those beginners to survive the mistakes that are made learning to make those nice, soft landings. The Navy version of the same airplane has a much sturdier undercarriage, as well as a more powerful engine.

Given their need to land on heaving aircraft carriers far from land, they do not have the luxury of stretching the landing distance to make nice, soft landings. It is their lot in life to fly to some point in the air above the flight deck, chop the power and crash, hopefully wheels first, onto the ship. Such technique by one of us would have seen us out of the gate by sunset and probably would have driven the wheel struts straight up through the wings.

Once we had achieved solo status, it took just a flight or two for our confidence to soar. There was no doubt in our minds that we were true hotshot pilots. Pinning on the wings was just a formality. Solo flying time was supposed to be dedicated to assiduous practice of air work and the perfection of flying skills. In truth, it frequently was devoted to general hell raising and rat racing, the sport of chasing each other around the sky in mock combat. Much as this might horrify the taxpayer, rat racing is to a fledgling fighter pilot what rough play is to a baby tiger. In both cases, their lives depend on the skills developed.

On one occasion a P2V, a twin engine Navy patrol plane, was passing through the area. It was promptly mobbed by four or five solo students in their T-28s. The exasperated Navy pilot called Hondo Tower on the radio and in a sarcastic tone of voice requested that the Tower advise all of the junior birdmen that he intended to make a left turn and that they had best get the hell out of the way. At the time, I was on a dual flight and could not join the fun. Mr. Anderson did mutter something about candy-assed Navy pilots over the interphone. It seemed that he was not above a little rivalry between the services.

On occasion, things went too far and punishment was swift and irrevocable. One afternoon two airplanes, piloted by a couple of hotshots, took it upon themselves to dust up a town about seventy miles from the base. In their minds, this town was far enough away that the helpless citizens would have no clue where the airplanes came from. They were very thorough in their buzz job. A frightened horse stampeded through the window of a hardware store, and in their fun and games, the lads failed to take notice of some high wires. They had a good head of speed up and the husky T-28s went right through the wires. Power was out to the town for about ten hours. The weather was hot and anything refrigerated or frozen was lost. Within minutes, the Base Commander was under siege by outraged citizens. Fearing the fate of the Alamo, he had an investigation underway before the culprits landed from their afternoon adventures. It wasn't difficult to identify the airplanes involved. Both had wire marks on the wings and one had leaves in the fins of the oil-cooler. It took less than an hour to process the paperwork that eliminated them from the cadet program. They also were punished under article fifteen of the Universal Code of Military Justice. This put a damper on some of the wilder cadets.

Whenever I got a little too big for my britches, Mr. Anderson's voice would come growling over the interphone, "Mister, you do not have this program made." The implied threat would always bring instant humility,

We cadets now were mixed with the student officers. They took the same academic and flying training that we did, however they lived a different life and were not held to the Honor Code as we were. It was assumed that, as Officers and Gentlemen, they were already imbued with the high ideals of the Honor Code. During academic exams, the proctor frequently left the room. The Honor Code was so powerful a tool that the cadets wouldn't consider cheating and would not tolerate another cadet who did. The Student Officers felt no such constraint and they freely "helped" each other. They were out of reach of the standards that we cadets were held to. Since we all were graded on the same Bell curve, this led to higher grades on the part of the student officers and hard feelings on the part of the cadets. The student officers were almost entirely products of college ROTC programs and they brought the relaxed test-taking standards of college life with them. It was about this time that word trickled up that Foxtrot Class had held an Honor Court. A cadet had been caught glancing across the aisle at another cadet's work during an exam. He was eliminated from the Cadet Corps for doing what the student officers did quite freely. Although we no longer had to shout the Honor Code or the Code of Conduct on the demand of an upperclass cadet, these codes were a part of us and we believed implicitly in them. These standards would be with us for the rest of our lives. The Code of Conduct, as written during the Eisenhower administration, was based on America's experience in World War II. Attempts by our POWs in Vietnam to live up to these standards led to the torture of most and the death of many of them.

The halcyon days following the Korean War were slipping away. The Russian bear was gaining strength and, unknown to us, the military was working desperately to build strength after the ill-advised disarmament following World War II and Korea. Although it seemed to us that the Air Force was doing everything possible to eliminate us from flying training, the planners had anticipated the tremendous need for aircrew and were frantically training pilots and navigators. It takes two years of training before a pilot is of any value to an operational unit. World War II was the last war that would permit us the luxury of time to re-arm. The age of both nuclear and so-called brush fire war allows for no such luxury, and the pool of pilots available after the Korean War were both aging and drifting into other work. Their skills, acquired by the constant flying of wartime, were growing dull. The six months of Basic flying passed and we moved on to Primary Flight Training and our first jet, the T-33.

After the country club life at the contract flying schools, there seemed a greater sense of urgency at Greenville. This was a flying school operated by the Air Force. We no longer had the insulation of civilian staff. The T-33 was a two-seat version of the F-80, which had been our first line jet fighter just a few years ago. The guns had been removed and lead weights replaced them to retain the balance of the airplane. The muzzle ports were closed over and the fuselage lengthened to accommodate the extra seat. It was a sleek airplane; its lovely lines a product of Kelly Johnson's famous Lockheed Skunk Works. The saying that an airplane flies the way it looks was born out by this pretty bird. In it we were to master new flying skills, including formation and instrument flying. But the deadly process of weeding out continued. Our flight room was a twin of the room we had operated from at Hondo. The pressure grew more intense and it seemed that my classmates were leaving at an ever-increasing rate. Don Hawley and I were assigned Lt. Bob Alexander as instructor. Pete Graff had come with us to this school but was flying with a different instructor. Pete's father was an Air Force General, which made failure for Pete even less of an option than for the rest of us. Everything seemed to move faster. The T-33 or T-bird was more than twice as fast as the T-28 and weighed nearly twice as much. It was a lot more airplane and we again had to achieve solo status within some mysterious maximum of dual time. As the hours of dual instruction accumulated, there was a sudden rash of eliminations. We would quickly check on the victim's amount of jet time and arrive at pretty fair estimate of what the allowed amount of instruction prior to solo was. This served no purpose other than to elevate the paranoia to near clinical levels for those approaching that level of dual time.

Our schedule alternated between academics and flying. For one week, we would fly in the morning and go to class in the afternoon. The next week, we would trade places with our sister flight and reverse the order of the day. When we were scheduled to fly in the morning, the time between the sound of reveille and cadet formation in front of the barracks was less than five minutes. In most cases, cadet officers conducted the formations. As soon as the squadron commanders reported "all present and accounted for," we marched off to breakfast. But every now and then, one of the TAC officers would conduct a surprise inspection. This not only would make us late for breakfast, but also led to my most spectacular entry on the weekly punishment roster.

In order to save a minute or two, it was our practice on the days that we went to the flight line in the morning to slip out of bed a little before reveille, dress in everything except our boots, then get back into bed with the covers pulled up to our chin in case of a surprise bed check. My roommate had washed out some weeks ago, so and I had to depend on my own mental alarm clock. One morning that mental alarm clock failed me and I didn't wake up until the bugle blew.

Disaster loomed. I now was a precious couple of minutes behind schedule. Frantically, I pulled on my flight suit and boots and raced to the latrine to empty a very full bladder. Flying suits are designed with one long zipper from the neck to the crotch. The zipper can be unzipped from either the top or the bottom. In my desperate haste, I unzipped from the bottom and strained to void as fast as possible. Time was pressing. I had mere seconds to be in formation in front of the barracks. I yanked the zipper shut and a blinding pain struck. I could hardly move but somehow, driven by the force of routine, I made it out of the barracks and into the back row of my formation. I could not stand at attention! I had no idea what I would do next, but when a TAC officer pulled up in a staff car, the problem was taken out of my hands. Upon seeing him, the Cadet Squadron Commander ordered "open ranks." I stood hunched in agony while the TAC officer walked back and forth inspecting the ranks. When he stopped in front of me, his composure was admirable. Since he had been a cadet himself less than a year ago, he had a fair grasp of the situation. With a perfectly straight face, he took a demerit slip from me and dismissed the formation. He had the compassion to drive me to the base clinic where a stone-faced medic injected the injured member with Novocain remarking, "Better things for better living through chemistry."

With that, he freed me from that hellish zipper and advised me to refrain from erotic thoughts for the next week. For the rest of my career in flying suits, I exercised extraordinary caution with the zipper.

On Friday, the punishment roster was posted. Since the tale of my adventure with the zipper had spread as only a story of that magnitude could, I received only minimal demands to explain the charge after my name: "uniform in disorder, i.e. pecker caught in zipper." The entire cadet corp had already had a great deal of fun at my expense with the usual question being "How could such a minuscule appendage become entangled in a flight suit zipper?" I did spend the weekend marching on the tour ramp and enduring the lingering discomfort.

Not all of my experiences were that traumatic. One afternoon, while flying solo on one of those routine-training missions, I was supposed to be practicing air work maneuvers but had grown bored with lazy eights and chandelles. I flew between two cloud layers that gradually closed in around me. They were thin enough for some sunlight to filter through and had occasional holes that allowed sunlight to stream in. In places, pillars of cloud connected the two layers, mimicking columns supporting an astral ceiling. The walls of this cathedral in the sky resembled mother of pearl. The only sound was the low whine of my turbine engine. I flew for miles through this beautiful and surreal place, winding around the giant pillars and skimming the alabaster walls. Finally, the fuel gauge told me that I had to leave this place and return to the real world.

Less than a week later, I paid for my joy ride in the clouds. Immediately after landing from an hour of formation flying, Lieutenant Alexander, my instructor, said, "That was a shitty performance. You got a pink slip for the flight."

There was no argument. A pink slip indicated unsatisfactory performance. Two pink slips earned you a check flight by a senior instructor. This check flight was supposed to be impartial, but was considered by all to be the kiss of death and was called a "wash out ride." A picture of gloom and despair, I trudged into the flight room and headed towards my table. The Flight Commander, Captain Killian, eyed my dejected march across the room.

"You, Mister!" he yelled. "Did you get a pink slip?"

"Yes, Sir," I answered.

"Get in my office!" he ordered.

I was sure that this was the end. I stood at the exaggerated position of attention called a brace as he followed me. In the corner of his office stood a large floor fan.

"Go stand at attention in front of that fan," he commanded.

Roy Killian liked cadets but kept us all terrified of him with a ferocious demeanor that barely concealed a grin that continuously wanted to break out. He had flown Thunderbolts in World War II and had been recalled for the Korean War. His call sign was Retread and he was not a man to suffer fools gladly. He walked over to where I stood close to the hub of his huge floor fan and turned the machine on high. The air blasted in my face and ruffled my crew cut.

"Mister," he snarled. "If you don't straighten up, all you'll see through your windscreen after you graduate will be a big fan like this one!"

"Yes, Sir," I answered. His words sank home. He wasn't kicking me out, at least not this very minute. He had said, "after you graduate." I struggled to keep an appropriately solemn expression as I nourished this glimmer of hope.

He called my instructor in. "Bob, what's the problem with this spastic cadet?"

"He won't fly tight wing formation, Sir. He does fine in trail, but I can't get him to close up when he's on the wing."

"Oh, is that so!" He roared at me. "You little candy ass! I'll cure you of that egg sucking shit! Go get your helmet. You and I are going to log a little dual time."

Cadets considered dual time with Retread as tantamount to the dreaded washout ride. He was the Flight Commander and, from his decision, there was no appeal. None of us were smart enough to take into account the fact that very few of the students he chose to fly with were eliminated. He had the hangman reputation. None of us would willingly stand on the gallows trap door to see if this reputation was deserved.

Minutes later we were racing down the taxiway after a flight of four that was just taking off.

"Bolero Flight, this is Retread. I'll be joining up as number five."

Startled, Lieutenant Pickitt answered, "OK, boss. We'll be making a left turn out for join up, echelon left. One, Two, and Three are solo, I'm in Four."

Roy slid the T-bird smartly into position on the left wing of number four. I thought he was awfully close. "Take the airplane, Mister, and hold this position," he ordered.

I started to drift out.

"Mister, you fly trail on his tip tank! Don't you think of anything but that orange tip tank! If you get one inch out of position I will kick your ass right up between your eyes!"

For the next forty minutes, that tip tank stayed framed in the center of the windscreen. When the formation went into trail, I stayed on Four's left, and when they formed right echelon, I flew trail on his right tip tank. Several times I was vaguely aware of the horizon turning as we went through formation aerobatics, but Four's tip tank was my whole world. I feared the wrath of Retread even more than an in-flight collision.

"Bolero, this is Five. I'm leaving position now and returning to base." Retread said suddenly over the radio. "OK, Mister, take us home. You've cleared the pink slip, but if you so much as fart sideways the rest of your time here, I will personally throw your sorry ass out the gate."

I backed off a few percent on the throttle and Bolero flight seemed to soar up from us as if lifted by an invisible elevator. With a quick look around, I found the confluence of the Arkansas and Mississippi rivers and banked away towards Greenville. Damn, would I be happy when I got back on the ground.

As Christmas approached, we stood down for the Holidays. Most of the cadets were able to get home for a short break. A Cuban cadet in our class, Jorge Requeny, went home to visit his family in Cuba. On New Year's Day 1959, Fidel Castro overthrew the Batista regime. Jorge did not return. We did not find out what became of him and the significance of the event was lost on us. It seemed just the fall of another unstable government in an unstable Central America.

We were scheduled to graduate on the twenty-eighth of January 1959, just a few weeks away. The dreaded sixty-dash-four check, along with the final flight check, loomed. They were the final obstacle to the coveted rating as an Air Force pilot. They involved a full day of written examinations and a flight check several hours long. We did not know it at the time, but we would have to face this same combination of examinations at least twice a year for as long as we were Air Force pilots.

I spent every free moment practicing in the Link instrument trainer, a device that one sat in that resembled the T-33 cockpit, complete with instruments and controls. When the lid was closed it was completely dark inside, with the exception of the instrument lights, and gave a good impression of flying alone at night. The instructor sat at a console outside and followed every movement on a tracking table. Each afternoon when I returned to the barracks, there would be at least one more forlorn bed with the mattress neatly rolled. Someone else had washed out at the last minute. The empty bed always seemed to have been occupied by someone that I thought was doing very well. Numbness overtook paranoia. We trudged along from minute to minute with the same mind-set as ranks of Civil War soldiers must have had as they marched into the withering fire of the enemy. It seemed ages ago that we had performed the fly-over for the graduation of class 59-Delta.

Then suddenly it was over. On a pleasant winter morning, we metamorphosed from lowly cadets to second lieutenants and pilots as class 59-Foxtrot thundered overhead in a mass formation. Two hours later, after a two-year engagement enforced by a rule that cadets must be unmarried, Carolyn and I were married in the Base Chapel. A classmate, Don Irish was my best man. He was destined for a fighter assignment and I for bombers.

Seventeen days later, two brand new Air force pilots took off from Greenville Air Force Base in a T-33. Don Irish and I both had a few weeks to wait before reporting to our next bases. What better way to spend these extra days than flying around in a jet plane courtesy of the Air Force? It was a clear February morning and we were having a great time. Our play was rudely interrupted when, with a rumbling grinding noise, the engine wound down to idle and refused further cooperation with the brace of neophyte aviators in the cockpit. Manipulation of the throttle brought ominous threats from the engine behind us. Our twenty thousand feet of altitude was shrinking at an alarming rate. An engine-out landing pattern at Greenville seemed the best choice. Neither one of us considered leaving the airplane via the ejection seats. We had no desire to practice something that one had to do right on the very first attempt, besides Roy Killian would skin us alive if we broke an airplane just because the engine wasn't performing. The control tower was quite laconic when we announced our plight and intentions. Overcompensating for our lack of power, our landing speed was a good deal faster than necessary. We used every foot of runway and finally stopped, with smoking brakes and the nose just a few feet from the end of the runway barrier net. This barrier is a device to keep errant young airmen, such as us, from roaring off into the weeds and beating the living hell out of a perfectly good airplane. Retread, as we fully expected, was not given to sympathetic commiseration but ordered us immediately back into the air. He reasoned that the Air Force would have wasted its money if we lost our nerve over this incident and decided to quit flying. That thought never entered our minds. Still retaining our cadet mentality, our worry was that we would somehow be blamed for the engine acting up. We were delighted to get off so easily and spent the afternoon happily flying out a full load of fuel. We both had survived the first of many incidents that go with the flying of airplanes. We did not know it at the time, but our days of youthful play were over. We had wanted those wings badly and had striven for them without a thought to what was expected of the men who wore them. Now they hung heavy on our shirts, and the marker was coming due. Although Don Irish would spend his career in fighters, our paths would cross a number of times in the next decade. Our final meeting was during the Vietnam War as eastbound passengers on a tanker over the Pacific. Don was on a rest and recreation break to Hawaii. He had been chasing MIGs but hadn't scored yet. That was the last time I talked to him and I have often wondered if he ever got his MIG.

THREE

◆ ◆ ◆ ◆ ◆ ◆ ◆ ◆ ◆ ◆

All are architects of fate
Working in these walls of time:
Longfellow

L t. Larry Talovich finished reading the taxi checklist to Major
Meeks. The B-47 waddled onto the hammerhead or holding area
at the end of the runway and stopped just short of the runway hold line.
It was a pretty Sunday morning. Damn, I hate Sunday flights, he
thought to himself. Everyone was behind in their quarterly training
requirements and the Wing was flying seven days a week trying to
catch up. This flight was primarily for the ATO take-off required once
a quarter for all combat ready crews, although the flight was scheduled
to last over nine hours.

"Lincoln Ground Control, Acorn Three Nine can you give me a
recheck on the temperature and pressure altitude?" Larry asked over the
UHF radio.

Presently the background hiss in his headphones was interrupted.
"Acorn Three Nine Lincoln Ground, Temperature sixty seven, PA
eleven hundred, wind three three zero at seven, altimeter two nine nine
eight, I have your clearance when ready to copy."

Larry clicked the transmit switch on the control wheel twice. This
unofficial shorthand told the ground control that he understood but was
busy and would call back shortly. Quickly he ran through the charts and
rechecked the take-off data. The airplane was heavy with fuel and the
rack of thirty ATO bottles strapped around the fuselage behind the

wing. They would have to carry the rack and expended ATO bottles to the gunnery range at Salinas Kansas to drop them. If this were a wartime take-off they would drop the rack as soon as they were off the ground, but in peacetime it was considered bad form to drop the damn thing through some farmers roof, especially on Sunday. He reviewed the fresh take-off data with Major Meeks. They would fire the rockets at seventy-five knots. That would also be their S-1 or decision speed. Once they were past that they would have to fly one way or another.

That done he called ground control back, "Lincoln Ground, Acorn Three Nine, I'm ready for clearance now.

"ATC clears Acorn Three Nine as filed. Climb on course to Minden VOR. Maintain twelve thousand, Expect higher altitude from Departure Control prior to Minden, contact tower two nine one point four." Ground control spouted the clearance at the speed of a cattle auctioneer.

Larry volleyed the clearance back word for word and advised ground control that he was switching to tower frequency. It was a matter of pride that a copilot could copy a clearance and read it back verbatim, without having to ask for a repeat, no matter what speed it was transmitted to him.

The scheduled take-off time was less than a minute away. "Tell the tower we're ready, copilot," Major Meeks said over the interphone.

"Lincoln Tower, Acorn Three Nine ready for take-off."

"Acorn Three Nine cleared for take-off, contact departure control two eight five point four when airborne." The tower responded.

Major Meeks started rolling exactly on time. Acorn Three Nine accelerated slowly at first. They had traveled well over three thousand feet before the airspeed indicator reached seventy-five.

"Seventy-five knots," Larry called over the interphone. He felt the sudden increase in acceleration as the pilot fired the ATO. The airplane surged ahead, its thrust effectively doubled. The airspeed indicator wound rapidly to take-off speed and the bomber lifted off.

"Gear up" Meeks ordered.

"Acorn Three Nine, Lincoln Tower. You appear to be on fire!"

Dumb shit, thought Larry. He's never seen an ATO take-off.

"Copilot, check the airplane. I'm getting nose heavy faster than I can crank in back trim," Meeks complained in a puzzled voice.

Larry glanced quickly at the engine instruments. All seemed well there. Then the parabolic rearview mirror caught his eye. It reflected nothing but fire. He felt his heart stumble and then start to race. In an instant he thought of at least a hundred places he would rather be.

"Boss," he said in a low voice. "The whole ass end of the airplane is on fire."

"Crew, prepare to bail out. I'll get us as high as I can." Meek's voice betrayed little strain even as he fought with an airplane rapidly going out of control. He needed every inch of altitude to give the Navigator a chance in his downward firing ejection seat.

"Bail out! Bail out! Bail out!" he shouted over the interphone.

The order was still sounding in his earphones when Larry pulled both yellow handles on his armrests up. The canopy disappeared, his seat bottomed with a thud and the seventy-five millimeter anti-aircraft shell that powered his ejection seat fired. He had no recollection of leaving the airplane or separating from his seat. The next thing he would recall was seeing his seat tumbling towards him.

"The fucking seat is going to kill me," he said out loud.

The seat sailed passed, missing him narrowly; the airplane impacted the ground and his parachute opened with a violent jerk all within the space of a second or two. Major N. V. Meeks died saving his crew. Larry glanced up at that beautiful parachute canopy. Some of the shroud lines were tangled. He looked down at the fast approaching ground.

"Better not fuck with those shroud lines," he muttered to himself and hit the ground with a crunch that knocked the wind out of him.

He was sitting on his butt in a freshly plowed field. It seemed quiet. He felt a little dizzy. An ancient pick-up truck was rattling towards him. Not far away the burning airplane sent a column of black smoke that drifted away on the gentle northwest wind.

Twenty miles away, Larry's wife was picking up after a late breakfast. The kids were in the living room watching cartoons on TV. She felt restless. It didn't seem like Sunday with Larry off flying. She glanced at the Sunday paper on the counter and thought about the Sunday School class she had been asked to teach this morning. Suddenly the kids started calling excitedly from the other room. Something about Daddy being on television. Mildly curious she walked into the living room, smiled at the excitement of the children, and looked at the TV. There was Larry grinning sickly from someone's porch. The camera panned away to a towering column of flame and smoke. The words of the commentator sounded like a distant echo.

Apparently the mobile news van had reached the farmer's place before the Air Force had thought to look there for survivors. She sank slowly to the floor on her knees and began to cry.

*****

The B-47 was the first all jet-swept wing bomber built in quantity. More than sixteen hundred were built. It was a strange looking airplane on the ground, but once in the air with the landing gear and flaps retracted, it had a sleek look and was faster than many of its contemporary fighters. If one looked closely, the B-17 in its ancestry would be seen in the sweep of the vertical tail. Pressured by Russian advances in nuclear technology and the growing intensity of the Cold War, The United States rushed production of this airplane. Its concept was ahead of the engineering technology of the day, but the perceived threat of a growing Soviet military and the insistence of the Strategic Air Command on an immediate all jet replacement for the B-29 and B-50, led to the production of an airplane with serious problems that were not resolved during its service life. Operated by Strategic Air Command at more than thirty tons over its original design gross weight, it was tragically underpowered by today's standards and required over two miles of runway to get airborne. To deal with this, when even two miles of runway wasn't enough, a rack called a "horse collar," which held thirty rocket bottles, was sometimes attached around the fuselage just behind the wing. This contraption would provide an extra thirty thousand pounds of thrust during take-off. That extra thrust lasted for just fifteen seconds, but once initiated could not be turned off, and the airplane was committed to fly. To add to the thrill of a rocket assisted take-off was the fact that this rack of thirty rocket motors was attached at a point that wrapped it around the airplane's aft main fuel tank. That fuel tank was separated from the rocket bottles by nothing more than the aluminum skin of the airplane.

The Soviet response to this fleet of high altitude bombers was the development of their Surface-to-Air Missile. This forced an airplane designed for high altitude flight down to tree top level for the attack portion of its mission. At about this time, thermonuclear deliverable devices were developed. These bombs provided an exponential increase in explosive power. Now the bomber crews had the problem of dropping a bomb from low altitude, the detonation of which would destroy the airplane making the attack.

Stuck with a fleet of airplanes unsuitable for the task at hand, the staff of Strategic Air Command was hard pressed to come up with solutions. The solutions turned out to be quite imaginative. The first attempt was to have this six-engine bomber make its bomb run at tree top level. At a predetermined distance from the target, the airplane would nose up sharply into the first half of a loop. At some point short of vertical flight, the bomb would be released in an attempt to lob it at the target. The airplane would continue its half loop maneuver and, when it reached the inverted position, perform a half roll to the upright position. In short it would do an immelmann turn. This ridiculous solution together with the unintended stress of flight at high speed and at very low altitude severely weakened the wings, and they soon began to fall off at inconvenient times.

But the determination of the planners to make this airplane work was undaunted. The entire fleet was rotated through a repair depot where the wings were strengthened in what was called the Milk Bottle modification, in reference to the shape of the pin that held the wing in place. This was enormously expensive and time consuming. The method of dropping the bomb and escaping by making an immelman turn was abandoned. The problem of escaping one's own thermonuclear blast was theoretically solved by attaching a huge parachute to the bomb and having the airplane pop up to an altitude high enough so that it could release the bomb, turn, and speed away, hoping all the while to get far enough away to avoid being destroyed in the blast. Of course, popping up to altitude over a defended target is a very good way to get shot out of the sky by missiles or anti-aircraft fire. We were burdened with a mission that promised scant hope of survival.

The B-47, designed to replace the high altitude bombers of World War II, became a hodgepodge of make-do fixes. We had built a lot of these airplanes and were stuck with them. Most crewmembers referred to them as "Widow Makers." Half a decade later, during the Vietnam War, some consideration was given to employing them as high altitude conventional bombers. I fervently prayed that this would not be, for I knew that the records would be combed for the names of any aircrew with experience in that airplane and I would again find myself flying an airplane that I loathed.

*****

A blustery east wind blew across the airfield at Lincoln Nebraska. I was in a foul mood as I finished my part of the walk-around preflight of the bomber. It seemed ages since I had actually operated an airplane.

Since graduation from Aviation Cadets last January, I had attended an endless series of schools. Survival school in the mountains above Stead Air Force Base, B-47 training at McConnell Air Force Base in Kansas, and gunnery training in Missouri. In all of those months it had been a struggle to get in enough flying time to earn my flight pay. And that flying time was usually as a copilot in some base flight bug smasher such as the C-45, a little utility twin that took forever to get anywhere. I glanced up at the cockpit of the six-engine bomber that towered over me, I won't get much stick time in this thing, I thought, It was obvious that my job during flight was to operate the guns and the electronic counter measures equipment, do all the paperwork, and worst of all, perform the celestial navigation since the navigator's position in the nose did not allow room enough for him to use a sextant. During the last two flights my control yoke had been unlatched and stowed, except for the take-off, in-flight refueling, and the landing; even then I didn't really get to use it. Things were not turning out quite as I had imagined they would during my cadet days, and it looked like a long journey from the copilot's position to the pilot's seat.

The navigator and I stood side by side in the preflight formation. The pilot stood in front of us and quickly checked our equipment. He also checked our hands to make sure that we had no jewelry on. Just a week earlier a crewmember in one of the other squadrons had slipped on the entry ladder, caught his wedding band and de-gloved his ring finger, leaving only part of the bone. We were now forbidden to wear rings while flying.

I didn't know either of the other two crewmembers. It had been just two weeks since I had reported to the 370th Bomb Squadron along with three or four other bodies straight out of flying school. All of us were armed with a colossal opinion of our value as aviators. These opinions had shrunk considerably in our first several flights. The copilot, whose place I was taking, was off flying status with a head cold. I was assigned in his place in hopes that it would speed up my own qualification as "combat ready," which did not seem to be proceeding at a notable pace.

Mindful of my duties, I spoke up. "Sir, just a reminder, with this fuel load we will have to start and taxi on the aft main tank to get the center of gravity in limits for take-off."

"Thanks, copilot," he grinned making me feel slightly patronized. "OK, let's get the interior preflight done and we'll have time for a quick smoke before engine start time." An efficient crew could get the preflight completed and have a few minutes before engine start time to walk out in front of the airplane for a cigarette, as long as nothing went un-serviceable during the preflight.

"Damn," I grumbled to myself as I climbed the entry ladder. "The only thing with a lower status than me is whale shit." I heaved my briefcase up beside the seat and dragged the parachute, handed up to me by the crew chief, up to my seat. It was pleasantly warm under the large Plexiglas canopy. I checked that both of the ejection seat safety pins were in place and then climbed into the seat. The seat cushion consisted of a survival kit and inflatable rubber raft that clipped to the parachute harness. This kit had to be compressed with a hydraulic ram when packed. The cushion part consisted of little more than an inch of tired foam. Those not equipped with well-padded backsides suffered after just a few hours strapped to that seat.

Once inside the airplane, each crewmember ran the first part of the checklist on his own, assuring that switches were in the proper positions before power was turned on. The B-47 was a slender airplane and did not have sufficient breadth for the pilot and copilot to sit side by side in the traditional manner. The navigator was isolated in the nose. His ejection seat fired downward. The pilots' seats were in tandem, with the copilot in the rear and the pilot in the front seat. Both of their ejection seats fired upward. There was no place in the airplane that a man could stand upright. Flights lasted from six to as much as seventeen hours, with nine being about average. During the entire flight each crewmember was strapped in his seat, sitting on that very hard survival kit and wearing a helmet, oxygen mask, and parachute. Bombers were not built with crew comfort in mind. Eventually, I finished positioning my switches and put the battery switch on. I selected 311.0 on the UHF radio and immediately heard the Command Post calling.

"Teapot Two One, Mable Control."

The pilot also heard the call. "Mable, Two One here," he answered.

"Two One, this is Mable. Scheduling wants to bump your copilot and put on Major Dowd. He needs an in-flight refueling by the end of the quarter, and this is the only flight we can put him on. He is on his way out now, and we have called Base Operations and changed the flight orders."

"Roger, Mable. Two One leaving your frequency for ground control. I'll check in with you airborne. OK, copilot, pack your gear and I'll see you on another flight. If you hurry you might be able to catch the staff car bringing Dowd out and save yourself the walk to Base Ops."

That was not to be. I hadn't quite packed all of my checklists and navigation tables when I saw a staff car off-load Major Dowd in front of the airplane and speed away. Resigned to a long walk lugging all of my flight gear, I handed my parachute, helmet, and briefcase down to the crew chief and climbed down to the ground. Major Dowd took my clipboard with all of the flight information and climbed the ladder. I started the long walk to Base Operations as the crew chief handed Dowd's flight gear up the ladder to him.

The engines were starting as I walked away from the airplane. I wondered what nasty little chores that Major Fish, the squadron operations officer, would have for me when I got back to the squadron. Non-combat ready copilots were given the title of S.L.J.O. or shitty little jobs officer and I was a non-combat ready copilot. Eventually, I reached Base Operations, housed in the building that formed the base of the control tower, and turned to watch Teapot Two One take-off. The bomber was just turning onto runway one-two, at the northwest end of the field. The wings sagged onto the funny little outrigger wheels, heavy with the weight of a huge external fuel tank hanging under each wing. The sound of the six engines coming up to power reached me and I saw the black smoke pour from the tailpipes as the water-alcohol mixture was injected into the engines to augment the thrust. The airplane accelerated, and I knew from the take-off data that I had computed that it would not lift of until long past my position. But something didn't look just right. The airplane seemed to be nose high, higher than normal. The strut on the forward main truck seemed fully extended. As the airplane reached a position directly in front of me, several thousand feet before it should lift off, the nose started rotating upward. In horror, I watched the nose gear come off the ground. The nose continued to rotate and the airplane came clear of the ground. There was no possibility that the six J-47 engines could generate enough thrust to overcome the more than two hundred thousand pounds that the bomber weighed. Teapot Two One achieved a near vertical position with its tail mere feet above the ground and all six engines howling at maximum thrust. In seeming slow motion it stopped, then backed down. The instant that the two twenty-millimeter cannon barrels in the tail touched the ground Teapot Two One exploded in a giant red and yellow fireball. A cloud of thick black smoke boiled upward. I stared and felt the impact tremor through my feet. The hot wind of the shock wave tugged at my flight suit. In the foreground, a pick-up truck was moving across the ramp, the driver not yet aware of the disaster unfolding behind him. The flight line fire station adjacent to Base Operations erupted into life. People were running and a siren started to wail. I felt a strange detached sensation as if I were watching from a great distance. Later, I would remember thinking that Fate had chosen to pass me by.

It was a quarter of an hour before I could get a ride back to the 370th's building with the Base Ops clerk. The Sergeant was taking a copy of the flight orders to the Squadron to get the names and addresses of the next of kin. Feeling lightheaded and a little sick to my stomach, I dumped my flight gear on a table in the mission planning room and walked into the crowded operations office. The talking stopped suddenly. Major Fish stared at me, his mouth hanging open and his face gone pale. As color returned to his face he stammered, "Where the hell did you come from. I just called the Chaplain and we were going to tell your wife that...."

I realized that the crew change hadn't had time to get back to the squadron. To them I had just returned from the dead. "Oh," I said. "I was bumped off the flight by some staff major named Dowd."

Frank Fish pointed to his telephone and said, "You had better call your wife. By now everyone in Lincoln knows there's been a crash."

*****

Nine years later I was the aircraft commander of a KC-135, bound across the Pacific to the Southeast Asian conflict. I made an overnight stop at Guam. Shortly after I had checked into the Bachelor Officer's Quarters there was a knock at the door. The major standing there looked vaguely familiar. He smiled and said, "I saw your name on the transient board at Base Operations. You owe me a drink. I thought I would stop by and collect it."

I stood aside to let him in. "I don't know what for but if I do, I'd better pay up." I unzipped the side pocket of my B-4 bag and retrieved a pint bottle of Jack Daniel's. The refrigerator grudgingly yielded a few ice cubes. In the bathroom, I found a couple of none too clean glasses that had migrated from the Officers' Club in the hands of previous residents, and poured the whiskey. The major took a swallow.

"Nine years ago, when you were a brand new shave-tail at Lincoln Nebraska, you were bumped off of a flight just before take-off. That plane crashed on take-off and all three of the crew died. I was the scheduling officer that bumped you off that flight."

For several seconds I stared at him, then poured the rest of the whiskey into the glasses.

FOUR

◆◆◆◆◆◆◆◆◆

*Beware of rashness, but with energy and
sleepless vigilance go forward and
give us victories.*
-Abraham Lincoln

The phone woke me. It was still dark. Carolyn stirred and rolled over as I got up and padded out to the living room. Without turning on the light, I answered the phone. A measured voice said, "This is a recall of all SAC personnel. Report to your squadron at once." The voice sounded as if I was not the first he had called, nor the last.

When events unfold that later become significant historical markers, it is not unusual for those involved to be only vaguely aware of what they might presage. The magnitude of America's deterrent ability was enormous, and we were used to our leaders drawing and cocking the weapon when a threat was perceived. I expected that some kind of trouble was brewing because of the grumbling from Washington over the build-up of arms in Cuba by the Soviets. To most of us this unrest was just another in a long line of alarms. We had regular intelligence briefings, but we were not told everything. Carolyn came wide-awake as I started dressing.

"What's going on?" she asked. "Do you want me to fix you some breakfast?"

"It's some kind of alert." I zipped up my flying suit and buckled my service revolver around my waist. "Don't get up. I'll get something at the base later on."

"Is it that Cuban thing?" She was beginning to look anxious.

"I don't know, it could be, but I don't think it's much."

"Will you be home for dinner?"

"I should think so." I retrieved a large brown briefcase from the closet. It contained all of the flight manuals for the airplane, as well as letdown plates for the world. It was bulging and heavy. "I'll call you as soon as I find out what's going on."

Gray light was struggling to penetrate the cold overcast as I left for the base. Someone must have alerted the local police. They were at all of the main intersections in town stopping traffic to give right of way to anyone in uniform. I was waved through several red lights in downtown Lincoln and reflected on the fact that we Air Force types had suddenly gained status with the locals. The barbarians must truly be at the gate. At the main gate, my base sticker on the windshield was not enough to pass me through. The young airman standing gate guard demanded my ID card and made a great show of shining his flashlight in my face and comparing my picture to my face. I didn't think that there was much of a resemblance but he passed me through with an exaggerated salute. Someone had convinced that kid that whatever was going on was important. The parking lot at the 370th Bomb Squadron was full, and I had to park off the pavement, a fair walk from the building. I debated on leaving my flight kit in the car and opted for that. I could come back for it later if I was going to need it. Inside, the place was a madhouse. Someone told me that there would be a crew briefing in ten minutes. I got a cup of coffee, it was too early for any donuts to be here, and found my friend Jerry Sparks.

"What's up, Jerry, have you heard anything?"

He frowned and rubbed the top of his crew cut. "Hi, Art. They may move the DEFCON up to three and maintenance is generating aircraft to try and get a head start on things."

"Well, if they recalled the crews, they must be thinking about putting a bunch of us on alert." I replied.

My assumption was correct. We were sent to the Intelligence Shop for sortie assignment and target study. As we crowded into the briefing room, a pair of armed airmen checked our line badges. This was unusual. As soon as we were assembled the door was closed, and the determined guards took position to block further entrance, their carbines at the port arms position. A rumpled major stepped up on the stage. His collar and tie were loosened and there were sweat stains under his arms. He looked as if he had worked the night through.

"Gentlemen," he began, "as your are aware, there is a large military build-up by the Russians taking place in Cuba. We now have intelligence information indicating that offensive, medium-range missiles and bombers are part of this build-up. We also suspect that SA-2 guideline missiles are being put in place and that an extensive, ground-control-intercept ability is developing. We have evidence that MIG 15, 17, and 19 fighters are being offloaded from ships at the port of Mariel. At this moment, U-2 flights are occurring to confirm the intelligence that we have. General Powers has decided to move SAC to DEFCON three. That is the reason for the recall."

He moved to the back of the stage and drew aside the drapes to expose a blackboard.

"These are your sortie and aircraft assignments. Maintenance is generating aircraft as fast as possible. For now, go the target study room and sign for your mission material. Get started on your mission study; we'll call you as soon as your aircraft is ready for preflight. We are working on room assignments. There are not enough rooms in the alert facility, so we'll be designating a barracks as an alert facility. That should be ready for crews to move in by this evening. That's if for now, gentlemen. We'll keep you informed as soon as we learn anything."

By mid-afternoon I was on alert and would remain there for thirty-three days. SAC was taking no chance on being caught unprepared, and neither did General Tom Powers. He was anticipating trouble and was rounding his crews up. By the third week of October, SAC had every available airplane on alert. They had even recalled the old, training TB-47s and the instructor crews from the training school at McConnell AFB and put them on alert. The staff was stripped of anyone who wore wings, and they were put on alert. In all, SAC placed nearly sixteen hundred B-47s on alert during the Cuban Missile Crisis, every plane able to fly. On October 22, the B-52s began airborne alert and by the next day the entire B-52 force was involved. Airborne bombers could not be destroyed by a surprise missile attack. As soon as one landed, another took off. This awesome force was added to the B-58s and all of the operational missiles. The Navy was doing their thing, as well. The ordinary Air Force crewmember was not aware of what strength the Navy could muster, but we were quite sure that it was equally overwhelming. To assure as much survivability as possible, SAC dispersed many of its B-47s to any airport in the country with a runway long enough for it to get off the ground at its warload gross weight.

As the Russian ships carrying ICBMs steamed towards Cuba and the waiting blockade, SAC advanced to DEFCON two. In Defensive Condition Two, we were sitting in the airplanes with power connected, ready to start engines. These long hours led to reflection. We worried about our families. They either lived in base housing or a few miles away in Lincoln. They were busy storing emergency supplies and making plans to leave in a group for the western part of the state. From the cockpit, we could not reach them by telephone.

Should we be launched with a "Go Code," we would not know whether we were being committed in retaliation or as a preemptive strike. Would the second seal be broken? Were our airplanes the manifestation of the red horse and we the riders that would be the executioners of Mankind? The long hours of sitting in a bomber waiting for war led to such surrealistic contemplation. But our minds could not accommodate the awfulness of our tasks for any great length of time. To do so led only to madness. When the Russian ships turned back at the blockade, we gradually returned to a lesser state of alert. We were allowed to leave the cockpits of our airplanes, and we returned to more normal thinking. Plans were made for Sunday dinner with our families, and some even talked of vacation trips when this crisis passed.

Slowly the tide of sanity returned. John Kennedy held four of a kind, Nikita Khrushchev, only two pair. His bluff had been called and he was too much of a poker player to bet the world on such a weak hand. The Russian Bear was allowed an avenue of retreat that saved face. Gradually, the terrible swift sword was sheathed, and for the men who had been the cutting edge of that sword, Thanksgiving Day that year meant more than it ever had in the past. The world had faced a doomsday event that exceeded any other yet encountered by man.

*****

The weather was turning colder. There was a lull in operations while everyone seemed to be catching his breath after the Cuban crisis. As 1963 began, we suffered a series of crashes that rivaled wartime activity. Even today, the wing history of this period remains classified. Details of accidents are not generally available. In all, Lincoln lost nine aircraft that year. A record that would have brought howls of outrage in present times, but the secrecy of the Cold War and the decades that followed obscured those losses from public scrutiny. In retrospect, this was probably reasonable. It would have posed a grave threat to the United States if public outrage forced the grounding of an airplane that had played a major role in the Cuban Missile Crisis and made up the primary bomber fleet of the United States. The concept of out-producing an enemy had served us well in World War II. In the case of the B-47, it also served. It was not the superior technology of the B-47 that was awesome to an enemy, the airplane was obsolete when the very first one flew, but the incredible number of them that Russia believed would overwhelm their air defenses. We can no longer count on numbers, for in the age of missiles it is technology rather than production that will prevail, and the patchwork make-do methods of adapting an unsuitable weapon to a task for which it was not designed could turn into a fatal weakness. To depend on sufficient advance warning to set production in motion and out-produce an enemy is naïve. We were stuck with the B-47 and had to make it work.

About that time, I was a guest of Britain's Royal Air Force at RAF Waddington, a Bomber Command base in England. There I had the opportunity to fly their magnificent Vulcan Bomber. The Vulcan was contemporary to the B-47 and first flew in 1952. Its performance was superior in every way. It could easily operate above fifty thousand feet and could cruise at a higher speed than the B-47. The huge delta wing allowed it to outmaneuver any fighter in existence at high altitudes. Its payload and range were exceptional and it was capable of in-flight refueling. On one mock combat flight, we engaged BAC Lightnings. The Lightning was the RAF's latest interceptor, capable of an initial rate of climb of fifty thousand feet per minute and speeds of Mach 2.3. On practice intercepts, at an altitude of fifty thousand feet, the Vulcan easily evaded the Lightning by making use of its superior turning ability. How I wished that we had this airplane for our fleet instead of the B-47. It would have been both politically imprudent and time critical to have built this airplane under license instead of the B-47. Had we done that, we would have had a far superior airplane that, like the B-52, would still be operational today, but we might not have had it in time. SAC needed a new bomber and once the decision was made to build the B-47, we were committed to an airplane with multiple faults, none of which were ever satisfactorily resolved.

In the not too distant future, Defense Secretary McNamara would commit a similar mistake by pressing for the TFX, a design concept intended to meet the needs of both the Navy and the Air Force. This made as much sense as designing a sports car that also functioned as a pick-up truck. The finished product would perform neither task well, and only by throwing incredible amounts of money at the project would the TFX finally evolve into the F-111, a useful airplane employed in a roll that had nothing to do with its original design.

It was the flight crews who endured the carnage of political decisions. Many flyers gained social standing by wearing the tiny lapel pin depicting a caterpillar dangling from a parachute. They were members of the Caterpillar Club, an exclusive organization; the membership prerequisite was that you had bailed out of an airplane to save your life. Not everyone was lucky enough to win that pin. Many died. The B-47 was unforgiving of any lapse of skill or attention. It was fatiguing to fly and a pluperfect bitch to land, especially from the back seat. Overweight and underpowered, every take-off was a crapshoot. Its loss rate had a deplorable effect on morale, and the ones who suffered the most were the crew's families. The B-47 loss rate in 1963 came perilously close to matching the B-52 losses of Linebacker Two nine years later. In Linebacker Two, waves of B-52s attacked North Vietnam over a twelve-day period against the most severe and concentrated anti-aircraft defenses ever encountered. But in 1963, we were at peace! I am sure that suppression of information about these accidents was justified during the Cold War, but there is no reasonable justification now. The Russians would have been delighted to know that American bomber crews were in as much danger from their own aircraft as they were from Russian Air Defenses.

*****

Air Traffic Control had cleared us for the Ironwood Oil Burner route. Oil Burner routes were designated for low altitude bombing and navigation practice. They were in the range of four hundred miles long and wound through sparsely populated areas. They could be quite a challenge for the navigator, as he had to guide the airplane on a specific track over the ground while traveling at five hundred miles per hour and at an altitude of a few hundred feet. At the end of each oil burner route, a radar station scored our imaginary bomb drop. For twenty seconds prior to "bombs away" a tone was transmitted over the radio. When the tone stopped, the radar that had been tracking us would mark that point as the point where the imaginary bomb was released. The bomb release was further complicated by the need to pop up from our very low altitude to a height that would theoretically allow us to escape the blast of a nuclear weapon. The optimism and gullibility of youth is boundless.

Don Hall's voice came over the interphone, "Copilot, this is the navigator. Two minutes to IP. Start the bomb run checklist, please."

A highway bridge over a creek flashed under the right wing. A glance at my strip chart confirmed that we were almost exactly on course. The heading indicator told me that we were carrying fifteen degrees of drift correction. There had to be a lot of wind. I could see streamers of snow streaking across the frozen fields. Naked trees huddled close to shivering farmhouses and barns. A thick, gray layer of clouds was just above us, broken here and there by shafts of weak sunlight.

I started reading the bomb run checklist over the interphone and Don answered each step as he completed it. The APS fifty-four, a radar receiver that warned us when radar was tracking the airplane, began to make the rasping sound of a tracking radar in my headphones. The threat light on the instrument panel was flashing "Forward." That would be the bomb plot radar starting to track us. I finished reading the bomb run checklist as we crossed the initial point or IP.

"Ironwood Bomb Plot, this is Patch Four Four, IP inbound. I have bombing information when you are ready to copy."

"Uh, roger, Patch Four Four. Wait one, please." That was unusual. The bomb plot would be anticipating the bombing information that they would need to score the release. We were rapidly approaching our "pop up point" where the pilot would apply full power on all six engines and climb to our release altitude.

"Patch Four Four, this is Ironwood Bomb Plot. Abort your bomb run, climb to five thousand feet and contact Air Traffic Control for further clearance."

Frank Hadl, the crew commander, took over the radio from the front seat. "What's the problem, Ironwood? We've come a long way and I'll have to give my boss a good reason for not completing this run."

"Patch Four Four, Ironwood. The aircraft making the run ahead of you, Patch Three Six, disappeared from the radarscope and we lost radio contact during his pop up. He may have crashed. When you get to five thousand, please attempt radio contact and advise us."

"Oh, shit!' Don said, "I hope to Christ we haven't lost another one."

At twenty five hundred feet we entered the overcast. I switched the UHF radio to guard frequency. "Patch Three Six, this is Patch Four Four on guard. Do you read?" Over and over I repeated the call and each time I was answered by silence. With a sinking feeling, I switched back to Ironwood frequency.

"Ironwood, this is Patch Four Four. No contact with Patch Three Six on guard frequency. We are leaving your frequency now for ATC."

"Roger, Four Four, thanks for trying."

In the time that it took us to climb to thirty three thousand feet and begin a high altitude navigation leg, the news that we had lost another airplane reached Lincoln. As usually happens when a disaster occurs, no one concerned knew for sure who was involved in the crash and whether or not there were any survivors. At the time of the crash, Lincoln had nine airplanes in the air. That meant that there were approximately thirty wives who braced themselves in anticipation of an Air Force staff car arriving in front of their home and a senior officer accompanied by the Chaplain coming to the door. These awful visits could not be made until the Commander was certain who had survived and who had not. That made the Wing Command Post a very busy place.

The Deputy Commander for Operations chewed on his frayed cigar. He glared at the mission board listing all of the wing airplanes that were flying today. "Was it Patch Four Four or Three Six?" he asked Major Allen, the duty controller.

"I'm pretty sure that it was Three Six, Sir. There was some confusion with Ironwood Bomb Plot, but I'm trying to get through to the ATC center up there."

"Stay on it. We have to start calling the wives of the crews not involved. The switchboard is getting swamped with frantic women and we need to let them know as soon as possible. How the hell the word gets out so fast, I'll never know."

The Chaplain buzzed the door and Major Allen pushed the button to unlock the door and let him in. He took a chair to one side and said nothing. Both he and the DCO were in for a bad few hours when they would have to make their grim rounds.

Major Allen turned to his Sergeant. "Make a list of all aircraft commander's home phone numbers so we can call their wives and put their minds to rest as soon as we know for sure which bird is down. You will also need to check the flight orders for any extra people flying. There's no way the AC's wife would know about extra people flying."

"Already working on it," Sergeant Davis replied. He was a Master Sergeant who began his military career in 1943 as a B-17 waist gunner for an Eighth Air Force bomber unit in England. He knew very well what it was like to have family wondering if you would ever come home again.

The phone console buzzed. Major Allen pushed the button for line one and answered. He listened for a moment, "Thank you," he said and hung up. "Colonel, it's Patch Three Six that is down. Four Four was seven minutes behind him on the bomb run. Four Four is on a high altitude nav leg now, according to ATC."

"Good, lets start notifying families of the crews not involved. Any word on survivors?" The DCO took the wet cigar stub out of his mouth, wrinkled his nose at it, and dropped it in an ashtray.

"No word yet, Sir," Major Allen replied. Wurtsmith has a team en route by helicopter, but it's a long way from there to the site. SAC headquarters is raising seven different kinds of hell demanding information."

"Well, that's the Old Man's problem. Damn, I'm glad I'm not Wing Commander today! I'd be thinking about a new job as laundry and recreation officer at Thule Greenland about now."

The DCO shook his head at the apparent injustice of replacing the wing commander whenever there was a crash. Lately, a Commander wasn't on station long enough for the crews to get to know him.

Sergeant Davis started calling the wives of all of the aircraft commanders, flying at that time, who were not involved in the crash. It was the custom for the aircraft commander's wife to call the wives of the other crewmembers when important crew information needed to be passed along. Sergeant Davis assumed this and did not remind anyone to call the other wives. In every case but one, the information was passed. In that case, the husband had just been transferred to bombers from a fighter unit. Neither he nor his wife was familiar with this custom. Thus the aircraft commander's wife of Patch Four Four was notified that her husband was safe, the two other wives of the crew were not notified.

Time crawled by. It seemed cold in the house. Carolyn shivered. She peeked out at Twenty Seventh Street through the blinds. The street was empty. Finally, she dialed Don and Marcie's number. "Have you heard anything, yet, Marcie?"

"No...nothing," Marcie replied. "You'd think they would have called us by now." The two young women talked aimlessly for a few minutes, but their minds were not on the conversation and the talk trailed off and finally stopped.

"I've gotta go," Carolyn said. "The kids are getting up from their nap." Another hour dragged by. Every sound was magnified. The two children ate their cookies and spilled most of the milk, then went off to play. Absently, Carolyn wiped the table off. The phone rang. The glass that she had been holding shattered on the floor. Terrified, she picked the phone up. It was Marcie.

"I can't stand it anymore!" Marcie sounded as if she had been crying. "I'm going to call Fran and see if she has heard anything and I'll call you right back."

In just over a minute the phone rang again. Carolyn snatched it up. "Hello."

"Carolyn, the guys are OK. The command post called Fran hours ago. She didn't know that she was supposed to call us. She thought that we had been called."

Patch Three Six had been proceeding along the Ironwood Oil Burner route seven minutes ahead of Patch Four Four. Upon reaching the pop up point, the pilot rapidly advanced all six throttles and began a maximum rate climb. Five J-47 engines responded to the throttle movements, one did not. Number six, the right outboard engine, started to accelerate but the fuel was fed too rapidly to the burner cans by the primitive fuel control unit. Pressure increased faster than the turbine blades could accelerate to accommodate the rapidly rising internal pressure. The engine was behaving much like a baby that had just stuffed a whole slice of bread in his mouth. It was choking. In the press of cockpit duties created by the rapid climb and the final seconds of the bomb run, the abnormal instrument readings for number six engine went unnoticed in the sea of engine instruments. The crew had less than a minute to discover the compressor stall and to correct it. They didn't make it. Number six engine exploded violently and took just over twenty-one feet of the right wing with it. Patch Three Six went into a violent right spiral. The two pilots were able to eject. The navigator and crew chief, riding in the jump seat, died in the crash seconds after the engine exploded. The parachutes of both pilots deployed as advertised.

The temperature was seventeen degrees below zero and the wind was blowing well over fifty knots. By the time they reached the ground, their hands were so numb that they could not squeeze the releases that would disconnect their parachute harnesses from the canopies. They both were dragged at nearly fifty miles an hour for almost a mile across the corrugated surface of a plowed and frozen field. Eventually the parachutes caught in a fence line and their brutal ride ended. Both men were beaten to death.

Some six months later, a modification started to appear on our parachutes. When the parachute opened, a wire loop about five inches in diameter popped out on each riser at just about face level. Pulling on one or both of these loops would release the corresponding riser allowing the parachute canopy to collapse. The risers could be released even if the aviator's hands were frozen.

Not long after the crash of Patch Three Six, it was my turn to look over the edge into the darkness. I was assigned to fly in the place of another copilot who had been taken off of flight status by the flight surgeon because of a head cold. Lieutenant Colonel Cragen, the Chief of Stanboard, was the pilot and Bob Morrissey was the Navigator. Everything was fine until we passed through nine thousand feet on the climb out. Without warning, the powered rudder failed. There was no way that even two pilots working together could move the rudder without that power boost.

"Copilot, see if you can troubleshoot that powered rudder," Cragen said.

I craned around in my seat and, with a sinking feeling, saw that we were trailing a long stream of brown smoke from the tail. That news just made Colonel Cragen's day.

"Just fucking great," he said. "and we have two full cans of twenty-millimeter ammunition back there. Call ATC and declare an emergency for a possible fuselage fire. Tell them we are going direct back to Lincoln. Then call the Command Post and give them the good news."

There are two things that truly put the fear of God in an aviator: structural failure and fire. I made the cryptic call and had just received clearance off Center frequency to call the Command post when number six engine failed abruptly and a spray of jet fuel came out of the air conditioning vent on the upper right corner of my instrument panel.

"Pilot, this is copilot. I'm getting soaked with fuel from the air vent," I complained on interphone. This one was not in the emergency procedure checklist.

"Son, you are just full of good news. I can smell it, too. Crew, go on oxygen and shut down all electrical equipment. Do it now before this fuel mist gets any thicker. One spark and we could go off like a bomb. Shut down everything. I'll keep the battery on so I can talk to you on interphone. Don't make any interphone calls that you don't have to."

This is just beautiful, I thought. Everything on this damn airplane is electric. My stomach churned as I shut down everything electrical, which left us without landing gear, flaps, or radios. The fuel coming in the vents suddenly intensified. It was now visibly trickling down every vertical surface. My eyes burned. I jammed my scarf into the vent and lowered my helmet visor in an effort to keep the fuel from spraying directly into my face. Only our oxygen masks allowed us to breathe. We continued our descent. Colonel Cragen had the throttles back to idle. I had no clue as to how the fuel was getting into the air conditioning system.

Cragen clicked the interphone on and held it. "Copilot, do not answer me. Turn your seat around and lower the landing gear manually. We'll be able to see the outriggers, we'll pray for the mains. This will be a flaps up landing." He didn't want to risk any more interphone calls than were absolutely necessary.

It took several minutes of heart-bursting work, bent over in my seat working the four long handles that lowered each of the landing gear. When I finished and had turned my seat back to face forward, I banged on the glare shield to let the pilot know that I was facing forward again. As long as my seat was not in the forward facing position, I could not eject. I could see him nod in acknowledgment.

The interphone came on one last time. "Crew, this is Pilot. Prepare to bail out."

Damn, I was scared. I bottomed my seat and stowed my control column in preparation. As I looked forward along the left side of the crew compartment, I saw Bob Morrissey stow all his equipment in his navigator's bag and zip it shut. He glanced back at me and must have known how frightened I was. He gave me the thumbs up and turned back forward. I knew that he was tightening his parachute harness and pulling his shoulder straps tight. His seat would fire downward and the lower we got the slimmer his chances would be of a successful bailout. Cragen would try to roll the plane on its side, as he gave the bailout order, to give us all an equal chance. I sincerely hoped he would not have to give that order. I followed the example and tightened up my chute and seat harness.

The geometric patterns of the Nebraska fields came closer. Farm buildings were very distinct. Patches of brown earth showed through the snow.

As Cragen made a descending left turn, I could see the base about four miles away. It seemed to be covered with flashing red lights. A tiny green light kept flashing from the tower giving us landing clearance. Little puddles of fuel had collected in corners of the airplane structure.

Colonel Cragen's touchdown was perfect. As soon as the main trucks were on the ground, he pulled the throttles to cut-off and held his clenched right fist up. I knew what he wanted and deployed the huge brake chute. At least that was mechanical and did not require electrical power. In moments, we were out of the airplane and well away from it. I must have looked a little shaken.

Bob clapped me on the shoulder. "How you doing? You look a little frazzled."

"I never knew that flying was so much fun," I answered.

Carolyn's first remark when I got home was, "Boy, do you stink. What happened?"

"I got fuel splashed all over me. I gotta take a shower and then I'll tell you about it." By the time I had showered and changed, the washing machine was sloshing away with all of my flying clothes in it.

*****

The interphone came alive and Don Hall said, "Art, end nav leg at three one past the hour. Score that for me, please."

I clicked the interphone twice and closed the box containing my flight lunch without having had a chance to eat a bite. I'd score the leg for him and might just have time to grab a sandwich before we rendezvoused with the tanker for refueling. At thirty-one minutes after the hour I would note our radials from two different radio navigation stations, or VORs, and plot them. I would then measure the bearing and distance from the planned position at the end of our celestial navigation leg and call that information to Don. Once I had done that, I noted the information on my flight log. Next to it, I wrote the time and date;

1931Z, 22 Nov. 1963. The local time was 1231. Don was very good and that point fell very close to his planned position.

The pilot, Frank Hadl, called the ATC center. "Fort Worth Center, this is Paddle Two Nine. We've completed our nav leg and would like a left turn and descent to flight level two eight zero. Our tanker is Fox Five One."

"Roger, Paddle Two Nine, left turn approved. Descend to and maintain flight level two eight zero at pilot's discretion. We're talking to your tanker and he will be on time. Er-ah, stand by one, Two Nine."

"I wonder what his problem is." Frank muttered over the interphone. "Every time someone tells us to stand by, the shit hits the fan and it usually blows our way. He's cleared us to turn and we have to start north or we'll be late." Frank turned the autopilot-heading knob and I automatically searched the sky to our left as the bomber began a graceful left turn.

"Paddle Two Nine, Fort Worth Center, we just received word that President Kennedy has been shot in Dallas."

"Aw, you Texans are all crazy," Frank replied. The news was so shocking that he thought the controller was pulling his leg.

"No joke, Two Nine, that's the straight truth and we have a message for you from SAC. You are to contact the nearest SAC command post. You are cleared off-frequency at this time to do that, report back on."

"Make the call, copilot. I guess he isn't joking."

I switched the UHF radio to 311.0 and, not bothering to look up the call sign of the nearest SAC base, used the general call sign for any SAC command post, "Sky Bird Control, this is Paddle Two Nine."

The answer was immediate, "Paddle Two Nine, this is Topkick control. Report ready to copy traffic."

"Go ahead, Topkick, ready to copy," I replied.

"Paddle Two Nine, this is Topkick Control with a priority message in one part, Delta Mike Zulu X-ray. How do you copy?"

Shit, this guy is serious, I thought and dragged my code tables out of my flight bag. "I copy Delta Mike Zulu X-ray. Authenticate, Alpha Mike."

"Authentication is Tango Sierra," he replied.

"Paddle Two Nine clear frequency," I answered. "Pilot, this is Copilot. The message decodes to "return to base" and the authentication is correct."

"Roger, call the center and get us a clearance home, present position direct, we'll stay at this altitude."

It took us less than two hours to get back to Lincoln. All I could think about was a recent movie I had seen, "The Manchurian Candidate," a story of a brainwashed POW trained as an assassin.

Lyndon B. Johnson took the oath of office aboard Air Force One before it left Dallas. Few anticipated how much this act would escalate our involvement in Vietnam and alter the course of history.

FIVE

◆◆◆◆◆◆◆

There is a destiny that makes us brothers;
None goes his way alone.
-Edwin Markham

I n 1961, John Kennedy had placed the Strategic Air Command on fifty-percent alert. He was reacting to Russian saber rattling and the rapidly shrinking response time that would exist should a preemptive nuclear strike be launched against the United States. To the American public, this may have seemed a good precaution, but it soon was forgotten by all except those who would have to carry out that order. This simple order meant that, at all times, one half of all SAC bombers would be manned, armed, fueled, and ready for an immediate take-off or, in some cases, airborne with weapons on board. That state of readiness also extended to the tanker aircraft that would support those bombers. The burden also fell on the people who would maintain these aircraft and those who would guard them. It altered the lives of everyone involved. That state of alert lasted for more than three-and-a-half decades, until President Clinton finally stood SAC down. It is remarkable that the Strategic Air Command was not only able to maintain this, but at the same time support the Vietnam War with the remaining B-52s and KC-135 tankers and phase out the obsolete B-47. Unfortunately, some of our political leaders today minimize this tremendous effort and see no need to maintain defensive abilities. This world could now very well be a radioactive dust pile had it not been for this deterrent effort. For the ground and flight crews that maintained this status, it was a long, dreary duty that stretched on beyond the foreseeable future with no hope of a transfer to other duty. Family life suffered and stress related disorders were common. Airline headhunters happily harvested the most experienced heavy airplane pilots. It was very difficult to stay on when a much better life was offered. Conventional wisdom said that the only way out of SAC was in a coffin.

In my memory, it seems that it was always winter when I was on alert. Perhaps that is because the SAC bases that I was assigned to were all so far north. It seemed that no matter where you were stationed, you had best be an avid hunter and fisherman because there wasn't much else to do in the scarce time off duty. SAC bases were positioned as far inland and as far north as possible, simply to buy an extra minute or so of warning time in case of a Pearl Harbor-style missile attack. That extra time would hopefully allow a few more of our alert bombers to get safely into the air before inbound missiles arrived.

It was just after six one morning and I was having a last cup of coffee with Carolyn. We both were tired. I had arrived home at seven the evening before from a terrible flight that seemed made up of endless weather and airplane problems. There was just time to meet the crew rest requirements before going on alert.

Our house on South Twenty-Seventh Street was a big, old, comfortable Midwest home. It had been built around the turn of the century and all of the wood in it was hardwood. I had absently wondered what it would cost to build this house with these materials now. Carol pulled her robe tight around her neck and looked up at the ceiling. Richard's room was directly overhead. He was nearing two and getting around pretty well. We could hear the sounds of childish feet overhead. Since it was not likely that Rick had escaped from his crib, it must have been his four-year-old sister. She was a bossy little thing and absolutely certain that her brother could not survive without her constant supervision.

"I'd better check on this," Carolyn said glancing up the stairs towards the small sounds, as she walked me to the front door. With a quick kiss, I was out the door with my B-4 bag and a cup off coffee in my hand. I hoped that our old Plymouth, which served as my "go to work car," wouldn't give me any trouble after sitting out all night in the cold.

It would be seven full days before I got home from that alert tour. Carolyn would have to deal with any household problems that arose. We were able to talk daily on the phone, but only something as drastic as a death in the family would have released me from alert duty, and even that was not a given. We usually were able to visit briefly on the weekend. This was complicated by the struggle of getting two small, squirming children dressed, and then driving fourteen miles to the Officers' Club where we would have dinner together. In all, that arrangement was about as satisfactory as a family visit at the county jail.

Alert was bad enough. Reflex was worse. That was alert duty at a forward base and involved flying to a base in England, Spain, or North Africa and standing alert there. The few SAC bases in the southwest reflexed to Guam. Those trips would usually last three-and-a-half weeks. We would make about five reflex trips a year, and it was common to spend every other week on alert while at home. In the time that remained, we were required to complete all of our quarterly training requirements, including all those "routine training missions" that seem to kill so many of us. Time studies demonstrated that, over a year, a SAC crew averaged ninety hours a week of duty. Leave was scarce and never more than two weeks long. This was a hardship for those whose families were more than a few hundred miles away. I frequently contemplated what our life would have been like had I remained with the Merchant Marine. I had passed my third engineer's examination and surely would have been first assistant by then.

I considered these things, as I had every time I drove to the base to assume alert. That morning seemed typical of going on alert. It was a dreary Nebraska day. There were no leaves on the trees and the countryside seemed raw. Slush was all around and there were patches of mud showing through the snow. It was just warm enough for other traffic to throw a muddy spray on the windshield, which froze immediately. My coffee had gone cold and I was in a thoroughly shitty mood. The guard at the main gate waved me through without bothering to salute. That made me feel a little better. Some other poor bastard was almost as happy as I was. At the entrance to the Hurry House, or alert compound, a shivering eighteen-year-old came out of the sentry box. He pulled off his mittens to accept my flight line badge. He had the sniffles and was having trouble with a runny nose. He looked as if he has been there in the cold for at least eight hours and would probably have killed for a plate of eggs and bacon and a big cup of coffee. He waved me through, trying to salute and pull his mitten on at the same time. I found a parking spot on the fringe of the parking area and left my flight bag and B-4 bag in the car. After the relieved crews went home, I would move my car to a more convenient spot and retrieve my baggage.

I had just ten minutes until "Change Over Briefing" would start.

A burst of laughter told me where my friend Jerry Sparks was. His effervescent personality attracted those of us suffering from the terminal depression of SAC crew duty and in need of a happy fix. He saw me in the hallway and waved me over.

"Art, Joan wants to know if we can get together for cards next Friday evening."

What we would be doing a week from then was a blank to me, but I seemed to remember that we were committed with Bob and Anne Morrissey sometime on that weekend.

"I'll have to check with my social secretary when I get a chance to call home. We've got something going on with the Morrissey's that weekend, but I'm not sure what day. I'll have Carol call Joan."

All of our social life was crowded into the two and a half days free after a week of alert. Since we were all about the same age and had small children, babysitters were very scarce. It was not unusual for two or three babies to be sleeping on a double bed at the end of an evening. A visit with Bob and Anne Morrissey was always pleasant. All of the kids got along well and David, their oldest son, had his father's strong sense of duty and kept the younger children occupied and safe. Anne was a great cook.

The hallway and briefing room were crowded and a fog of tobacco smoke hung head-high throughout, completely defeating the ventilation system. Off-going aircraft commanders kept strange looking aluminum boxes close at hand. Either their navigator or copilot stayed close to their sides. These boxes, about the size of a small toolbox, were riveted soundly together and adorned with two large combination type padlocks. They contained the Go Codes or "tickets" and the necessary code tables to validate them. A nuclear strike could have been launched with the contained information. They were under the two-officer policy; that is, no one person could be alone with the box. The pilot and the navigator each had the combination to one of the locks. During the changeover, the tickets and code tables were inventoried and the oncoming aircraft commander would sign for them. It was at this point that the new crew assumed responsibility for the alert sortie. Once the sortie was relieved, the off-going crew was free to leave. They wasted little time, for they now were off until the following Monday morning, barring some other international uproar.

Each crewmember had to be certified on any sortie that he stood alert for. To be certified meant that he had spent a full day studying that sortie and had satisfactorily briefed either the wing commander or vice wing commander on all phases of that mission. I have never heard of a crewmember that failed his certification briefing, no matter how hard he tried. It was considered wise not to be certified on too many sorties, as that would make one too vulnerable for substitution for someone who might have contracted some dreadful disease that temporarily grounded him, such as a head cold or terminal clap. It was not unusual for a crewmember to finish one seven-day alert tour and continue on for a second week. On one occasion, I had just returned from a reflex trip to Spain. I got off the airplane at Lincoln after flying across the Atlantic and half of the United States, visited Carolyn and the kids for a few minutes at Base Operations, got onto another B-47, and returned directly to Spain and the same base I had left some twenty four hours earlier. To be fair, that incident was unusual. In most cases, after alert or reflex, we were home by noon Friday and were not called on until Monday morning.

Once the off-going crews had left, we sat through what was called "Daily Briefing." This was conducted by staff officers. These individuals worked a reasonably regular schedule. They could plan on weekends and holidays in most cases and would fly once a month or just enough to qualify for flight pay. Their positions were both envied and resented by the flight crews. This resentment grew from the practice in SAC of moving an individual who was unable to perform crew duty into a staff position. To protect their non-flight crew, and nine to five status, they often felt compelled to appear important at these briefings and would compete with each other in relays to heap as much meaningless detail as possible on us, especially if anyone from the "Head Shed" was present.

Eventually, this marathon briefing would come to an end and we would find our alert vehicles, usually a double cab Dodge pick-up, and go out and pre-flight our airplanes. The tickets would be stowed on board and the airplane "cocked," or brought to the point on the checklist that would allow an immediate engine start. Once this was done, we would leave the aircraft sentries to their frigid pacing and spend the rest of our day devoted to target study, tactical doctrine revue, and the numerous, required written tests.

In reality, we spent most of the required study time telling "war stories," exchanging gossip, and pursuing the scientific investigation of making paper airplanes. Should a senior officer enter the building, extraneous materials disappeared and an air of engrossed study prevailed. In truth, we had spent so much time on alert that we knew this material very well. It might have been fascinating information to the civilian on the street, or perhaps an ill-informed spy, but to us it was like reading the same book over and over again. There always was one curious fact that popped up each year when the new SIOP, or Strategic Integrated Operations Plan, came out. The SIOP was SAC's whole war plan in a nutshell and showed all of the routes, targets, and the enemy order of battle on a single huge map. Inevitably, we would have to come back within four or five weeks and study the revision. Every single one of the original routes of attack would show clusters of mobile surface-to-air missile sites along them, and we would have to study the new ones. I am sure that this caused our military leaders a lot of lost sleep, but it provided job security for the spies on both sides.

The Target Study Officer came by our table passing out well-worn five-by-eight-inch cards. "OK, gentlemen," he said, trying to talk over the conversation of a group that was paying no attention to him at all. "Please, revue and update your emergency data cards and make sure that you have memorized your authenticator number."

This information was supposed to assist in our rescue or recovery should we find ourselves captured or stranded in hostile territory. Apparently, the plan would be for us to stomp our authenticator number in the snow of Siberia or send it by carrier pigeon, and that would immediately bring a team to our rescue. Older crewmembers viewed this plan with a good deal of cynicism.

"Hey, Gene, how are all these rescue folks supposed to get this information if it's so secret you have to burn it before reading it?" And this round of Friday harassment of the Target Study Officer had begun.

Gene was a thin and fussy man. He hated Fridays. Alert changeover put him into all-day contact with the alert flight crews and they took out their hostilities on him. His rank protected him from the younger ones, but the others did not spare him. When he arrived home on Friday evenings, he would head straight to the bar in his den. He seldom drank during the rest of the week.

"There will come a day," he answered above the din, "when you will wish that you had paid more attention to me!" His headache was getting worse. He wished that these rowdies would take their study more seriously.

"Gene," someone called. "Tell us what the big boys in Omaha think the attrition rate will be if we launch with a go code."

He cringed. He had seen the number and it was over ninety percent. "That's information you don't have a need to know," he answered.

"Why not? We're the guys who have to go," a thirty-year-old Captain with streaks of gray in his hair asked.

Gene retreated to his office. He knew they were right. In a nuclear exchange, none of them would come home. There would be no home to come to. In a lesser war, those personal authenticator codes would be forgotten by all except some poor desperate devil chained to the wall in some unspeakable prison.

From time to time, the alert force would be exercised. Most of us have seen the documentaries showing the flight crews racing to the aircraft with klaxons blaring in the background. We truly did not know if an exercise was a drill or for real. In the early days there were four kinds of practice alerts. An Alpha alert required only that we answer roll call on the aircraft radio; a Bravo alert meant engines were started, but the aircraft were not moved; a Cocoa meant start and taxi and we must cross the runway hold line within fifteen minutes of the klaxon sounding; a Juliet alert meant that we would actually launch. This type of alert was wisely abandoned early on. It just didn't seem provident to have a bunch of psyched up young men in bombers milling around our peaceful skies with nuclear weapons on board. Besides, the B-47 had a well-demonstrated reputation for crashing, and this would be exacerbated by rocket-assisted take-offs at war load gross weights. We had trouble enough flying at training mission weights. Also, any wing that launched its alert force for training was out of the alert picture until the airplanes could be recovered and regenerated, which was no small task.

SAC was very sensitive about these nuclear weapons. The awesome fact, manifested by think tanks such as the Rand Corporation, was that the potential for an accident was so very great as to border on the inevitable. To their credit, the military commanders kept the genie in the bottle. Enormous pressure was kept on the flight crews and other personnel responsible for these weapons to ensure that the cap remained on that bottle.

Even with such intense safety efforts, there were a few very bad scares. During that time, the B-52 was going through teething problems and seemed to have a lot of trouble with leaks in the fuel tanks in the wings. This is was to be expected because those enormous wings were capable of flexing some thirty odd feet at the tips. One evening on alert, while watching the evening news, we were galvanized by the news commentator's announcement that a B-52 had exploded in flight. In the breathless manner that commentators use when trying to hype a story, he continued: "The airplane had been carrying two nuclear weapons, and although one had fallen to earth, it had been a dud. Fortunately, the gallant crew had managed to safely parachute the second bomb to earth." There was a horrified silence for several seconds.

Then a voice said, "Holy Shit! Can you imagine looking up at that humungous parachute with that ugly fucking bomb hanging under it? Can I run fifteen miles in seventy-five seconds? Let's try!"

The fusing and firing circuits had been designed with such a possibility in mind, but in this case, only luck prevailed. It is unavoidable that airplanes do suffer mishaps and occasionally crash. If they are carrying bombs, the bombs get to crash, also. The weapon that free-fell could not detonate because the deploying of the parachute was a necessary step in the firing sequence. The man who speculated on his ability to run miles in seconds knew that the second from the last step in the fusing and firing circuit was the deployment of that parachute. The second weapon descended with the parachute deployed. There was the horrifying possibility that the weapon had correctly completed the steps necessary to arm it. The final step would be for the contained altitude radar to indicate the selected airburst height or for the nose to touch the ground, and that is what prompted his remark. Some believe that the fusing or arming sequence occurred in the proper order and only a faulty battery prevented detonation. We came very close to a thermonuclear explosion in a heavily populated area.

We spent a great deal of time sitting in classrooms studying these weapons, and we had confidence in their safeguards. Even so, we treated them with enormous respect.

Once all of the first day duties were completed, usually by late afternoon, things settled down to dreary boredom. Alert klaxons were mounted on poles along specific alert routes and in the Officer's and Enlisted Clubs in order to give us reasonable run of the base. Any movement outside of the Hurry House required that the crew go as a unit or arrange rides with other crews. We were careful not to abuse our limited freedom. We knew that a foul-up would restrict us all. Most of our reoccurring ground training was scheduled during the weekdays. That helped to pass the time. Thursday was almost always devoted to mission planning for a flight on the Monday after we got off alert. We would go to the mission planning room at the individual squadron buildings to do this.

Winter dragged on. Spring was cold and wet, but gradually the sun crept towards the solstice, and its greater declination forced the bitter winds and snow back to their hiding place in the far north. My chances of advancing to aircraft commander seemed faint. There still were majors riding in the copilot seat and they were far ahead of lieutenants in the line for advancement to the front seat. In desperation, I applied for transfer to just about every airplane the Air Force had. I especially wanted to fly the big transports of Military Airlift Command. But each application was returned to me disapproved by the Deputy Commander for Operations. My requests were not even getting off the base, and the remarks scribbled across the returned requests were growing steadily terser. I did not know it, but the winds of change were stirring with the seasons.

SIX

♦♦♦♦♦♦

They gave their merry youth away
for country and for God.
- Winifred M. Letts

Take-off performance was critical for the B-47. As seemed to be military habit, the weight of the airplane was increased dramatically over its design weight. Originally, the B-47's designed maximum take-off weight was165,000 lbs. That weight limit was raised to 221,000 lbs. during the Cold War by installing a stronger landing gear and other make-do fixes, in all an increase of nearly a third. Power was slightly increased, but the airplane still required several miles of runway to stagger into the air. A heavy weight take-off on a hot summer day would bring even the most agnostic airman closer to God. The basic airplane structure suffered. In-flight structural failure was not uncommon, especially after the airplane's design mission was changed from a high altitude bomber to a low level bomber following the Russian introduction of the SA2 surface-to-air missile. During an attack, bombers would be forced to fly under radar coverage. Russia's ability to shoot down highflying aircraft was dramatically demonstrated on May 1, 1960 when they shot down Gary Francis Powers in a very highflying U-2. During high speed, low-level practice flights, the B-47's thin and flexible wings were severely stressed. Huge, external wing tanks, added to increase range, exacerbated the stress problem.

*****

On a warm and humid July morning, three bomber crews gathered in Base Operations. They had completed the major portion of the mission paperwork several days earlier while on alert. It was their intent to take off one minute apart and fly in cell formation to meet three tankers some hour and ten minutes after take-off. Upon completing in-flight refueling, the cell would break up, and they would go their separate ways. The mission also included an annual flight check for the navigator of the lead airplane.

The copilot of this crew was a young Lieutenant who had not completed his training to combat ready status. During the flight preparations, he seemed unsure of himself. It was one of his tasks to compute the take-off data. In the several days between the mission planning and the flight, the aircraft had been changed and the planned fuel load increased several tons over the planned take-off weight. Added to the increase in weight was a radical change in the predicted weather. A warm air mass had moved over the eastern portion of Nebraska and the temperature was fifteen degrees higher than anticipated. For any practical purpose, the take-off data that the Lieutenant had computed several days earlier was useless. He was caught completely unprepared, and he wasted precious time trying to salvage his computations when it would have been much easier to discard them and start fresh. He did not ask his aircraft commander for help. His AC, a Captain, was concentrating on briefing his flight for the departure, join up, and refueling formation. The other two copilots in the flight were experienced. They quickly corrected their computations and went for coffee.

A disaster seldom is the result of a single incident. Almost without exception, a chain of events precipitates a catastrophic accident. The aircraft change was one of these events. At the last minute, maintenance workers had found an electrical problem on the airplane intended for the flight. Another airplane was substituted. It was SAC practice to keep all airplanes fueled when on the ground. This saved both tank space for fuel storage and time should aircraft be needed for an emergency. The substituted aircraft had a fuel load three thousand pounds heavier than the planned aircraft. It also had a history of problems with the water-alcohol injection system, which injected a mixture of water and alcohol into the engines during take-off and made a significant difference in the amount of runway needed to get off the ground. There was no time to defuel the bomber before the flight. The aircraft commander accepted the heavier fuel load and informed the copilot of the change in both the basic weight of the aircraft and the increase in fuel. The copilot now had to re-compute both the weight and balance or form F and the take-off data. He was not up to the task in the allotted time and was too embarrassed to admit this. The increase in weight precluded a take-off without water injection. The system had to work or the airplane would not take-off from the runway available. The other two airplanes, with their lighter fuel loads, could just make the take-off using dry thrust. For them, the water-alcohol provided a safety margin.

On the crew bus that took the three flight crews to their airplane, the young copilot attempted to compare his take-off computations with one of the other copilots. He saw that the older copilot had written a second set of numbers in the margin of his work sheet and he started to copy them onto his notes, but the bus arrived at his airplane before he could complete the notes. It was his unfortunate luck that his airplane was parked close to Base Operations and, as a consequence, the first stop for the crew bus. He also failed to notice that a lighter weight was used for the computations of the other airplane. Two more seemingly inconsequential events were in place.

The instructor navigator, who was to check the crew navigator, must have noticed the copilot's confusion. He was assigned to the Standardization division, and it was his job to observe and evaluate the navigator. He was also trained to be a keen observer of all of the crews' activities. It is almost certain that he intended to inform his boss that this copilot would not be ready for his check ride two weeks in the future. It would be far better to delay the copilot,s check flight and provide further training than to allow him to proceed with a check flight that seemed certain to end in failure. It takes a long time for a crewmember to live down that sort of a black mark on his professional record. He must have made a mental note to ask that the copilot's training records be reviewed. Apparently, the aircraft commander had also assumed that his copilot knew what he was doing, for he had made no attempt to check his work.

The wind was light and variable when the three airplanes assembled at the northwest end of the runway. They would take-off to the southeast, as the wind seemed to favor that direction. The instructor navigator sat on a jump seat just aft of the entrance hatch and about level with the copilot's rudder pedals. He could see nothing but sky from this position, and then, only by looking straight up through the top of the canopy. After the airplane was off the ground, he would move to a forward position just to the left of the navigator.

At exactly the appointed time, the bomber began its take-off roll. The pilots in the other two airplanes saw and heard the power come up and then abruptly return to idle. They heard the pilot announce to the tower that he had aborted the take-off because the water injection failed to start. They also heard him announce that he would "go dry." Both of the other crews were aware that they had the ability to make a dry take-off, if necessary. They were not aware that the lead airplane was carrying a heavier fuel load. The lead airplane turned off at the first taxiway and returned to the end of the runway. The tower had cleared him for a second attempt. The hammerhead, or waiting area at the end of the runway, was wide enough to allow the lead airplane to pass the other two and roll onto the runway. They noticed that he was taxiing fast and completely compressed the left outrigger strut as he turned onto the runway. As he started his take-off roll, the pilot of the second airplane noticed that the windsock alongside the runway was indicating a slight wind from the northwest. The light and variable wind had now become a tailwind. The final factor was in place. Disaster was assured. One can imagine the feelings of that crew when the last runway marker flashed past and the airspeed indicator told them that the airplane could not fly. In desperation the pilot tried to force the plane into the air, but the increased angle of attack as he raised the nose also increased the drag. The airplane staggered off the ground, cleared the perimeter fence, bounced once and, at eighteen minutes after eight on a pleasant summer morning, crashed and exploded into an ugly black and orange fireball. All four men on board died instantly.

The Supervisor of Flying was ordered by the Command Post to check the runway for debris. When none was found, the remaining two airplanes of the flight were ordered to take-off. Their flight path took them through the black smoke cloud boiling into the sky from the crash site. They did not get credit for an on time take-off. The crash trucks had trouble reaching the site of the crash. Curious citizens had blocked the only dirt road that came near the scene with their cars. Four men and a multi-million-dollar bomber passed from the Air Force rosters into the dim and forgotten history of the Cold War.

SEVEN

◆◆◆◆◆◆◆◆◆◆

A politician thinks of the next election;
a statesman, of the next generation.
-James Freeman Clarke

Two and a half weeks later, without warning, I received orders transferring me to the 28th Air Refueling Squadron at Ellsworth Air Force Base in South Dakota. For three months I would be TDY, or temporary duty en-route, at the school for KC-135 training in California. I could not believe my incredible good fortune.

Some months before, I had been sent to Spain on a reflex trip. Since the airplanes stayed at the forward bases longer than the crews did, we did not always fly our own airplanes over. That was the case on that trip. With a number of other crewmembers, I made the trip as a passenger in a KC-135. During the flight I wandered up to the flight deck. The aircraft commander was a young first lieutenant; the copilot was a second lieutenant. The cockpit was spacious. The two pilots went about their duties in a quiet and relaxed manner. I reflected on how little chance I had of advancing to aircraft commander of a B-47 and was instantly consumed with envy. I went back to my seat in the passenger compartment thinking just how small the chances were for me to fly a fine airplane such as this one. Now I had the orders in my hand assigning me to that airplane. It seems that the 307th Bomb Wing had been tasked by SAC personnel to supply several copilots for training in tankers. My guess was that, because I had made my wishes known far and wide that I wanted to fly anything other than the B-47, the decision was made to get rid of such an unhappy person. Within a couple of weeks I loaded three little kids (one in diapers), a three-month-old collie pup, and a very exhausted wife (who had done all the packing and dealing with movers, while I spent my final days at Lincoln on alert), into the car and headed for Merced, California. I left Lincoln behind without a single regret.

In the usual manner of the military, I was allowed just adequate travel time, no extra for finding a house or other family needs. At this time in military history the prevailing attitude was, if the government had wanted you to have a family, they would have issued you one. The country was just two decades out of World War II and poised for World War Three. There was little time or patience on the part of the military commanders for families. No matter what the needs of my family were, I had a specific reporting date at Castle Air Force Base and, come hell or high water, I had best be there. To the scheduling staff at Lincoln I was just another copilot and they utilized me as a body to fill an alert sortie until the last possible minute.

As we made our way across Utah, we met with an enormous piece of luck. Somewhere in the long stretches of that state filled with eye-aching sunshine, I stopped at a remote gas station for fuel. It was a typical desert gas station set a hundred yards back from the two-lane highway. An eastbound car pulled in on the other side of the pumps. It was not difficult to recognize a military family traveling. Several kids were bouncing around in the back seat and the wife had that vague look of just barely being able to hold things together. When the driver got out and started filling his own tank, his close crewcut confirmed my guess that he was in the military. In a moment, I struck up a conversation with the friendly driver while his wife shyly nursed an infant.covering the baby and her breast with a baby blanket. The young lieutenant had just graduated from the school I was on my way to attend. He had rented a three-bedroom, furnished house about a mile from Castle Air Force Base. That sounded too good to be true. He gave me the owner's name and phone number and I called from a dust-clogged pay phone before I left the gas station. The owner promised to hold the house for me for three days. That gave me enough time to get there.

Colonel Hauser was a retired flight instructor from Castle. He understood that the military was unable to provide housing for the hundreds of students passing through the training pipeline and had bought up several houses as rentals. He had furnished them completely, including dishes, pots and pans, and he rented only to students going through the school. His rent was no more than the housing allowance provided by the military. His tenants stayed three months at the most, which was the time it took to complete the training, but he never had a problem with a renter and his houses were seldom vacant for more than a few days. I have always been grateful for his resourcefulness. He understood the demands made on SAC aircrew and how valuable time was that could be spent with families.

*****

I began my love affair with a great airplane. The KC-135 was developed from the Boeing 707 airliner series. It had been designed with the intention of extending the range of strategic bombers. Its outline was the same as the 707 except that it had what looked like a long piece of four-inch pipe attached at the aft end of the body underside. The end of this pipe had a set of vanes on it that resembled small wings. This was the flying boom and the reason for the airplanes existence. It allowed fuel to be transferred, in flight, to another airplane. Few had any idea of the many tasks this airplane could perform. Like many other airplane designs, the KC-135 would find itself employed in tasks that had not been anticipated during its gestation. Although built by the same company that designed and built the B-47, it had none of the bombers bad habits. The tanker came on line in 1956. It is still in service today although none have been produced for decades. Some of the crews flying tankers today were not born when I flew those very same airplanes. None who flew this airplane disliked it. It is strong, safe, and reliable and would get you home when other airplanes would fail. It is very easy to fly. Several times the airplane did scare the cockiness out of me, but I brought those situations on myself.

The meager flying skills I had graduated with as a cadet had suffered after more than four years in the B-47. I had to relearn a lot of stick and rudder. More than four years in the back seat of that bomber, with only an occasional take-off or landing, had eroded my sparse flying skills. On one occasion I was starting an instrument approach and, for some reason looked back over my shoulder at the vast cargo deck stretching into the distance, andI wondered how the hell I was going to get all this stuff back on the ground.

The instructor noticed my concern and said, "Don't worry about all that trash. Just take that steering wheel wherever you want to go. All the rest of this junk is attached and it will just follow right along."

I was pretty sure that there was a little more to it than that, but it turned out to be almost as easy an airplane to fly as he alleged.

My three months at Castle were a pleasant interlude. I soon regained enough of my skills to do a passable job of flying the tanker. The instructors were accustomed to B-47 copilots being short on most flying skills, and wasted little time getting their skill levels back up. They understood that these copilots might excel at gunnery, electronic countermeasures, and navigation but had little opportunity to actually fly an airplane during their stay in the B-47 program. The academics were easy after having had to learn the bomber's systems. There was no alert to stand. We did do some night flying but for the most part it was a vacation after crew duty in a bomber.

As I approached the end of my training and was occupied with exams and check flights, Lyndon Johnson defeated Barry Goldwater in the 1964 presidential election. The country feared the hawkish stance of Goldwater. Meanwhile, until the election was over, the Johnson camp furiously tried to keep the lid on the escalation of hostilities in Vietnam and the active part U. S. forces were taking. Two U.S. destroyers, the Maddox and the C. Turner Joy, were churning up the waters of the Tonkin Gulf in a furious battle with shadows. No enemy was ever sighted in this night engagement. Johnson, eager to retaliate against this non-attack, asked Congress for and received extraordinary powers in the Tonkin Gulf Resolution.

The intentional paucity of public information set the stage for the awful struggle in Southeast Asia. Johnson, unenlightened in the skills of foreign policy, heeded poor counsel and led us into a needless war that was micro-managed to an insane degree. A war that would cost America more than fifty five thousand lives, untold treasure, and international credibility, all in the sacred name of his personal political power.

All too soon my happy time at school came to an end and I was granted a thirty-day leave before reporting to my operational squadron. This was the only leave longer than two weeks that I enjoyed in my entire Air Force career. Since both my family and Carol's lived in the same New England town and the holiday season was approaching, there was only one thing to do: drive all the way across the country to Boston and then a drive two thirds of the way back to western South Dakota where my new base was located. And the driving would be done in wintertime with three small children and a dog in the car. What incredible optimists the young are!

Time seemed compressed as I worked my way through my final flight checks and written exams, while planning the trip. It became obvious that I would have to drive all the way south to Bakersfield to get around the Sierras. The highway over Donner Pass closed early that year, which should have warned me that I was in for an unpleasant trip. With all of these things on my mind, I paid little attention to the pot beginning to boil in Southeast Asia. I would have been uneasy had I known some of the places that I would have to take the airplane that I was growing to think so much of. I assumed that once I left the bomber force MIGs, surface-to-air missiles and anti-aircraft guns would no longer concern me. Combat was not on my mind. I had visions of clear skies, long runways, and pleasant bases in friendly parts of the world. I had had a career's worth of excitement and close calls crammed into the past four-and-a-half years and I was looking forward to some plain flying. I was blissfully unaware that just three months before I entered this school, KC-135s operating out of the Philippines had begun supporting tactical air operations over Vietnam, and that these tanker operations were to grow at an exponential rate. With this rose-colored view of the world, I stuffed kids, dog, and household goods into the car and with a slightly rested wife, headed for New England.

That next month passed with what seemed like a never-ending series of storms, icy roads, sick kids, and indifferent motels. Out of the month, we managed to spend eight days visiting families.

The snow squeaked under my tires as I finally drove into the transient-housing parking lot at Ellsworth Air Force Base. It was late in the afternoon on a clear, cold, January day. The air was still and very dry. Clouds of condensed breath hovered about our faces. The shadows were beginning to grow long as the sun descended behind the Black Hills. Rapid City lay fourteen miles away. I hoped that I would be able to get rooms for the night on base. Luck was with us. I checked into a double room on the first floor. We stuffed the children into their snowsuits and wrapped the baby in blankets for the short journey from the car to the transient quarters. One problem presented itself. Pets were not allowed and the temperature was heading for twenty below that night. The little collie mix might not survive the night in the car. As soon as the sun had set I went out to the car, got the dog, and passed him through the window to my wife. He was a well-behaved animal and slept quietly on the floor next to our bed. In the morning, after I had taken the family to breakfast and returned them to our rooms, I reported to the squadron and got most of my in-processing done. Within a few days I had found a little house in town and was settled into the 28th Air Refueling Squadron. Carolyn was busy setting up our home. It was fiercely cold but no different from the Nebraska winters that we were used to.

While I learned to work with my new crew, two major tanker missions were growing in Southeast Asia: Arc Light and Young Tiger. Arc Light supported the B-52 bombing raids that originated at Guam, and the Young Tiger missions supported tactical air operations that involved all of the Air Force strikes against the North. Both missions involved every SAC crewmember and all of the maintenance people for the next seven years. This tremendous buildup of air operations would sorely tax the six hundred and twenty-five-odd tankers that the Air Force had, for they still were committed to supporting the strategic war plan. The crews of the 28th ARS soon realized that they would either be on alert at Ellsworth or flying missions in Southeast Asia.

Summer was just starting to get pleasant when I found myself headed west across the Pacific. At the same time, my cadet classmate, Don Hawley arrived at Hurlbert Field to begin training as a Forward Air Controller. He would be in Vietnam in a matter of a few months. He would not return alive. As in all wars and great battles, I had no more idea of the "big picture" than some young soldier had trudging across the Wheat Field at Gettysburg. But like all the others in uniform, I was a full-time soldier, and once you have "taken the King's Shilling," you no longer get to choose your war, no matter the stridency of the college demonstrators.

*****

The Rockies were soon behind us and Neil Voshell began the descent that brought us over Lake Tahoe and the familiar Sierras, heavy with the past winter's snow, to Castle. He was my aircraft commander, a tall lanky man with straight, blond hair and a friendly manner. He walked in a casual way, as if all of his joints were just a bit loose, and he was not given to an excess of military protocol or too much in the way of idle chatter. Somewhere on his person he usually had a rumpled package of Redman chewing tobacco. He also was an excellent pilot. We would stop at Castle long enough to refuel and file our flight plan to Hawaii. Besides Neil and myself, the crew consisted of Second

Lieutenant Joe McNeil, our navigator who was fresh out of the advanced navigation school at Mather Air Force Base, and Sgt. Bill Web, our boom operator.

The voice of approach control on the radio jarred me out of my sightseeing. "Banjo three seven, right turn now to heading two seven zero, descend pilot's discretion to three thousand two hundred, expect localizer intercept in one six miles, cleared ILS approach to runway three zero, report established on the localizer."

I glanced at Neil to see if he had understood the clearance. He spit a stream of tobacco juice into the paper cup sitting in front of the rudder trim knob, shifted his plug of Redman to his left cheek, eased the throttles back and nodded. This cryptic message directed us to an altitude and heading that would intercept an electronic flight path which, if properly flown, would lead us to a point over the end of the runway and at just the right altitude to allow us to simply close the throttles and land.

"Roger, Approach," I answered, "out of seven for three point two, will report localizer inbound."

I wondered how he kept from splattering tobacco juice all over the cockpit. The ground crew back at Ellsworth routinely made a fifteen-foot detour when working under the nose of the airplane whenever Neil was on board. Two months ago while on a trip to Alaska, our navigator decided that if the "big man" could chew that stuff, he might just give it a try.

"Hey, pilot," he had asked over interphone, "can I try some of that Redman?"

Neil absentmindedly reached into his right leg pocket, pulled out the battered pouch and handed it back to Joe. That was the last that we heard from our faithful navigator for the rest of the trip. I used the radar repeater scope by my left knee to find our way to King Salmon VOR, and from there on into Eielson, it was pretty straightforward. After we landed I got a look at Joe as I was getting out of my seat. His normally healthy complexion had turned a sickly, sage green. He was doubled over, hanging onto the edge of the navigation table, with a cold sweat covering his skin.

He looked up at me as I went by and in a shaky voice asked, "Hey, Art, what do you do with the juice? He apparently had not taken notice of the paper coffee cup that Neil kept handy in front of the rudder trim knob.

Joe had long since recovered, although he had been quiet a full twenty-four hours after that incident. As we made the approach, he was his busy self, calling off the altitudes and stowing away his navigation equipment, including his huge, brass alarm clock, complete with two large bells on top. I don't know if he used that monstrosity instead of the chronometer he had been issued for navigation or if it just was some sort of talisman, but every once in a while the alarm would go off with a shattering clamor that sounded very much like our bail-out bell. Neil had protested on the grounds that the similarity had an unsettling effect on the crew, especially himself, but Joe refused to yield and went into some harangue about the mysteries of navigation being far beyond the understanding of a mere pilot. Overwhelmed by this amount of brass from a very young second lieutenant, Neil had retreated, muttering, to his throttles and fuel valves. Joe was a good navigator and those were a bit hard to come by, so he rated a fair amount of slack in the military department; besides, Neil wasn't a recruiting poster model for the Air Force Academy.

Neil eased the throttles forward slightly and clicked the stabilizer trim button on the control yolk. The altimeter settled on three thousand two hundred. "Flaps thirty," he said, not bothering to spit.

The localizer needle, which represents an electronic projection of the runway centerline, trembled and moved off of the left side of the instrument case. Neil rolled into a gentle right turn and caught the needle in the center of the case with the heading on three hundred.

"Castle Approach, Banjo Three Seven established on the localizer," I reported. The white tower of the Tioga Hotel, in the center of Merced was directly ahead.

"Roger, Three Seven, contact Castle tower two nine four point one when you have the runway in sight."

"Switching now," I said and reached up to the overhead panel and switched comm. one radio to tower frequency. "Castle Tower, Banjo Three Seven, ILS inbound, approaching the outer marker."

"Roger, Three Seven. Have you in sight, cleared to land runway three zero, wind three three zero at eight, altimeter two nine nine four."

The glide slope needle started down from the top of the case. "Flaps forty," Neil said and shifted his plug to the right cheek. As the flaps extended further, he clicked in a little back trim and wiggled the throttles back a little. The outer marker light, which marks the beginning of the final approach, flashed and its beeping tone filled our headsets as the airplane settled into a three hundred and fifty feet per minute descent, on speed and with both ILS needles centered. I checked my ILS instrument for off flags and called out altitude and airspeed. Neil concentrated on instrument flying. No matter what the weather, whichever pilot flew the approach would fly on instruments down to "decision height," while the other took care of checklist chores and kept a watch outside as a safety observer. The altimeter wound down steadily. As it passed through four hundred feet, toward the decision height of three hundred and eighty-nine feet, the rapid beep of the middle marker came loudly through the headphones, as the panel light flashed in sequence with the sound.

"Decision height." Joe, who was monitoring the descent on his own altimeter, echoed my report.

"Going visual, runway in sight, I will land, flaps fifty," Neil said as he shifted from flying by instruments to visual flight. He followed the procedure for this type of instrument approach as if he were in actual instrument conditions. When we reached the point where he must either go around or land, this announcement made his decision clear to the crew and ordered the final flap setting for landing. Again he added some back trim to compensate as the flaps moved to their maximum extension. With a rush, the end of the runway slid beneath the nose. There was a momentary increase in engine sound as it echoed off of the pavement. Neil held the power a few seconds longer as he gently raised the nose to stop the descent. With the airplane in the landing attitude, he moved the throttles back to the idle stops and the wheels rolled onto the ground as the one thousand-foot marker flashed past the wing tips. The engine sound faded to a low whine as he lowered the nose wheel onto the runway and raised the speed brakes. The tankers did not have the engine thrust reversers that the airlines had. To help slow the tanker on landing, large panels on top of the wings were raised to provide some aerodynamic braking. The airplane decelerated steadily with little braking and we turned off the runway at the mid-field taxiway. Neil called for the after-landing checklist and steered to fall in behind the pick-up truck with a large "Follow Me" sign facing backward that scooted in front of us. The Follow Me busily led us to the Base Flight parking area in front of the tower. He seemed awfully redundant, as there wasn't a tanker pilot in the Air Force that hadn't trained at this base and we all could find our way around blindfolded, a frequent occurrence in the winter fog season.

Should we ever land at a base that we had never been to before, there wouldn't be a Follow Me for miles.

Our stop at Castle was planned for two hours. We were informed that we would meet two F-4s over the Farallon Islands forty miles west of the Golden Gate and escort them to Guam. So, we had to calculate our fuel load at the maximum fuel weight for a safe take-off. This was an exercise that I had worked any number of times as a student at this same base, just a few months ago. In ten minutes I had the figures and called the fuel load to Transient Maintenance. As I worked at the flight-planning table rechecking the radio frequencies that I would need, it seemed strange to see instructors that I knew herding students around and checking the accuracy of every calculation they made for their local training missions. Now I understood why these instructors were so fussy over details which, at that time, I had considered trivial. Three airplanes and three flight crews depended on the calculations that I was making to get us across a lot of ocean, and there were no handy alternate airfields should I make a serious mistake or should other problems arise.

Just two hours after our landing we lifted off, cleared by Air Traffic Control, to climb on course directly to San Francisco. Our climb would take us through the descending flight path of all of the civil aircraft arriving at San Francisco from the east. That would make for a busy time for some controller in the Oakland Air Traffic Control Center at Fremont, California. Only the importance of the mission and the tight fuel consideration had justified this direct routing.

We had not quite reached our cruising altitude as we crossed the California coast with its white stripe of surf. Oakland Center advised us that Pablo Flight was one hundred and twenty miles south of us and Joe was watching for their beacon on radar. He had no time for sightseeing as he tried to affect the rendezvous with the two F-4s and get a departure fix from the Farallon Islands as we passed over. Once we were out of range of the TACAN station on the islands, we would have nothing but our sextant to get us to Hawaii. The TACAN station would provide us electronic range and bearing information for about a hundred and seventy-five miles, depending on how high we were. We would be expected to make good our time and position at the ADIZ, or air defense identification zone, a line drawn around the Hawaiian Islands that no aircraft could cross without being positively identified. They still were a little touchy about strange aircraft approaching.   I switched comm. two to the assigned interplane frequency and called up Pablo Flight. Pablo One answered immediately and said he had us on his radar and would fly a pursuit curve to join us—the same curving approach that he would use if he were attacking. That would save us at least one orbit over the islands. Pablo One agreed on a single altitude for our formation. The weather was excellent and we would have no trouble maintaining visual separation. Oakland Center was grateful to hear that we were not going to ask for a block of several thousand feet of altitude in this busy stretch of airspace. Several minutes later an F-4 slid into position just off each wing tip. When the pilots were sure that we had seen them, they slid back into a loose trail, which they would maintain to Hawaii, except for occasional refueling. Joe announced that he had his departure fix and gave me an ETA for one hundred and thirty degrees west longitude. In a minute or two, I had established contact with McClellan Air Ways on our powerful High Frequency radio and closed out with Oakland Center. I acknowledged McClellan's routine order to report every ten degrees of longitude and we were on our way.

Nothing was visible in front of us except the hazy blue line of the horizon. Below, the sea had taken on the deep blue of the open ocean on a sunny day. This close to the entrance to San Francisco Bay, an occasional white line on the surface betrayed the passage of a ship. I finished the level-off check and set the fuel panel. The fuel remaining showed that we were about a thousand pounds behind on the "how goes it graph" but I was sure that we would make that up in our second or third hour. Neil was tinkering with the throttles and trim, trying to find that sweet spot on the step that always gave us just a little better fuel performance than the charts promised. We were still pretty heavy and I didn't think he would be happy until we had burned off another eight or ten tons. Bill Webb got out the sextant stool. He and Joe were already working on the first sun line. They would be busy at their celestial navigation until we made landfall on radar.

More than twenty-three hundred miles of ocean lay between us and Hawaii. Joe would have to hit the ADIZ on the money. He had very little slack in either time or position. It was not unusual for a crew to be returned home as passengers on an east bound tanker for a serious violation of the ADIZ. There were no landmarks that could provide a fix to passing aircraft except Ocean Station November, a ship stationed about halfway between California and Hawaii. Since we were crossing during daylight, Joe would have only sun lines for his navigation, unless he was lucky and either the Moon or Venus were visible to provide him with that vital second line of position. Navigators would much rather make ocean crossings at night when they have a huge selection of stars to choose from and can shoot and plot as many three-star fixes as they need. I would make position reports every ten degrees of longitude, or about every hour and twenty minutes. The UHF radios that we normally used were only practical for line of sight transmissions, so I would have to make my reports on our HF radio. This was a powerful monster that would have launched most amateur radio operators into a fit of ecstasy. But it could be cranky, depending on conditions such as sunspots and time of day. It was not unusual to be unable to work a California station from five hundred miles away, yet still relay clearly through Guam or Alaska.

Pilots on long ocean flights were often bothered by a poltergeist.

It was the "automatic rough syndrome," a term borrowed from airplanes powered with piston engines. As soon as land dropped below the horizon behind the airplane, all four engines would start running rough. Not rough enough to turn back, but just enough so that the roughness could be felt through the throttles and be worrisome to the pilots. Strangely, even jet engines would do this. One of the engines would develop a faint vibration that could be felt in the throttle. No amount of fiddling with engine controls would cure this and it would disappear as soon as land was once again in sight. This phenomenon was not limited to engines. Even the best-maintained airplane would develop strange groans and moans. Creaking sounds would come from the wings and you would be sure that you just saw number four oil pressure gauge flicker, but no matter how long you stared at it, it would not move until you looked away. This was especially true for us, as none of us had crossed the Pacific before and the leg from California to Hawaii was the short leg.

Pablo lead appeared off of our left wing tip. When he could see that Neil was aware of his presence, he made a drinking motion with his right hand and slid back out of sight.

Neil clicked his mike button twice on the UHF radio to indicate that he understood and on interphone said, "Hey, Boom, our chicks want a drink."

"Roger, Sir," Bill replied. "Off interphone and going to the rear." Sergeant Webb disconnected his interphone chord, put on his helmet and connected to a walk-around oxygen bottle. Half a minute later he reported on interphone in the boom pod. We quickly ran the refueling checklist.

"This is lead, how about eight each?"

"No problem," I answered.

"Pablo Two is in pre-contact position," Bill advised over interphone.

The amber light on my fuel panel winked on. "Tanker contact," Bill reported followed at once by "Receiver contact." from Pablo Two.

I started the aft body tank pumps, and in just short of two minutes, he had his eight thousand pounds. "You have eight grand, Pablo Two," I said over UHF.

The amber light flicked off as he disconnected. These guys were not given to a lot of chatter on the radio. Less than a minute passed and the amber light came on again. Again the boom operator and receiver pilot reported contact and again I transferred four tons of fuel. The two big fighters slid back to their silent vigil behind us. Other than acknowledging the positions that Joe radioed to them each time he completed a fix, they were silent.

Sometime past the halfway point, my fuel calculations showed that we were passing the point of no return. We no longer had sufficient fuel to return to the West Coast with the two F-4s. All three airplanes would have to make it to Hawaii or ditch in the ocean.

Far below, cruising slowly in an assigned patch of ocean called Station November, a trim and handsome ship idled along at endurance speed. The original task of these ships was to gather meteorological data. But some years back at an Atlantic Ocean Station, an airliner had run short of fuel and had to ditch in the ocean. It managed to perform this unpleasant feat in close proximity to the U. S. Coast Guard manned Ocean Station vessel on duty in the Bravo area. All eighty-nine aboard the airplane were rescued. The pilot had performed a near impossible feat of ditching a large airplane in the open ocean without injuring anyone on board. Since then the Ocean Station vessels were the sweethearts of airplanes crossing the oceans and their duties evolved into providing navigational fixes to passing aircraft. I called Ocean Station November on UHF and got an answer on the first try. The radio operator on November was used to chatting it up with passing aircraft. Station November lay under the direct route from San Francisco to Hawaii, so he got a lot of business. We talked a minute or two and then

I handed him off to Joe. They chatted for several minutes about bearings and distances. Joe must have been satisfied that November's opinion of our position agreed with his celestial navigation as he made no comment. Joe was doing very well on his first ocean crossing.

Later, when we hit the ADIZ as planned and Honolulu had us on radar, Neil smiled and said on interphone, "Joe, you no longer are restricted to a fifty-mile radius of the base flagpole."

"Thanks, boss. You are most kind." His answer was laconic but I think that he was very pleased with himself.

Radar guided us to Honolulu International Airport. Hickam Field no longer had operating runways. Air Force aircraft shared the civilian runways and taxied the mile or so to Hickam. We landed in formation as a flight of three. This allowed Air Traffic Control to treat us as a single aircraft, which helped with congestion problems and thrilled the tourists as the big tanker and two F-4s touched down together.

A couple of hours later we met with our fighter crews at the Officers' Club. In the course of the usual "do you know so and so" conversation, I learned that Don Irish, whom I hadn't seen since our engine-out landing at Greenville, was in F-4s somewhere and I was able to report on a few of their friends that were in SAC. The fighter jocks treated the news of their friends as if they had been banished to the high arctic and assigned duty driving snow blowers. Assignments to SAC, especially for bombers, were very undesirable; but the voracious appetite of SAC for aircrew kept the pilots of Tactical Air Command on edge. It was a common weapon of TAC squadron commanders to threaten troublesome pilots with a transfer to SAC.

The following morning we were on our way again, our two silent friends ghosting along with us. We had agreed the night before on the amount of fuel to be transferred on each top-off. Whenever they wanted fuel, Pablo lead would appear off the left wing tip. As soon as he saw Neil had noticed him he would make a drinking motion and slide back out of sight. When conversation was absolutely necessary, their speech was reduced to two clicks of the mic button for yes, OK, I understand, I agree, and a whole range of affirmative remarks. When there was nothing for it but to speak, their remarks were masterpieces of monosyllables.

So in this smothering atmosphere, we continued on. There were no more Ocean Station Vessels. Only Wake Island lay under our route. Wake was almost two-thirds of the distance from Hawaii to Guam. We would top off Pablo flight with fuel over Wake and they would proceed on alone to Guam. We would land at Wake and take on about fifty thousand pounds of fuel, since after refueling Pablo flight we would not have enough to make it to Guam. I was looking forward to this stop. The history of the World War II battles at Wake fascinated me and I hoped to get a chance to look around.

Wake island is actually three small islands, but the channels between these islands are so narrow that it appears as one horseshoe-shaped island with the runway of less than ten thousand feet along the longest side. The area inside the horseshoe forms a lagoon. The island is so small I wondered how the American military and civilian defenders found room enough to fight the invading Japanese in December of 1941. The VORTAC, a combination of VOR and TACAN, began to make the needle on our instrument panel nervous as we came into extreme range. After a few uncertain movements, it spun full circle once and stopped, pointing straight ahead. Shortly, the distance indicator locked on at one hundred and seventy-five miles. Ten minutes later the fact that an island was ahead of us was confirmed as a startling white cumulous cloud began to climb above the horizon ahead of us.

As we slowed in the landing rollout, I could see the carcass of a burned out KC-135 lying just off the runway. It appeared to be a fairly recent crash and I had heard nothing about it. Sergeant Webb and I assisted the ground crew with the refueling. They did not have single-point refueling fittings at Wake Island so we had to climb all over the airplane to refuel the tanks individually. Fortunately, we only had to fill the four main wing tanks.

While Neil and Joe were off taking care of the paperwork, I walked out onto the beach and stood next to a bullet-scarred Japanese pillbox. It didn't amount to much more than a piece of three-foot concrete pipe set upright in the ground and covered with a cast concrete top shaped like a hemisphere. It was just big enough for one man to stand inside. I looked out over the ocean and wondered at the emotions of the men who had fought so desperately for this tiny sand spit in the middle of this great ocean. The sun sparkled off the water. The wind was soft and pleasant. In my mind I could see the great armada of Japanese ships coming over the horizon, propelled by the blood lust of a fantastic string of victories. How lonely and desperate the defenders must have felt in December of 1941. For a long time after the capture of this island, the American battle cry had been "Remember Wake Island."

The present returned. I walked back to Banjo Three Seven. Bill Webb was sitting in the shade with his back against the nose tires. The pilot and navigator would be returning soon, and we would have to be on our way to another war, an undeclared war that just didn't seem real. Although its objectives were unclear, even to the politicians directing it, many of us would find out that the bullets were very real. I was eager to get on with it and get it over with. It seemed that, with the forces that we were mustering, it would be a very short war. I had not yet seen the stifling restraints of the insane rules of engagement, rules written by men in pinstriped suits who had not learned that strategic planners had best leave tactics to the generals who spent their lives studying them.

Less than four hours later we landed at Anderson Air Force Base on the north end of the Island of Guam. It was from this island, along with Tinian and Saipan to the north, that the final bombing assault on Japan was made. Anderson now was a busy stop for all air traffic moving between the United States and the Far East. Most of the airline traffic landed at the civilian field outside of Agana, but occasionally a contract carrier, wearing Pan Am or Eastern livery and carrying a load of troops, would be parked in front of Base Operations. There was a great deal of aircraft movement at this base. It seemed that the further west we traveled, the more intense things became. Military aircraft of all types were parked on the ramp and most were bound for Vietnam. We would leave Pablo flight here and, in the morning, we would head northwest to Okinawa.

A little after noon the following day, Kadena Approach radar picked us up over Miyako Jima and we started our descent for landing. As we flew along the West Coast of the island of Okinawa, I stared at the beautiful green landscape that just twenty years earlier had been a savage killing ground. Minutes later the gray beach, where Marines had walked ashore almost unopposed on April Fool's Day, passed under the nose and we touched down on the runway at Kadena Air Base.

For the next three days, we suffered at the hands of the Staff Weenies who made a lie of the word "briefing." In endless and minute detail, they lectured on every aspect of operations in Southeast Asia. After the first hour or so, the newly arrived aircrews sat in numb stupefaction as these staff types worked in relays to smother us in a tsunami of trivia. A ten-minute coffee break was announced when it was obvious that the percentage of aircrew lapsing into a coma exceeded fifty percent. Where they found the material to sustain this effort is one of the mysteries of life that still eludes those who have endured it. One topic was emphasized: prohibited activities. It seemed that any independent thought or action that might be necessary to complete a mission would lead to at least a court-martial, possible loss of career, and certain disgrace. Mission profiles, including routes, altitudes, timing, and fuel off loads, were dictated by the Pentagon whiz kids in Washington. It sounded very different from my ideas of winning wars. In 1942 we were handicapped in the Pacific theater by the unexpected technical superiority of Japanese torpedoes and aircraft, as well as the fact that some of our submarine commanders were not aggressive. The doctrine of the times saw submarines as nothing more than scouts for the fleet, they were not intended as aggressive warships. Peacetime Navy response was harsh if one showed signs of independent thought or even scratched the paint on a warship. This changed rapidly and the more timid submarine commanders were quickly replaced, but it took a little longer to catch up with the very superior Japanese Long Lance torpedoes and some very fine Japanese aircraft. On our trip across the Pacific, I thought of these issues. Surely our country had studied the mistakes of earlier wars and would not repeat them. After graduation from cadets, much of my working hours had been spent in study of the order of battle of the Communist countries. I was confident that we had both technical superiority and superior force. However, the constraints that had been dictated to us seemed to cancel our advantage. I had a very bad feeling about this.

The Officers' Club at Kadena might be likened to Times Square. If you sit there for any length of time, everyone you have known in Air Force aviation will pass through. We occasionally took our meals in the main dining room but our all-out favorite was the Stag Bar. A huge tropical fish tank set in the wall separated the Stag Bar from the main dining room. The bar was in front of the fish tank and supposedly kept it safe from the more exuberant clientele. However, the atmosphere was somewhat diminished when some fighter jock, passing through, dropped a live piranha in the tropical fish tank and the following morning there was nothing but pink tinged water and one piranha in the tank.

Hanging at the end of the bar was a large brass bell, very much like a ship's bell. Should someone enter the stag bar with his hat on, anyone handy to the bell would ring it and the offender would be obligated to buy a round for the house. Should a person, whose inhibitions might be slightly relaxed, ring the bell just to hear it ring, then he too would be obligated to buy a round. There was a row of slot machines that actually paid once in a while, along one wall. A blue fug of tobacco smoke hung constantly in the air and at least one poker game was always in progress.

Dress code did not apply in the Stag Bar so flying suits were common. Women were not welcome; hence the language tended to be on the colorful side. Such barbaric practices were allowed in those days. The menu was the same as in the main dining room but the hours were longer to accommodate the irregular schedules of flight crews. After flights of fifteen hours or more, these flyers disposed of enormous amounts of alcohol along with a killer diet of steak, French fries, and rolls crammed with butter. Should one arrive in the morning hours, an omelet could be had that weighed at least three pounds, one pound of which was cheese. In short, it was an outstanding hangout after many hours in the air.

Finally finished with our arrival briefings, Neil sat at a table in the Stag Bar with several other pilots that he knew from his days at Barksdale. As a mere copilot, I was tolerated and knew enough to keep my own counsel.

"Are they serious with all these restrictions?" Neil asked in a puzzled tone of voice.

"You better believe it!" The man who answered was a large fellow named Alvin, with a face that looked as if he had been standing out in a storm all of his life. Apparently he and Neil had been copilots together at Barksdale Air Force Base. "We got a crew here right now that has been under house arrest while they worked up court-martial paperwork on them." He wiped a beer foam mustache off of his upper lip for emphasis.

"Court-martial? What the fuck did he do, piss in the punch bowl at the base commander's social?" Neil asked in a puzzled voice.

Alvin waved a hand the size of a ping-pong paddle at a couple of others who tried to tell the story at the same time. "No, he saved the ass of a 104 jock that got hit over Haiphong. Seems this guy took some hits at low altitude and started losing fuel. Them 104s don't hold much more fuel than a small dog can piss, so he was hurting bad and hollered for a tanker. The Navy heard him on their radar picket, Red Crown, so they called up for any tanker in the gulf. This guy was the only one up there that day with a basket on the boom, you know 104s aren't set up with a receptacle, just a probe. So our boy figures this guy is going to have to punch out over downtown Haiphong unless he does the job he's there for. There was all kinds of TAC air in the neighborhood, so he whistles up a couple of fighter types that are only too happy to fly cover for him and goes after the 104. The dude is down to only a few thousand feet, so every kid with a twenty-two is shooting at them along with all the heavy stuff. He finds the 104 and gets some go juice to him and they get the hell out of there. He then flies with this guy all the way back to Danang and drops him off. When he gets back to Kadena he spills his guts at intelligence debriefing, thinking he'd done what he was supposed to do. The next thing he knows, he and his crew are restricted to quarters pending court-martial for violating the rules of engagement."

"That's fucking insane," Neil gasped. "How'd he get out of it?"

Alvin tipped his head back and swallowed two thirds of a glass of beer; "The TAC general back stateside got wind of the story and called SAC headquarters. I guess he wanted to hang medals all over this guy and that kinda put the legal beagles back at Fort Fuckup in an embarrassing position so they just decided to drop it."

"What the hell are we doing over here, anyway? You mean to tell me someone gets in trouble and we can't help?" Neil asked angrily.

"Old son," Alvin said solemnly, "let me tell you just where the bear shits in the buckwheat. Nobody does nothing without the man in the oval office or his whiz kids giving permission. By the time you get permission, the guy you're trying to help is either dead or a POW, which is about the same thing. To make it worse, they pretend that there ain't no such thing as POWs. It is embarrassing to those pinstripe-suited bastards if you get shot down and captured. You remember that code of conduct crap you had to memorize in cadets? Well, my friend, that applies to you and God help you if you fail it, but it don't mean a damn thing to some piece of shit politician chasing pussy all over Washington."

Alvin was on a roll. Several others tried to agree but he talked right over them. "If you stay here at Kadena you're in good shape because you'll be flying ARC Light missions, which is almost like stateside flying except they still are using that damned point-parallel rendezvous. That's a major cluster fuck when you got thirty bombers and thirty tankers trying to refuel all at once in the middle of a herd of thunderstorms. But if you go to Thailand, you will be flying Young Tiger missions. That means refueling Thuds and F-4s. These guys are getting hurt on a regular basis, especially the Wild Weasels, and there are a lot of times a tanker can save someone's ass. You do what you gotta do but keep your fucking mouth shut about it or your balls will be nailed to the flagpole while some asshole plays 'To the Colors' on a bugle." The bartender had heard this topic argued many times and was on his way with a tray of drinks for the table when Alvin finally stopped for breath.

Busy with my own problems, I had not paid much attention to politics beyond the homogenized, fortified, and filtered versions provided by television news analysts. I went to grade school on Bunker Hill and still felt the influence of the ghosts of that forgotten battle. Someone from my family had fought in every war this country had engaged in and I was very much aware of this. To imagine national leaders acting with less than honor was unthinkable. The discussions I heard from those involved in this war seemed to border on blasphemy, but I still could not understand why we were in a war that Congress had not declared. I thought we had learned our lesson in Korea. It seemed that the Johnson administration was having trouble with that question themselves. I had a lot to learn.

EIGHT

◆◆◆◆◆◆◆◆◆

A little group of willful men, representing no opinion but their own
have rendered the great Government of the United States helpless
and contemptible.
-Woodrow Wilson

Takhli Royal Thai Air Force Base lies one hundred and twenty-five miles north of Bangkok, not far from the area where allied prisoners of World War II were enslaved by the Japanese to build a railroad. The radio code name of the base, King Cobra, was quite apropos. As the monsoon season of 1965 drew near, construction to expand the base went on at a furious pace. All this activity disturbed the indigenous fauna, which consisted mainly of snakes that frequently found their way into unlikely places in search of new homes. Takhli, a former Japanese fighter base, now hosted the F-105, a big single engine jet originally designed to deliver tactical nuclear weapons. As so often happens with military equipment, the Thud was put to a use that it was not intended for. Its new role was that of a low-altitude fighter bomber much like that of it's grandfather the P-47 Thunderbolt. Republic called this airplane the Thunder Chief; the pilots, who as usual ignored the public relations efforts of both the manufacturer and the Air Force at naming airplanes, called it the Thud for the sound it made as it hit the ground, but Thud aircrews were intensely loyal to their airplanes.

The area all around Hanoi harbored intense concentrations of anti-aircraft weapons. To the northwest of Hanoi was a ridge of hills that had a particularly intense concentration of anti-aircraft batteries and missile sites. Losses were very high in this area, and the pilots named these hills Thud Ridge. Although the F-105 weighed as much as a loaded Flying Fortress of World War II, the Thud had just one engine, an engine that could be sensitive to damage. In some cases a hit led to progressive destruction of the engine and rapidly turned the airplane into a lead sled.

Those who flew the Thud from Tahkli had a difficult mission, for this was the first Southeast Asian home of the Wild Weasels. It was the lot in life of these men to go into unfriendly places in their airplanes, seek out surface-to-air missile sites and anti-aircraft batteries, and attack them in advance of other strike aircraft. I suspect that the genesis of the Wild Weasel mission was the roving attacks on German flak towers by allied fighters in the European theater during World War II. Such tactics and technology, at this early stage of the war, were quite primitive and the loss rate for the Wild Weasels was horrific. The technology may have been primitive for the job but it was what they had. It was a new concept and we would pay for its advancement with the lives of the crews.

Aircrew who found themselves afoot in hostile areas were hunted assiduously by enemy forces. An enormous effort, called a RESCAP, was set in motion to rescue the downed airman. All of our parachutes had a built in radio that started transmitting a siren sound as soon as the parachute opened. The distress signal was on guard frequency, which all airplanes monitored. The sound resembled the whooping siren that Naval Destroyers use. It was a powerful sound that reverberated in headphones, invoked instant attention, and haunted the dreams of those who had heard it for the remainder of their lives. Tankers had a radio receiver originally intended to home in on the radio signals of other aircraft for refueling operations. It turned out to be ideal for homing in on the distress signal from a descending parachute. Any navigator within range and worth the title would have a couple of quick bearings turned into a fix by the time the distressed pilot reached the ground. The problem was that tankers were not supposed to enter hostile airspace. Tankers did not have armor plate or self-sealing fuel tanks and were considered by SAC as too valuable to risk. Developed solely to refuel long-range strategic bombers, they too would evolve to play a role that was not contemplated during their conception.

All of our training in air-refueling tactics for both bombers and fighters was rigidly outlined in what was called Tactical Doctrine. This was published in a red covered book with the word SECRET stamped prominently on both front and back covers. Each training quarter we were required to record a certain number of hours spent in diligent study of this document. It was the most incredibly boring collection of pages covered with print and diagrams that I have ever encountered. The chapter covering refueling procedures was filled with intricate diagrams of orbits and little tiny airplanes arriving at rendezvous in perfect formation. Some staff officer had spent a great deal of time writing this, but he had not anticipated the tactics of this war. It was mandatory in application and bereft of practical guidance for such contingencies as turbulence, horrible weather, battle-damaged receiver aircraft, wounded pilots, and such distractions as anti-aircraft missiles and artillery or, Heaven forbid, hostile fighters. In short, it had nothing to do with the war that we were involved in. Thus, when we took our tankers to war, we were on our own, and as frequently happens, had to develop tactics to meet the needs of the present situation.

It was a stroke of good fortune that promotion-seeking staff officers sought positions in the bombing side of SAC operations. Having a record of staff duty on the tanker side was not very glamorous and lacked the benefit of medals and ribbons, thus was not desirable for one seeking the recognition of promotion boards. Our happy command situation prevailed until 1970 when the bombing operation became burdened with a surfeit of colonels seeking a star. SAC colonels needing combat time on their records began to seek staff positions in tanker operations. Until that time the highest-ranking people in tanker operations were lieutenant colonels. Most were squadron commanders and operations officers who deployed with their squadrons and frequently flew missions with their crews. They knew what was going on and knew that it was best if they used a trick of their political masters and retained "plausible deniability," so they simply were "unaware" of our stretching the rules of engagement. It was this unusual military situation that allowed the tanker force to evolve into the powerful force multiplier that it has become.

Since fighters normally were not shot down in friendly areas, the pilot fortunate enough to make it safely to the ground depended on rescue from above. It was imperative to get air cover over the downed pilot before hostile troops reached him. Once on the ground it would be very difficult for a fast-mover, as the fighters were called, to see him, especially as he would have to make himself quickly inconspicuous.

Once aircraft were overhead protecting him, they would use up their fuel at a rapid rate. Jets just are not very fuel efficient at low altitudes. Time was critical. Tactical Air Command pilots would go to any length to get their man back, but they couldn't do it without fuel, and flying back to the sky over Thailand to meet a tanker took an unacceptable amount of time. The choice was simple. The tanker aircraft commander could ignore the pleas of the fighter pilots trying to protect their downed comrade or he could ignore the rules of engagement. The first choice would almost certainly lead to the capture or death of an American airman. The second choice could very well lead to the rescue of that downed airman, but if discovered by Washington would lead to the possible court-martial and loss of career for the tanker crew. Few tanker crews anguished over this decision for any length of time, they simply did what was necessary.

The genesis of this mind-set arose from an incident that occurred on the 6th of June, 1964. An RF-8A Crusader of VFP-63 from the carrier Kitty Hawk and piloted by Lt. Charles F. Klusmann was shot down while on a photo-reconnaissance mission. This was not Lt. Klusmann's first encounter with anti-aircraft fire. Two weeks prior to this incident his F-8 had been hit, but he had managed to nurse the damaged airplane back to the Kitty Hawk. However on this encounter his luck ran out. The airplane was struck by 37mm anti-aircraft fire over the main supply road leading from North Vietnam westward into the Plain of Jars. He managed to limp along for a few miles, but finally ejected. His wingman, Lt. Jerry Kuechmann called for help and flew cover until driven off by anti-aircraft fire. A rescue force was launched from the U.S. fleet in the Gulf of Tonkin and was driven back. Admiral Harry Felt, commander of the U.S. forces in the Pacific during the build up, notified then Secretary of Defense, Robert McNamara, that he was launching a second attempt to rescue Klusmann. McNamara directed Felt to stand down. Admiral Felt refused, and with the courage of his convictions, demanded to speak with President Johnson. To Johnson's credit, he overruled McNamara and gave Admiral Felt the go-ahead to try to get his pilot out. It was too late for Lt. Klusmann. During the delay of the second attempt, he was captured by Pathet Lao forces. The unstoppable Klusmann, not happy with his accommodations, escaped three months later, and after two days of hide-and-go-seek, was rescued.

When word of the attitude of McNamara and his advisers towards the first RESCAP of the war spread, it did little to win the affections of the men that they had sent to war. It was plain to all of us that we were simply assets to be expended as necessary, much as a gun or a tank could be consumed, and when damaged, simply abandoned. This kind of thinking led to an "us against them" attitude that endured long after the end of the war.

The Tactical fighter-bombers were held in rigid control by the Johnson administration. McNamara and his whiz kids determined their targets, routes, and altitudes and they were very unimaginative in their planning. Day after day they would order strikes at the same time, at the same altitude, and on the same routes. Commanders in the field were not consulted and many a pilot had his airplane shot to pieces trying to hit a free-standing privy surrounded by anti-aircraft artillery and missile sites that were manned by troops who knew not only what time the strike would come, but at what altitude and from what direction. When the mistakes made in Washington were brought to the attention of those in power, they would demonize and discredit the messenger, then lie to the public and the president.

The aircrews' determination to leave no one behind no matter what the rules said became thoroughly entrenched. In the years that followed, it developed into a rapid and efficient rescue operation. It is to the everlasting shame of the government that this loyalty and determination was not embraced by the political leadership and extended to the hundreds who were abandoned to endless captivity after the war.

We had not been long at Tahkli before a mission supporting fighters put us to the test of action

*****

Orange Anchor three one climbed sluggishly in the humid tropical air. The big tanker, glutted with fuel, was accompanied by four Thuds. They were working hard to climb as each was carrying a huge load of ordinance. Our northeasterly heading would take us to the Orange Anchor refueling area on the Mekong River just east of Vientiane. Pre-strike refueling was planned for fourteen thousand feet. Mid-level cumulous clouds appeared with bases at about ten thousand feet. As our formation reached the height of these clouds, we picked a path through them with a series of S turns. The minor maneuvers were of no consequence to the four Thuds who flew, two on each side of our tanker, as if attached by some invisible means. It is unlikely that the heavily loaded airplanes would be able to get much higher by the time we reached the assigned anchor. Off to the east the radar site "Brigham" idly noted our passage.

"Take the airplane, Art." Neil turned the flight controls over to me, fiddled with the throttles for a moment or two, then slid his seat back and put his feet up on the rail under the instrument panel. He yawned and reached into his leg pocket for his pouch of Redman. Joe applied himself assiduously to his charts and did not ask for any of Neil's chewing tobacco. His talisman, the huge brass alarm clock, sat incongruously on the nav table. Its large hands were just indicating noon.

The fighter flight leader's voice came over the UHF radio. "Hey, Orange Anchor, our heading at end AR will be zero four five."

Neil reached forward and clicked his mic button twice. He said nothing.

"Looks like those boys are going to the big city," Joe said. "Boom, it's getting to be that time."

Sergeant Webb checked off interphone for the rear of the airplane. Neil stretched, slid his seat forward, and took back control of the airplane. We quickly ran the refueling checklist, and the first of our fighters moved into pre-contact position. The boom operator lay on a pallet near the aft end of the cargo compartment. He reached up and moved a lever that raised a section of the underside of the airplane giving him a clear view behind and below. The refueling boom was lowered from its stowed position against the underside of the airplane and a set of small, wing-like vanes, operated by the boom operator, controlled its movement. As the receiving airplane moved into position with its slip-way doors open to expose the refueling receptacle, Sergeant Webb carefully extended the boom, guided by the vanes, into the receptacle where a set of latches held it in place. Once contact was established the copilot controlled the flow of fuel from the fuel panel on the flight deck.

"Pilot, we are at the anchor, you can start your left turn to two one zero." Joe said. This would establish the airplane in the racetrack pattern called Orange Anchor.

"Negative, Nav, I'm coming right to zero four five. These guys are going to be hurting before this day's over. We'll run in another fifty miles with them."

I glanced across at Neil. He said nothing. I pointed at a line of blue-gray mountains ahead of us and said, "Those top out at a little over nine thousand."

The "contact made" light came on and I started the fuel transfer. The other three fighters huddled close just off each wing tip. As each one replaced the fuel used since take-off, they changed places with one of the others in the flight. There was no talk on the radio. We must have been making an enormous radar return but there wasn't any need to advertise further with a bunch of radio chatter. It took just about fifty miles to top off all four of them. They pulled out ahead of us and sped off to the northeast in a finger four formation. Neil slowed the airplane to an economical cruise speed and turned back towards the southwest. The sky to the north was clear with just a little haze. The fair weather cumulous that we had wound our way through ended at the Mekong River, and below us, the land was a startling green with patches of brown where jungle had been cleared. A dirt road wandered off to the east. There was no other sign of life and the land seemed very peaceful. Since we were scheduled to refuel the same Thuds on their way home, I assumed that Neil intended to orbit in the Orange Anchor area until our boys returned. But about ten minutes before they were due, he spit his chewing tobacco into a paper cup and without a word left the orbit once again to take up a heading of zero four five.

A minute or so before we reached the point where we had turned back earlier some broken speech started coming in on refueling frequency. I could pick out the words, "....engine...hit...fuel...can't." We were obviously too far away for good reception.

"Nav, get on that." Neil ordered.

I reached up and switched the ARA-25 onto comm. one. The number one needle immediately swung to just left of the nose. Neil turned to put the needle on the nose and Joe scribbled furiously trying to plot bearings. I could see across the hills now to the Plain of Jars. Neil pushed the throttles up, and we started making speed straight north. Suddenly voice transmissions on comm. one started coming in clearly. We could here number three of the flight talking to the lead. His engine was hit and was rapidly turning itself into expensive scrap.

"Three, this is Lead, can you make it back to the river?"

"No chance, boss, I'm going to have to punch out now. I have an engine fire warning light and the mill is winding down."

"OK, Three, this is Indian country. We'll cover you as long as possible." Seconds later the siren sound of a deployed parachute blasted over guard frequency.

"Four, this is Lead. He has a good chute. You head south and see if you can raise our tanker on the radio and ask him if he'll come north a bit. We're all going to need fuel bad. Two and I will cover Three. Call Brigham and tell them we're gonna need some help up here!"

Neil broke in on the radio, "This is Orange Anchor Three One. We are due south of you, just coming over the Plain. Where do you want me to park?"

"Son of a bitch! Am I glad to hear your voice. Four, continue south and join up with the tanker. Cover him and see if you can get him in orbit about ten clicks south of us. Orange Anchor, none of us will have enough fuel to get home if we cover Three. How much have you got to spare?"

Neil eyed the fuel totalizer. "What do you think, copilot?"

"It's just about four hundred miles from their position to Takhli," Joe added.

With a quick check of the fifteen-thousand-foot range chart I said, "At the weight, we'll be down too and at this altitude we'll need fifteen thousand pounds to get home with no reserve."

"OK, that'll be our bingo fuel. If we get into trouble we'll plan on Ubon as an emergency field." To the Thuds he said, "We're fat on fuel for now, but let's get things going and get this guy out."

A new voice broke in on the radio. "Orange Anchor, this is Dodge lead, flight of four pre-strike F-4s. Can we assist?"

"Yes," Neil promptly answered. "Switch to guard and talk to the dude on the ground. He'll FAC himself and he needs help now. Hope you have some anti-personnel stuff with you. Can you take over the RESCAP? I'm going to be busy refueling these Thuds; they're all dry."

Neil was getting his hands full as a 105 slid in behind us with the frantic urgency of a small schoolboy that needed to go to the bathroom. He didn't seem at all concerned that we were twenty knots off of the refueling speed for a 105 and banking steeply.

"Roger, Orange Anchor. Where's our boy located?"

"Drive straight north," Neil answered. "There is a road running off to the east. He'll talk you in on guard frequency."

Four minutes flying time north of us, Captain Robert Campbell crouched in a clump of bushes on a small rise. He could see a dirt road about a quarter of a mile north of him. A plume of dust to the east drew closer. He had made contact with Dodge lead on his survival radio. As he watched, the F-4 rolled out on a west to east pass along the dirt road. As the airplane flashed past Campbell said, "Now" into his radio. "I'm a click due south on that little knoll."

"Gotcha marked, old son." Dodge lead's drawl sounded like West by God Virginia. "There's a couple of truckloads of pissed off people coming up the pike. I'll just run over and attend to that."

A minute later there was a rumble and the rolling orange and black cloud of napalm rose to the east. Campbell called Dodge lead. "Did you get them all?"

"Sorry, old son, they saw me coming and six or eight got away into the bush before I could drop. I expect they'll be coming your way. We don't have guns, but your buddies can hose 'em down with their cannons."

Campbell felt the hair on the back of his neck move. His back ached from the powerful thrust of his ejection seat. He had a deep scratch on his left arm, but otherwise seemed to be all in one piece. He did not want to be captured. Downed pilots were often shot or hacked to death with machetes if captured. This early in the war, Hanoi had not yet made it a policy to capture American airmen alive if possible. A wave of fear almost overwhelmed him. He felt very thirsty. He reached into a pocket of his survival vest and found the plastic baby bottle full of water. He drank it down and wondered if they would be able to get a helicopter this far north. Almost every pilot flying over the north had learned that the first desire of anyone who made it to the ground was water. The common plastic baby bottle made an ideal canteen. It could be carried in a pocket and was rugged enough to survive an ejection and landing.

Overhead a gaggle of Thuds and F-4s flew cover. He wondered how long they would be able to stay. Where the hell were they getting fuel? They couldn't be going all the way back to Thailand. There was some movement along the edge of the road to the north of his position. He called lead on his radio. Half a minute later, two of his buddies swept the road with hellish storm of cannon fire. The thunder of their passing stunned him. He had never been that close to the death that he controlled.

While this battle escalated just to our north, I worked fuel computations and was busy with radios. Neil carried a mental plan of where the airplanes needing fuel were and maneuvered to shorten the distance. The rock-steady air refueling platforms of stateside practice were forgotten. These pilots seemed able to park in the refueling position no matter what maneuvers the tanker made. More and more aircraft converged on the area and it seemed that they all wanted fuel. The first helicopter rescue attempt had been turned back by small arms fire. As the afternoon wore on, I became a miser with the fuel, trying to transfer to as many airplanes as possible without running ourselves out. Of course, everyone that pulled in behind us wanted to fill up. At that rate, we would long ago have been out of fuel. I told each receiver pilot that we were getting "scoshi" ourselves and to take the minimum he could get by on. This they did and returned to their bases in Thailand as soon as their ordinance was expended. Joe and I collaborated on possibilities and tried to anticipate any questions that Neil might ask. The nearest runway that we could use was Ubon, not far across the Thai-Laotian border. We knew that if we used that option, the fat would be in the fire and we would have to 'fess up to where we had been. If we could make it back to Takhli, the base where we were stationed, we probably would get away with this. The afternoon was aging fast. The "contact made" light blinked off and an F-4 dropped away. The fuel totalizer read eighteen thousand pounds. I added up the individual tanks and got the same amount. Just as I started to call this to Neil's attention, Dodge lead came on the radio with a jubilant shout.

"We got him! We damn sure got him! The chopper slipped in right after we all just laid down a shit storm of everything we had left and snatched his young Yankee ass right out of there. Orange Anchor, you guys are number one. Let's get the fuck out of this neighborhood!"

Neil was rolling left and heading south. "Heading for home, Nav?"

"Two zero eight, Pilot." Joe looked proud enough to swallow his damned alarm clock.

A little over an hour later, we braked to a stop in our parking spot at Takhli. The cockpit sliding windows had been opened about ten miles out from the base. The air conditioning system was useless at low throttle settings and in our long fuel-conserving descent with the throttles at idle, heat had built up inside the airplane. Neil looked out his side window with a puzzled expression. A group of pilots were pushing an aerostand up against the nose. This large set of collapsible steps is usually pushed up to the cargo door. Several pilots rushed up the aerostand and pushed a large beer pitcher through the window. I thought it was filled with ice water, a real luxury in these parts. It was filled with Martinis. And so the party began.

In these early years of the war, the rescue of downed airmen was a spontaneous affair and would involve just about anything airborne that was in the area. As time brought experience, we learned quickly. GCI sight Brigham at Udorn Royal Thai Air Force Base managed most RESCAPS and, after February of 1966, the GCI sight Invert at Nakhon Phanom RTAFB handled operations further to the southeast.

With darkness came monsoon rain. It was steady, unremitting, and incredibly loud. It rumbled on the sheet metal roof of the Officers' Club with a subdued roar. There was no wind with this rain, and even though the screened walls of the hooch that served as an Officers' Club were open to the outside, the air was stagnant and thick with tobacco smoke. It seemed that the only air that moved was the hot air from the war stories being shouted by all and heard by none. Even that had little effect on the thick and humid air. Recovery of the downed Thud pilot fueled the party.

The small amount of ice, flown in that afternoon on the courier from Bangkok, had long since been consumed. We were down to drinking salty dogs without ice. I sat unsteadily on a barstool that was kept from floating away by Bob Becker, a Thud pilot who sat on the floor holding the stool down with an arm around one leg. Whenever his glass was empty he would hold it straight up in the air and I would pass it to the overworked bartender for a refill. In a more lucid moment it occurred to me that, if I continued on with this party, the hammers of hell would be beating on my head in the morning. Mustering all remaining equilibrium, I climbed down from the barstool, stepping on Bob's hand in the process and, with all the stately aplomb I could muster, marched to the door.

Outside it was very dark. My imagination, made excessively acute by an overabundance of salty dogs, attached horrible importance to the many jungle sounds. A boardwalk stretched off into the night towards the hooch where I lived. At infrequent intervals, a light bulb with a green metal shade made a small pool of light on the boardwalk and made silver streaks out of the rain. This only served to emphasize the surrounding darkness. I recalled that we had been instructed not to be out after dark without a flashlight. Because of all of the construction, there were a lot of snakes about, and the brown brush cobra was known to be very aggressive. Just two days ago someone driving along the river of mud optimistically called a street had picked up a Banded Krait with the front wheel of his jeep. Through some unfathomable mystery of physics the snake was hurled into the front seat of the jeep. Understandably angry at this rude interruption of his affairs, the snake expressed its anger in unmistakable body language. The driver, not given to arguing with inarticulate beasts, promptly bailed out leaving the snake to manage the jeep as best it could. Since the snake did not have a valid military driver's license, the inevitable happened and the jeep came to rest partially submerged in a water-filled excavation. The snake, fearing punitive action, fled the scene and was not seen again.

I had no flashlight, and there was nothing for it but to make my way along the boardwalk as fast as I could and hope for the best. With my usual luck, my hooch was the very last one. As I proceeded at best speed, I failed to notice that the Engineers, who had been constructing God knows what during the day, had left a fire hose lying across the boardwalk. It was partially full of water and covered with mud. I did not see it but I did step on it. The fight or flight instinct flashed on with heavy emphasis on flight. A massive jolt of adrenaline smashed into my system, instantly burning off any blood alcohol. Nothing short of an air-to-air rocket could have caught me. In my mind I was running from the biggest damned snake in the world. I did arrive safely at my hooch and as I lay in my bunk looking up at the rafters, I was absolutely certain that should a snake poke his head over the edge of the bed I would be in those rafters in a single bound from a resting position flat on my back.

*****

About four hundred miles to the southeast, at Tan Sun Nuht Air Base, luck was running out for my classmate from cadets. Don Hawley reported to Lieutenant Colonel Gene McCutchan, the commander of a FAC, or Forward Air Control, unit attached to the Vietnamese Airborne Division. It was the 29th of September 1965. There were four pilots in this tiny unit. They all used the call sign Red Marker. Gene McCutchan was Red Marker One. Don, the newest of the group, was Red Marker Four. Their airplanes were tiny Cessna O-1s, the smallest and lightest of airplanes doing duty as forward air-control airplanes. If a pilot was lost, his replacement took over his call sign. The Vietnamese Airborne grew to know the men who were their FACs and were fiercely protective of the men who were their eyes in the sky. The American pilots were attached to the Vietnamese Division but remained under the

U.S. Air Force chain of command. The U. S. Army provided an advisory team for the Vietnamese Airborne from the famous 82nd Airborne Division. The FACs wore the same uniform as the Vietnamese Airborne troops, complete with the red beret, the idea being that should a FAC be on the ground with the Vietnamese troops, some sniper would not single him out. This was an enviable situation for the independent and self-reliant pilots. They were far out on the chain of command and seldom bothered by the brass. They flew when necessary and were not terribly concerned with paperwork.

As only happens among men who face great danger together, a strong personal bond existed among the four men who flew the tiny Cessna Bird Dogs. This bond is the stuff of legends. It is the bane of wives and lovers. Books and movies have attempted to portray it and psychologists nod wisely when discussing it. It crosses all lines of race and creed, and should one attempt to discuss this characteristic with a soldier, he would dismiss you with a self-conscious smile. Many have attempted to label this strange cohesion but it defies description. In all of the filth and ugliness of war it is probably the only noble attribute, for it is the unselfish expression of man's love of his fellow man and is the driving force of so many brave deeds in battle, the majority of which pass unnoticed except by those affected directly by them.

Del Fleener was assigned to the Division as a forward air controller at about the same time Don was. He carried the call sign Red Marker Three. He was a few years older than Don, and they became good friends who often worked together in relays. Several months into their year-long tour, a battle developed northwest of Saigon between the Viet Cong and some South Vietnamese troops who, at that time, were short on American advisors. Don took off in O1-E #57-2873 from the air base at Bien Hoa to direct air cover. Del would follow later and relieve Don. It was December 17, 1965.

Red Marker Four turned west, leaving Bien Hoa Air Base behind. Don tried several times to raise the advisors for the Province troops on his radios. Several bursts of Vietnamese were all that he heard. Skimming the trees, he found the area of the engagement identified only by thin smoke occasionally rising above the trees. He dropped lower, banked around some tall trees, and zoomed right over a fire-fight on the ground so suddenly he couldn't tell one side from the other. The troops on the ground were heavily engaged. Finally, he contacted an American advisor on the ground. The Province troops had stumbled into an ambush and needed help. Don called for air support and circled back to the scene of the ambush. He would have to sort out who was who on the ground before the air support arrived. He spotted troops on the ground. Who were they? He banked and dropped lower, skidding the airplane and twisting to avoid Viet Cong guns. The O-1 staggered as small arms fire tore into it. Smoke poured from the engine as it seized. Wracked with pain, Don instinctively rolled the wings level. The Bird Dog smashed into the ground. A wing crumpled as the crippled plane slid to a stop. Dazed, Don unbuckled and tumbled out of the plane. He had to get away before the Viet Cong got to him. Which way were the good guys? The darkness came over him and he sank to the ground next to his ruined airplane.

Del listened to the confusion on the radio as he headed to the site to relieve Don. This was sounding like a major cluster fuck. Del called back to Bien Hoa for help. Red Marker Two was rolling in minutes. He arrived in time to see Del circling the crash site. Del could see Don on the ground next to the airplane. He hadn't moved since getting out of the plane. He could see men in black pajamas working their way towards the downed airplane. There was an open area not far from Don. He might be able to squeeze in and out of it. He pulled the throttle to idle and raised the nose to kill off speed. With flaps full down and airspeed just above a stall he pushed the nose over, dropped like a rock and flared at the edge of the open area. The Bird Dog landed with a solid thump. With the engine idling, Del rolled out onto the ground and started for Don. Small arms fire ripped through the brush and into the plane. Del hit the ground as something tore into him, knocking the wind out of him. It was too late. The Viet Cong had overrun the crash site. Del had to run. Dodging and weaving, he got his plane between himself and the gunfire and staggered into the brush. He was lucky. He ran straight into friendly troops. Furiously, they fought to get to their downed FAC. Eventually they broke the Cong, but it was far too late for Don. Joe Granducci, Red Marker Two, known to the Vietnamese Airborne as Captain Mustache, identified Don's body. It is the hope of all of us that Don left this life before the Viet Cong over-ran his crash site. Don was the third Forward Air Controller attached to the Vietnamese Airborne Division to die in 1965. All of them carried the call sign Red Marker Four.

My days of pretending at war were over. The dreary routine of alert, waiting for the horn to call us to the apocalypse that might or might not be real, were behind me. I thought that I was leaving the active business of war for more passive pursuits when it suddenly became real. Men flew missions and did not come back. Napalm rolled in searing horror over the ground. Missiles turned airplanes and the men that flew them into flaming trash. Young soldiers suffered the awful pain of hand-to-hand combat and pilots that became POWs endured tortures refined through all of human history. Students demonstrated and politicians lied. America writhed in agony

*****

Takhli was a primitive base in 1965, capable of handling only a single tanker due to lack of parking space. Other tankers supporting tactical air operations had to make the round trip from either Formosa or Okinawa. This allowed little time on station and limited the fuel available for transfer. While construction proceeded at a rapid pace on a base capable of handling both tankers and B-52s south of Bangkok, some tanker operations were conducted out of Bangkok International Airport. Not long after our arrival at Takhli, we were rotated to Bangkok. All four of us considered this an excellent decision on the part of our commanders, as living in Bangkok was far more agreeable than spending the monsoon season in a wood and canvas covered hooch in the jungle. U. S. military air operations were relegated to a far corner of the Bangkok International Airport, the intent being that we remain as far from sight as possible and have minimum impact on civil air operations.

It was in Bangkok that I met the Combat Ready Dog. He was an ugly beast of truly international heritage, about medium size for a dog, with scruffy gray and black fur and huge master sergeant stripes painted with some sort of permanent dye on each side of his body. His hide was covered with scars and one ear was badly torn. Obviously, he had no fear of mortal combat. Frequently, he sported a prominent erection, much to the delight of the young Thai boys who swarmed all over the Air Force ramp attempting to sell anything from some long lost jade antiquity to their sisters' virginity. I wondered at the deference shown by both locals and flight crews to this battered canine. It seemed that when U. S. air operations started here in the previous year, this derelict dog had attached himself to tanker crews. He ignored flight crews from other types of aircraft and would choose a single tanker crew and follow them wherever they went for several days, then he would move on to a different crew. It was considered bad form and bad luck not to offer Sergeant Dog whatever hospitality he required. At the end of each day he would follow his chosen flight crew and ride with them on the crew bus to their hotel in Bangkok. There he would spend the night, either whoring about town or sleeping on the floor of one of their rooms. Always in the morning, no matter what his nocturnal activities had been, he would be on the crew bus and return to the flight line.

His duties were not limited to ground operations. He would frequently board a tanker when it was preparing for flight, without a care for its destination. His sortie count was higher than that of many of the air crew, and he had visited every base in the western Pacific that tankers operated from, sometimes staying a week or more at a base that struck his romantic fancy. Then he would board another tanker and eventually find his way back to Bangkok. All this travel he accomplished without passport, visa, or military identification card. More than one startled fighter pilot pulled up into the refueling position behind a tanker only to see this scruffy beast peering out of the boom pod window next to a grinning boom operator.

Eventually, his fame spread to the exalted halls of Strategic Air Command Headquarters, and he was featured in the SAC safety magazine, Combat Crew. Of course, his picture graced the cover. I don't know what became of him, but I am sure that he retired in some warm stateside climate, drew a Master Sergeant's pension and kept track of the local young female dogs in his neighborhood for the remainder of his days.

NINE

◆◆◆◆◆◆◆◆

> *They have learned nothing*
> *and forgotten nothing.*
> *-Talleyrand*

T he anti-war movement in the United States, vital to the North Vietnamese, was growing rapidly. When a small nation is engaged in conflict with a powerful nation, the public opinion generated by propaganda is an enormously powerful weapon for the smaller nation. This propaganda is often amplified by entertainers who are convinced that their popularity is a direct indicator of their wisdom. Their high visibility and notoriety lend an undeserved credibility to their opinions (some of which are based on very little knowledge of the facts), which are often accepted without question by a public informed only by sound bites and catchy slogans. The powerful nation is portrayed as a bully, and the natural instinct of the followers of the self-appointed expert is to cheer for the underdog, no matter how outrageous its behavior. Opinion, created by the demonstrations seen on television worldwide, is difficult to overcome. The impact is powerful, and to self-righteous public figures and campus radicals, it does not matter who is responsible for the suffering.

Feelings were running high between the anti-war protesters and the military. Confrontation with those in uniform was unproductive at best. Soldiers cannot have much say about the policies that the government adopted. We could vote, but that was about it. Political activism is rightly prohibited for those in the military; however, defending political disagreement is a primary duty of the armed forces, a duty that was hard to embrace by the soldier who felt he was being placed in unnecessary danger by his fellow citizens.

At one time during the late 60s when I happened to be in Rapid City in uniform, a young woman of about twenty blocked my path, shrieked into my face, "Baby killer!" and stalked off accompanied by her giggling friends. I felt her vitriol should have been directed at the government and thought that her attack on me was misdirected. She would go about her life never knowing or caring that her safety was paid for by others, and as long as the Barbarians never breached the walls, she would despise those of us who paid the price.

Until the horror of war arrives on our doorstep, most American people hold the military in low esteem. Should we not prevail in the Vietnam War, the battlefield would surely move into our homes. While that young woman's action offended me, it could not compare to the suffering and death that Jane Fonda's actions brought to American POWs as she was manipulated like an unthinking propaganda puppet by the North Vietnamese government. The plight of American prisoners held by North Vietnam was an embarrassment to the Johnson administration, which they dealt with by trying to ignore the POW problem entirely. There was no outcry from human rights activists on their behalf, and not until the wives of captured Americans banded together and formed The National League of Families was the Administration forced to offer at least the appearance of taking action. This organization soon came under the control of the government and its effectiveness withered.

This strange attitude prevails to this day. Ill-informed, self-appointed intellectuals commonly provide aid and comfort to our enemies, not because of their sincere beliefs but to attract attention to their otherwise dull selves. When the conflict is over, they quickly return to the comforts and safety of the country that they had loudly and publicly vilified.

The enormous pressure of the anti-war movement, the Johnson administration's inability to make difficult and potentially unpopular decisions, and the government's fear of provoking Soviet or Chinese intervention, left the military blundering about in a war and projecting an uncertainty that emboldened the enemy to carry on. This was further exacerbated by reluctance of the military leadership, at the Joint Chiefs of Staff level, to take a stand against asinine tactical policies. Instead, their fear of loss of position and power paralyzed them. The siege of Khe Sanh during the 1968 Tet Offensive emphasized the cost of such policy. Widely claimed as an American victory, it is difficult to justify this point of view when it was the Americans who finally withdrew and the North Vietnamese who occupied Khe Sanh. As is usual, when generals lose battles, it was called a strategic withdrawal.

No general or politician ever admits to a defeat. With few exceptions, the flag officers that we counted on to speak for us and to protect us from the needless waste of our lives failed us. There were no George Pattons or Hap Arnolds in this war. The few that were worthy of such a comparison were banished to the anonymous footnotes of history. Tactical Air Command had General Jack Lavelle, who fell from grace with the Washington bureaucrats and the entrenched military good old boys by defending his fighter pilot's right to return fire. The Navy had Admiral Harry Felt who had the courage to go over the head of the Secretary of Defense directly to the president for permission to attempt the first RESCAP of the war. Navy Captain Eugene "Red" McDaniel, shot down on his 81st mission and a prisoner of war for six years, founded The American Defense Institute. This non-profit organization does much to inform the public of the governments constant redefining of the role and mission of the armed forces. He also is a champion of the prisoners that we left behind after the war. Men such as these are few and far between. They are seldom mentioned in the mainstream press. Few Americans are aware that even these few lived, or what they stood for, but within the shrinking circle of people who fought in Vietnam, these leaders are known and honored.

TEN

◆◆◆◆◆◆

Knowledge comes but wisdom lingers.
-Tennyson

Henry Miller was the Squadron Commander of the Twenty-Eighth Air Refueling Squadron. Of all the commanders I served under, he was my favorite. He was honest, consistent, and had no special pets. Lieutenant Colonel Miller was a big man with a commanding presence. He was bald but I don't think that he was aware of this. He was one of those men who can get along very well without head hair. He seldom displayed anger, but if one were foolish enough to annoy him beyond his personal threshold, he gave fair warning of the imminent explosion with a rising tide of red that began at his collar and rose much like the liquid in a thermometer. When it reached the top of his head, it was best that the source of his annoyance be far removed from his sight. Copilots were especially eager to remain in his good graces as it was his decision that would determine who would upgrade to Aircraft Commander and when. Any pilot who has had to serve his apprenticeship as a copilot will quickly agree that there is only one good seat on a large airplane and that is the front left seat.

Hank, as we called him amongst ourselves, had devised a system to establish the order that copilots could begin upgrade. A very fair man, he allowed no special consideration, and he kept score himself. It was rather a complicated system that consisted of points allowed for total time, time in type, annual check flight scores, time in the Vietnam area, actual combat time, and whether or not you picked your nose during squadron briefings. There also was a system for taking away points for such indiscretions as poor performance on a check ride, screwing up during an operational readiness inspection (ORI), or being the cause of any disagreeable communications from wing headquarters; in short, just about anything that might make his lunch unpleasant or otherwise disturb his serenity. He had very little trouble with copilots who had any career ambitions.

Those of us suffering servitude in the right seat considered all possible ways of influencing this score in our favor. High score on check rides was good, but that could be a two-edged sword, for if one had a bad day and demonstrated something less than maximum-magnificent performance, it would cost points—and one didn't volunteer for extra check rides. It was possible to increase total flying time but the days of going to Base Flight and checking out a trainer to buzz around in were long gone. That left one possibility. The B-52 Squadron on the base was supporting Chrome Dome operations, or airborne alert in a B-52 carrying a load of nuclear weapons. Crews stayed aloft for over twenty-four hours, a frightful burden on the bomber crews, as there were not enough bomber pilots to send an extra one on a Chrome Dome mission. The bomb squadron had indicated that they would be happy to accept pilot volunteers from the tanker squadron if they had bomber experience. Copilots who chose this method of increasing their flying time would have to do so during their very limited time off, for Henry was not likely to diminish his crew availability to help out the bomber types. In desperation, I did what is never wise to do in the military, I volunteered.

On the appointed day, I arrived at the bomber briefing room and took a seat with the crew I was to fly with. The serious briefing room atmosphere of my former bomber days surrounded me, including the aluminum boxes with the tickets and go codes inside. Most of the aircrew had strapped on sidearms. I had always wondered what the hell we were supposed to do with a snub-nosed .38 in an airplane. Perhaps it was to put everyone in a proper warlike mood. The briefing was long and tedious. Much of it covered detail over which I would have no control. I was riding along to give the primary pilots an occasional break.

Eventually, a crew bus took us out to the bomber flight line. After a nineteen-year-old guard carefully checked our names against an access roster, we were allowed to disembark from the bus and unload our equipment. Piled in front of the airplane it looked quite enough for a three-month expedition to the Arctic.

It was just coming on daylight. The B-52 loomed over us. It is a huge airplane, and loaded as it was, it weighed nearly four hundred and fifty thousand pounds. The main tires were squashed nearly flat even though they were inflated to well over two hundred pounds per square inch of air pressure and the wings sagged near to the point of collapse. The outrigger struts for the little training wheels were almost completely compressed. Tanker crews referred in jest to the B-52 outriggers as training wheels. I could see that if they were not there, the wings would fold wearily to the ground under the enormous weight of fuel that each wing carried. It did not comfort me at all to know that each wing tip was capable of flexing through an arc of thirty-seven feet before it would fail. The forward fuselage and flight deck projected far in front of the forward main truck. It sagged so much that there were huge diagonal wrinkles in the skin from the bending stress. The vertical fin soared like a skyscraper. Beneath the tail plane, an aerostand was in place to allow the gunner access to his lonely station in the tail turret. Once in the air he had no access to the rest of the crew except by interphone. He would be wise to have plenty to read with him because this was going to be a long ride.

Preparation for this odyssey seemed interminable. I was already tired by the time we were ready to start engines. I had drunk too much coffee while the bomber crew went about their preflight and I had a sour taste in my mouth. Finally, they got the airplane powered up. There were eight engines and it took time to get them all running with the associated sub-systems operating. I sat in the jump-seat just behind and between the pilots. The ATC clearance for such a long flight was brief; "ATC clears Acorn Two Nine for Chrome Dome five routes and altitudes."

The copilot called for taxi clearance and we were herded out of our parking spot by two members of the ground crew with lighted wands, one at each side. The pilot advanced the forest of throttles that sprouted out of the center console. Reluctantly, the airplane began to move and we lumbered off towards the end of the runway. Again, I thanked the gods of aviation for my release from bombers and my assignment to a gentleman's airplane. In due time, the take-off roll began. I still recall the impression of enormous weight and a very long take-off roll. The effect was much like driving an apartment building down a long wide highway, but eventually the wings flexed upward and lifted all that weight off the ground in the typical nose-low attitude of a B-52. The two pilots went through the procedure of cleaning up the landing gear and flaps in a businesslike manner as we accelerated to climb speed. There was a noticeable easing of tension once we had reached a relatively safe altitude and airspeed. Our course was easterly toward New England. We would continuously monitor both the UHF command frequency and the shortwave frequency for the half hourly Foxtrot broadcasts on which we would receive the coded message that would mark the beginning of Armageddon. I fervently hoped that we would not go to war that day. I pondered the horror of the four, long, olive drab shapes suspended in the bomb bays, then pushed the unthinkable from my mind.

Boston passed beneath. Several hundred miles further east we met our first of three tankers. Both pilots were working hard to maneuver that heavy beast into position for hook-up with the boom that would physically connect the two airplanes and allow the transfer of more than three tons of fuel per minute to the B-52. Twenty minutes later, we were topped off. The tanker headed for home and we still had better than eighteen hours to go. The AC's flight suit was soaked with sweat from the exertions of refueling. He climbed out of his seat and motioned me to take his place. Once I strapped in, my duties consisted mainly of babysitting the autopilot while the copilot managed the complicated fuel panel. Idly I listened to the crew chatter as they went about their various duties. The EW, or electronic warfare officer, was doing the sextant work for the navigator and there was a lot of information exchanged between them, as well as traffic on the several radios that I was monitoring.

Each crew station has a radio-mixing box that allows the person occupying that station to select, from the many different signals, those that concern him. He will not hear the signals that are not selected. Of course, the person in command is concerned with almost all of the signals and must have most of his switches in the on position. This can create a terrible uproar in his headphones during busy times, and frequently, someone else on the crew interrupts with an interphone call, unaware that he has cut off some other message. It takes practice, but eventually one gains the ability to sort the pertinent information out of all of the talk and noise feeding into the headphones. Hollywood conveys the impression that flight crews spend most of their time in the air telling jokes and making brave statements on the interphone. Good crew discipline requires otherwise, but in defense of film writers, it would make a dull movie if several hours of flight went by without a word spoken.

The gunner's voice caught my attention, "Pilot, this is guns, permission to test fire?"

This caught me off guard. What the hell does he want to fire the guns for, I wondered? I glanced at the copilot. He nodded. Well, I guess this is what these guys do.

"Guns, Pilot, permission granted," I answered.

Apparently he test fired the four fifty-caliber machine guns in the tail, but I heard and felt nothing to indicate this. Shortly, he advised me that the test fire was complete. To prevent confusion for the crew, the three pilots use different interphone calls. The aircraft commander answers to AC, the copilot answers to copilot, and I answer to pilot. It did not matter where we were in the airplane. That way each crewmember knew just whom he was talking to.

We turned north. Hour after long hour passed. The AC and I changed seats several times and he would move over to the copilot seat to give him some rest. Extra pilots who went on the Chrome Dome missions had to have B-47 experience, but were not familiar with the engineering procedures that were managed from the copilot's position. The checkout for these tanker pilots was limited to left seat duties so we did not relieve the copilot. The aircraft commander, however, was qualified in both positions.

The second in-flight refueling took place somewhere off the west coast of Greenland. Time dragged. Helmets and oxygen masks chafed and itched. The straps from the parachute harness and shoulder straps rubbed skin raw. Muscles ached. The D model B-52 was not built for crew comfort. The only place a man could stand upright was on the ladder between the lower deck and the flight deck. One person could just stretch out on the floor forward of the Electronic Warfare Officer's position. We took turns stretching here and tried to nap. The dry air of high altitude dehydrated us. Eyes itched and mouths tasted sour. After eating my flight lunch, I felt as if I had swallowed a rock and regretted every bite.

Again, it was my turn in the seat. We were far north. The sky was stark and very blue at an altitude well over forty thousand feet. The sunlight seemed watered down this far north, and below, a vast field of white spread in all directions. The navigator called, "Pilot, we are at latitude ninety north." We were over the North Pole. I stared down at the white desert. There was nothing remarkable about the North Pole. A blinding white desert stretched as far as I could see. We were just at the halfway point of this odyssey. It had become a struggle to endure. The good-natured atmosphere of the earlier hours was gone.

Now we headed south, but every direction was south. It was imperative that we choose the right south. Navigators solve this dilemma with a technique called polar grid navigation. Their charts are printed with an overlay of a grid system. By applying a grid convergence factor and orienting the aircraft gyrocompass to this new system of coordinates they are able to ignore the problem of converging lines of longitude in the Polar Regions. The arc of our passage swung to the left to carry us down along the West Coast of Alaska and into the gloom of the night that waited to the south. There we rendezvoused with a tanker from Eielson Air Force Base at Fairbanks for our final refueling. In the dark, the weary pilots worked for the fuel that would see us back to South Dakota. I looked up through the eyebrow windows at the underside of the tanker. The underwing and body lights, along with the pilot director lights, or "Christmas Tree," could be seen from several miles away and flooded the underside of the tanker with light. I had turned those lights on many times and had seen them from a B-47 during refueling. I had forgotten what a display they created. I did not know it at the time, but those lights would very much affect me just a little more than a year later, on a night rescue in the war that I had temporarily escaped.

With tanks full again, we pressed on through the night. It was necessary to always have enough fuel to fly a war mission from wherever we were in this long flight. Thus, we now had far more fuel on board than we would need to get back to Ellsworth AFB. I took my final shift in the pilot's seat during the dog hours that come just before the first hint of light shows in the eastern sky. That is an awful time to have to fly an airplane. The autopilot does the work, but you still have to stay awake and your body is in a full state of rebellion demanding that you relax and sleep. Only the brain keeps you aware of the consequences of surrender. Over the Seattle area, we crossed the coast and turned east to the Dakotas. Just a few more hours to go. About an hour out from Ellsworth, the Aircraft Commander returned to the pilot seat as refreshed as is possible under the circumstances. He was required to make the landing and had been awake for at least thirty-five hours. We began a slow en-route descent. The copilot had radioed for landing weather and worked out the necessary landing data. The Bighorn Mountains passed below us and we continued our en route descent towards the Black Hills of Dakota. The sun came up and we flew directly into it. It seemed that whenever I was flying in the early morning or late afternoon, the direction of flight was always straight into the sun.

There was a crosswind at Ellsworth, not an unusual event. The wings of the B-52 are so long that the slip or wing-low technique of crosswind landing cannot be used. The problem is solved by setting the crosswind crab into the landing gear. The entire main landing gear re-orients itself so that the wheels all track straight down the runway while the airplane itself is cocked into the wind. For me, not used to this technique, it was very uncomfortable to touch down with the nose of the airplane pointing somewhere other than straight down the runway. It seemed to work. The landing was uneventful, the huge brake chute deployed, we slowed and turned off the active runway. The parachute was released and we taxied back to the same parking spot that we had left twenty-five hours and fifty minutes earlier. Eventually, the post-flight paperwork chores were completed, and I had added significantly to my total flight time, but I felt very tired and much as if I had a nagging hangover. This is the result of the mild hypoxia of high altitude for long hours, for the B-52's cabin pressure is not kept at as low an altitude as that of the airliner-like KC-135.

At the same time the next day, I would go on alert for another week-long stretch. At that moment other bombers were in the sky continuing the airborne alert that this DEFCON, or defensive condition, calls for. It is the way of the world that I will have the opportunity to make this flight again, as often as I wish.

Just a little over a week later I found a message in our crew mailbox. Colonel Miller wanted to see me. Silently, I reviewed my activities for the past few weeks and concluded that I was guilty of nothing that he was likely to know about. With a fairly clear conscience I reported to his office.

"Come in, Art," he said, following my knock at his door.

He waved me to the chair opposite his desk, known to his subjects as the hot seat. "I've got a deal I want to offer to you. You're getting close to the top of the upgrade list.... along with a couple of others."

I had the distinct feeling that I was about to strike a deal with the devil, but I just nodded.

"I know that you've only been back from Southeast Asia a few weeks but I have to send Dave Huff over. He will soon be going to an air staff position in Saigon. SAC wants him to have some time in the area before he goes.

My heart sank. I was about to be screwed by the fickle finger of fate. He was wording this as a request, but I knew an order when I heard one.

"If you'll do this for me and I get a good report from Dave Huff, I will assign you to an instructor pilot as soon as you get back and you can start upgrade. You will pick up enough extra flying time to put you in first place so I won't have to field any flak from those other eager bastards." He smiled at me with all the sincerity of a department store Santa Claus.

There was no way out. If I pitched a bitch, he would send me anyway and I'd be in the cellar, as far as the upgrade list was concerned.

"OK, sir," I said, "I'll go if I am physically able."

"What the hell do you mean, physically able?" The dangerous red tide was well above his collar.

"Carolyn will break every bone in my body when I tell her you are sending me back over." The red tide subsided.

"I'll have the flight surgeon patch you back up. Thanks, Art. I'll make it up to you."

With that I was dismissed and tried to think of some gentle way to break the news to Carolyn. The fact that I would have to go one way or the other would make little difference. It seemed that I was seeing less and less of my family.

In the armed forces, if one were sent to Southeast Asia, it was for a one-year tour. Once a person had completed this one-year tour, he could not be sent back unless he volunteered. Strategic Air Command was tasked with both B-52 and tanker operations in the war in Southeast Asia. They also had to support the Strategic Integrated Operations Plan, or the fifty-percent alert, that we had been on since the start of the Cold War. The SIOP was intended to deter the Soviet Union from an attack on the United States and NATO. SAC did not have enough crews to do both if a man could be sent overseas just once for a year and not sent back unless he volunteered. It was with the use of a legal loophole that this shortage was circumvented. In these regulations, there was a provision that if a man was assigned duty away from his home base for less than one hundred and eighty days it was called TDY, or temporary duty, and it was not considered a transfer or change of station. By assuring that he was out of the overseas area by the one hundredth and seventy ninth day, he technically had not served an overseas tour and could be sent back immediately for another one hundred and seventy nine days. The lack of a declaration of war combined with a limited number of aircrew made this unintended use of TDY regulations necessary. Those of us who survived often accumulated more than three years of duty in Southeast Asia and several hundred combat missions, but our records show no overseas assignment.

The toll on family life was appalling. The divorce rate among crewmembers was something that Air Force recruiters were reluctant to mention. The almost universal lack of support from the American population, together with years of family disruption without an end in sight, proved more than many relationships could endure. Had we been involved in a declared war, such a silly commuter situation would have been unnecessary. Aircrew training would have been rapidly increased and those sent overseas would be there for a single tour of duty. Since the Vietnam War lasted almost twice as long as World War II, an accelerated flight-training program would have poured out all of the aircrew needed.

*****

When I called "Rotate!" Dave Huff smoothly moved back the yoke of Brown Anchor Two Six. The big tanker lifted its nose gear off of the ground and pointed towards the dark and rainy sky. Trailing the black smoke of water injection, she lifted from the runway and disappeared into the overcast. At Dave's relaxed orders, I raised the landing gear and cleaned the flaps up. Presently, the supply of water injected into the engines was exhausted and the EPR gauges dropped abruptly.

"Set NRT for climb," Dave said.

I consulted the outside air temperature gauge and then my checklist for the desired power setting. Normal-rated thrust was the maximum-continuous-power setting allowed for the engines and it was frequently used for climbs when the pilot was not in a hurry. I made the power adjustment.

Humming to himself, Dave calmly regarded the instrument panel. It was time to start the left turn that would reverse our course and take the airplane out over the Formosa Straits and onto a southwest heading. He applied slight pressure to the yoke and thumbed in a single click of back trim. The inboard ailerons responded, the left spoiler lifted imperceptibly and a jackscrew far back in the empennage turned and moved the leading edge of the stabilizer down a fraction. In the rain-filled clouds, only the instruments indicated a climbing turn to the left. Presently, he rolled out of the turn on the desired heading. The rain diminished, then stopped, and the clouds grew lighter. Mainland China was an invisible but perceived presence to the right. The clouds grew even thinner. The airplane broke into sunlight and climbed above the now gleaming white clouds. Brown Anchor Two Six would skirt south of Hainan Island and then turn north into the Gulf of Tonkin. Her duty today was to serve as the emergency tanker for U.S. aircraft coming off of a strike on Hanoi. Some would be damaged and all would need fuel. There would be other tankers scheduled against specific aircraft. Two Six's job would be to go to the ones who couldn't get back to the rest of the tanker fleet.

Soon we passed over the southern edge of the rain and bad weather that covered Formosa and the straits that separated that island from the mainland. Twenty-four hours earlier it had covered Hainan, but now the Gulf of Tonkin and Hainan were reasonably clear. As Two Six turned north to parallel the southwest coast of Hainan, I could see faint, brown smoke trails over the island. They were MIGs climbing to altitude to be in position should any U.S. aircraft intrude on Chinese airspace. Recently, they had scored two A-1s that had wandered too close in the recent bad weather.

As Two Six approached its anchor point, we began to hear radio chatter from far inside the Gulf. The anchors were a series of geographic points stretched east to west across the mouth of the gulf. The plan was for the tankers to be at these points to meet the strike aircraft as they exited the gulf. Brown Anchor Two Six was assigned the most easterly anchor. It was just outside of Chinese territorial water.

"Red Crown, Red Crown, this is Baxter lead. We need help. Send the emergency tanker north...hell, send them all north!" The strike leader was calling the Navy ship that served as a GCI sight in the Gulf of Tonkin.

Dave sat up straight. He clicked off the autopilot and took control manually. "Copilot, set military thrust. Nav, get me bearings on whoever that is talking."

"Brown Anchor Two Six, this is Red Crown. Vector three four five, angels base plus two zero, Buster. He is a Mayday. All other Anchors, move your points two five north. Stand by for vectors." In that short sentence the floating radar site had given us the heading towards and the altitude of the distressed F-4 and his use of the word "Buster" told us to stoke up the boilers and get going.

"Attention all aircraft, this is Big Eye. SAM launch, SAM launch."

Big Eye gave coordinates for just north of Vinh. The North Vietnamese were firing off a few expensive Russian surface-to-air missiles just to muddy the water. None of the tankers were in range, but the orbiting C-130's alarm blasted over guard frequency and blocked a lot of other frantic messages.

Dave concentrated on getting as much altitude and airspeed as he could out of the straining engines.

"Pilot, this is Nav. Our first receiver is two three nautical and five degrees left. Expect a left turn to one eight seven in thirty..."

"Brown Anchor Two Six, this is Red Crown. Come starboard to one five zero." The transmission was extremely powerful. It blocked everything else.

Dave looked at me and saw my horrified expression.

"No fucking way! Turn left! Turn left!"

Dave had already started banking left. "That's right where we're going, son. Don't get your knickers in a knot." Before the turn was completed, an F-4 slid into position behind us and the boom operator hooked him up. The radios were swamped with shouted instructions and demands for fuel. Red Crown managed to break in.

"Brown Anchor Two Six, I have another Mayday. He is two zero north of you and is at base plus three two. I am vectoring him to you in a dive. He is just about dry and has a few holes. If he doesn't go in the drink, he should be with you just about the time you drop off your current chick."

Dave nodded at me as I busily juggled the fuel panel. "We'll take him, Red Crown," he answered. "But if he is that dry, he will take us down to bingo fuel."

"No problem, Two Six. We have the rest of the tankers here now, and if you can get that guy to Danang, you are clear to return to base."

The first F-4 no sooner dropped away beneath us than a second moved into position. A mist of fuel trailed out behind him. Brown Anchor Two Six headed south with a leaking F-4 chasing after her like a thirsty calf chases its mother. At the rate he was leaking, it took a lot of fuel to get that bird close enough to Danang to drop him off, but eventually he turned away and descended to the west. We turned to the east and headed back to Formosa.

"Nav, pass me up your plotting board," Dave said. He studied it for a minute or two and then said to the crew, "If we had fallen for that phony call to come starboard we would have been in Chinese airspace before we rolled out of the turn. But we got two confirmed saves in seven minutes. That's four men and two airplanes and we get to go home early. Good job, guys."

On an easterly heading, Two Six passed south of Hainan and climbed to forty-nine thousand feet. Below the South China Sea was a deep purple. The shadows of the fair-weather cumulous clouds made dark patches on the sea. Behind us a thick white contrail formed that seemed to stretch back to the troubled land fading to the west.

As Dave let down for a landing at the base in Formosa, we entered the bad weather again. Rain slashed at the windshield and small hail made a rushing sound on the skin of the airplane. As we descended lower, the wet humid smell of the island filled the cabin. Through occasional breaks in the clouds, mountains loomed on either side of the airplanes path. We hated letting down in terrain such as this, no matter how much we trusted the instruments. The base on Formosa always seemed damp and cold. Today was no exception. After a detailed intelligence debriefing over the bogus radio call using Red Crown's call sign, a crew bus took us to our quarters. The hovels we lived in were the poorest in the theater. We would have preferred the wood and canvas hooches of the forward bases. At least they were warm.

Eventually the six months passed. Shortly after our return I found orders in our crew mailbox relieving me of duty with Dave and assigning me to Jim Loosley's crew. Jim was the senior squadron instructor and the man that every copilot wanted for his upgrade instructor. I thought I had died and gone to heaven until I found out that, in a little over a month Jim's crew, including me, was scheduled for a six-month tour in Southeast Asia. Our youngest son had been born six weeks prematurely. He was struggling to catch up, but still had some of the difficulties common to premature babies. After being home less than two months, I would again have to leave Carolyn to deal with these problems.

I started my time on Jim's crew by going on alert for a week. I was anxious to get to flying, but it was just as well that I had a little time to learn Jim's methods. The first day of alert was taken up with the usual routine. We finally got to sit down and talk over my upgrade training on the second day. The plan was straightforward.

"You will act at all times as if you are the pilot in command," Jim began over coffee on the second morning. "So, in addition to the normal copilot chores, you will take over the aircraft commander's paperwork and flight duties. I will fly in the copilot seat and perform the copilot's flight duties. You will make all decisions and I will not override you unless I have to. If the need for a decision comes up that you feel uncertain about, I will offer advice in the same manner that you smart-ass, old-time copilots like to do when you have no responsibility for the outcome of the decision. I will not interfere unless you set out to do something that is unbearably stupid.

"As far as the other crewmembers are concerned, your supervision of them will extend only to mission planning and flight duties. They are not students, but are instructors in their own specialty. They also will help you as much as they can. I will be available to you at any time, day or night. If something is on your mind or you have a question that you need my help to work out, feel free to call me even during our off time. I know that you have a fair idea of how to fly an airplane. Henry Miller would never have put you in the upgrade program if you did not. I'll teach you the tricks that I know, but the most important thing is to learn how to make decisions that do not end in disaster. The best guide for that is to remember that rules are meant to be interpreted with intelligence and followed blindly by fools. Is that agreeable?"

"Sounds fine with me," I stammered, somewhat surprised by his all business approach. It seemed out of character for Jim who was a constant source of jokes and stories with the squadron.

"OK, we'll see how it goes," he said with a smile. "Our first mission is next Monday. Bring me the completed mission package for my signature by two o'clock Thursday afternoon. Until then, don't bother me with it."

The paperwork was not a burden, as the copilot did most of it anyway. There were some timing errors in the mission profile as published by scheduling, but this was not unusual considering the amount of material that they had to crank out each day. These discrepancies were easily worked out with a phone call or a trip up to the scheduling office. Of course, I was vain enough to enjoy my newfound importance and the envy of the other copilots waiting their turn to move to the left seat. The fact that I would be back in the right seat until the end of time if I botched this chance lingered in the background of my thoughts. It also was in the very forefront of the thoughts of those other eager wolves, one of whom, should I fail, would move into my place. The pressure had not increased yet to the point that this troubled me. That would happen on my first flight with Jim.

Monday came. It was the kind of pretty morning that sometimes happens in South Dakota. The sky was so clear it made your eyes ache and there was very little wind. Jim and his crew were relaxed and joking with each other after their weekend free. I was nervous. I wanted to make a good impression, not only on Jim, but also on his navigator and boom operator, for these men could easily make my training a pleasant task or a miserable experience.

Jim offered little tips throughout the flight. He needed to evaluate my ability and things seemed to be going pretty well until I made my first landing. Only the fact that Bill Boeing and his boys had built an airplane that one could take the wings off and use for a railroad locomotive saved us from disaster. Final approach seemed fine, but I flared too late and the airplane hit the ground with what could only be called an arrival. The startled airplane leaped thirty feet back into the sky. No chance of saving this landing! Nothing for it but to put on power and go around. Humiliation overwhelmed me. I didn't dare look at Jim.

Don Morris, the boom operator, pulled a first aid kit from its storage place on the flight deck bulkhead and tossed it up between the pilot's seats with the comment, "Everyone is all right in the rear."

Ron Dufresne, the navigator, added to my embarrassment. "Can I get combat pay for this?" he asked over interphone.

Jim took the airplane from me on downwind. "Sit back, Art, and cool off. You're trying too hard to impress me. The only time you are supposed to make landings like that is when you have generals on board. That way they won't fly with you again and you don't have to carry on with all that ass kissing."

He called the tower for a touch and go. When he had rolled out on final, he started talking his way through the landing. As the flaps were extended in steps, he showed me just how much back trim to put in and how. When the airplane was properly trimmed, it only took two fingers to hold the yoke. These were things I already knew but had forgotten in my desire to show Jim what a great pilot I was. With his easy chatter, I felt the tension easing. He rolled onto the pavement without a bit of fuss and said, "You have it. Go around and then make a full stop."

I took the controls, determined to exonerate myself. "Flaps twenty. Speed boards down," I recited. Jim positioned them and repeated my commands. "Stand up the throttles," with a glance I checked the engine instrument panel. All four were spooling up properly. "Set take-off EPR, please."

"Rotate," Jim called as we passed take-off speed.

I was almost afraid to raise the landing gear for fear that it might fall off after the beating I had given it, but it worked fine. The final landing was acceptable and I had learned a lesson. Self-confidence is important if you are going to fly heavy jets, but too much self-assurance will lead to trouble.

In the three weeks that followed, we flew several more times. Jim backed off from helping me as he gained an assessment of my abilities and I became more comfortable in the left seat. He expected me to be fully prepared for each flight and to brief him on each maneuver that he was going to teach on that particular flight. The decisions that had such obvious solutions when I was not responsible for their outcomes were now much more difficult to make. I was suddenly aware of how little I really knew about flying when Jim told me that I had best be up-to-date on international procedures. He indicated that he had no intention of being much help to me crossing the Pacific, and if I busted an Air Defense Identification Zone or did some other stupid thing, he would see that I didn't drive anything bigger than the base garbage truck.

Upgrading was turning out to be an awful lot of work and not nearly as much fun as I thought it would be. Jim kept increasing the pressure by pretending to be an exceedingly dumb copilot. If I called for the landing gear to be put down, he would reach for the flap handle. Should I fail to catch his intentional error, I would get an unpleasant lecture on who was responsible for everything that happened on an airplane that I commanded, and the fact that the copilot might be a moron would excuse nothing. I had no idea that in two years Jim would move up in the world and I would be the instructor pilot filling his job.

That event was far over the horizon when we once again loaded our baggage on top of all kinds of cargo, filled the remaining space in the airplane with maintenance troops, and headed west across the Pacific Ocean. That was a terrible departure. The day before we left, our youngest son was admitted to the base hospital with pneumonia. Carolyn was torn between seeing me off and getting back to the hospital. There is a lag between deployment and the start of regular mail delivery. It was almost two full weeks before my first letter from Carolyn arrived, dated the day I had departed. It was several more days before a whole bundle of mail arrived. I arranged them by postmark dates and read the last one first. Bob was home from the hospital and doing well. Now I could read the rest of the letters at my leisure.

ELEVEN

♦ ♦ ♦ ♦ ♦ ♦ ♦ ♦ ♦ ♦ ♦ ♦

'Tis education forms the common mind;
Just as the twig is bent, the tree's inclined.
-Pope's Moral Essays

The larger islands of the southwest Pacific have their own character. In the vastness of the Pacific they call out their location to the sailor or the airman with a tall crown of clouds. From an airplane, their landfall is foretold by what appears to be a single distant cloud in an empty sky. It breaks the clean line of an otherwise pristine horizon and, as approached, seems to spread and climb steadily into the heavens. The cobalt blue of the open ocean changes to a lighter blue, then green and there, just beneath the edge of the cloud, a yellow band of beach can be seen fringed with white surf. The landing direction seldom changes, as it is determined by trade winds that have kept their direction since long before man came and borrowed their power to drive his wind ships.

Approaching Guam from the east, we flew inland south of Anderson Air Force Base for a right turn onto a long final approach over jungle covered hills that seemed to reach up for us as we sank lower towards our landing. As we drew closer we could see that the airfield was covered with B-52s and teeming with activity.

Even with the intense activity on the base, Guam had a somnolent air that one can only experience in the tropics. It was mid afternoon. The temperature was in the low nineties and so was the humidity. The effect was oppressive. As soon as the hatches and doors were opened, and the pressurized and refrigerated air of the aircraft interior vented to the atmosphere, it became unbearable inside the airplane and our clothing was immediately saturated. There was some speculation on the availability of cold beer as we left for operations. It is easy to understand why even the most urgent activity is carried out at a slower pace than its importance might deserve.

But maintenance and ordinance troops didn't seem to have that option as they swarmed over the bombers in preparation of a strike. Small tractors pulling trains of little trailers, each carrying a five hundred pound bomb, delivered their cargo to the waiting bombers. Dark blue step-vans and pick-up trucks hurried about on busy errands.

Just over twenty years ago America's young men had carried out this same activity on this same airfield. Only the airplanes were different. Our arrival at operations confirmed that a strike was pending. We were informed that our airplane was being refueled and we were to report for mission briefing at three thirty the next morning, then preflight our tanker for strip alert. Strip alert meant that we would remain at the aircraft with the radios on and ready to take-off within minutes of being notified that one or more of the bombers needed extra fuel. We might have to fly far west of the Philippines or meet the bomber just offshore from Guam. There also was a chance that we might not be launched at all. A stop at the Base Exchange for reading material was in order. It could get very boring sitting in an airplane parked in the sun for an entire day.

After we had completed the paperwork for our strip alert duty, we left Operations and checked into our quarters. Jim and I shared a room. Ron roomed with another navigator and Don Morris went to the NCO quarters. Knowing what a bunch of dog robbers they were, I had no doubt that theirs were the most luxurious quarters on base. We shared a bathroom with the adjoining room. A window air conditioner, installed through the wall, wheezed and rattled in its contest with the humid tropical air. Water, leached from the saturated air, ran down the outside wall beneath the air conditioner and stained it a permanent rust color. Several geckos patrolled the walls and ceilings. We did not disturb the geckos, for it was their vigilance that kept the population of exotic bugs at manageable levels. A double wardrobe stood against one wall, and inside each half, a light bulb burned constantly. Without the heat from the light bulbs anything stored in the wardrobes would grow green mold overnight. Flying suits hung in the wardrobe would emerge dry the next day, but would sport huge white stains where the sweat had dried and left the owner's body salts. If flying suits were hung anywhere other than in the wardrobe, they would not dry at all. A battle-weary refrigerator occupied a corner of the room. It was fully capable, given enough time, of lowering the temperature of beer from hot all the way down to tepid. Through the window I could see a weary palm tree that leaned away from the constant trade winds and rattled it's few remaining fronds in weak protest. Guam is a pretty island, but the air base falls short of being a tropical paradise. The hallmark of the Pacific islands is the endless sound of surf. Anderson is situated on a promontory five hundred feet above the sea, which mutes the sound of the surf. What surf noise remained was quite overcome by the continuous roar of jet engines and the strident sound of some neighbor's stereo.

We immediately stripped off our soggy flying clothes, opened a beer still somewhat cool from the Base Exchange, and stretched out on our bunks dressed only in our undershorts. The mattress had that damp and well-used feeling, common to a rundown Mississippi motel that rents rooms by the hour.

Jim took a long swallow of beer, trying to drink it while it still retained some vestige of coolness and said, "Well, it's plain to see that nothing is too good for the troops and that's just what they get." A loud belch punctuated his philosophical observation.

I watched with scientific detachment as a gecko stalked some sort of huge winged insect, captured it, and ate it directly above my bunk. He swiftly cleaned his chops with a single sweep of his tongue. "Dear God, Jim. How do those bomber crews manage a six-month tour here? The boredom must be mind bending."

His response was maudlin with sympathy. "Aw, fuck them. They're always whining about something."

With that he drained his beer and hurled the empty can in the general direction of the wastebasket. Another belch ended the conversation. He rolled over on his side and presently began to snore. His comment reflected the low regard for the bomber force held by both the tanker crews and the fighter aircrew more directly engaged. The bomber crews lived on this island thousands of miles from danger, and occasionally flew a mission at very high altitude and south of the DMZ. The frustration for these crews bordered on unbearable. The war would have ended years earlier and countless lives been saved had they been properly employed. Not until Nixon finally committed them, during the Christmas bombing of the north in 1972 against what had grown to be the most heavily defended targets in the history of air warfare, would they be vindicated. Within two weeks, North Vietnam demanded a return to the peace talks.

I lay on my bunk reflecting on my responsibilities during strip alert, trying to imagine various situations that might arise and just what my response should be. Presently I dozed off into that half awake, half asleep state that lasted until a loud plop on my pillow brought me fully awake. The inverted gecko of a few minutes ago had lost his grip on the ceiling and fallen next to my face. He eyed me for a moment or two then, with a disgusted look, as if I was to blame for his sudden fall, stalked away.

"The hell with it," I muttered and got up and opened another beer.

A quarter of an hour before the scheduled mission briefing, a crew bus stopped in front of our quarters with a loud squeal of brakes. We stumbled aboard, dragging our canvas bags of flight gear and leather briefcases of let-down charts and tech orders in what is known throughout the Air Force as a "bag drag." A few minutes later we were delivered in front of the operations building. The briefing room was the size of a modest movie theater. Bomber crews consisted of six men per airplane, and judging by the number of people milling about, this was to be a large strike. As the appointed hour approached, the crews sorted themselves out and found seats. A major in rumpled suntans stood near the door at the back of the briefing room. With nervous movements he kept opening the door a few inches and peeking outside. Obviously, his task was to announce the arrival of the Commander by calling the assembly to attention.

Presently he bellowed, "Room, ten-hut!"

With much banging and scraping of seats, the assembly rose and assumed various positions of attention. Aircrews are not noted for military bearing. The door was flung open with a bang and the Wing Commander stomped down the center aisle, a large cigar protruding from his mouth, his face a mask of determination, and several of his staff trailing behind. He evidently had served his apprenticeship under General LeMay. His staff also stomped, but not quite as ferociously as their leader. This little ceremony followed the form of every mission briefing I had ever attended, except those conducted by the Royal Air

Force. Their briefings were blessed with a paucity of ritual and took the word brief literally.

After a little over an hour of non-stop details, the Chaplain came to the podium and invited us to join him in prayer, while he beseeched the Almighty to bless us and our undertaking of dropping over three thousand bombs on other human beings. His plea to the Supreme Being made me a little nervous, as I felt we might be pushing it a little asking favor of Him in order to wage war.

We learned that thirty B-52s would take off and fly to an area over the Ho Chi Min trail and carpet bomb an area where concentrations of trucks and troops were suspected to be. En route, they were to meet a like number of KC-135s over the South China Sea and top off their fuel tanks. Round trip distance for this mission was approximately forty-eight hundred miles. No refueling was planned for the return trip. Fuel consumption decreased dramatically once an airplane was rid of its bomb load; however, we would remain on strip alert until the Bomber Task Force Commander reported to Port Wine (the radio call sign for the Air Force Command at Guam) that no bomber needed an extra refueling. We could reasonably expect twelve hours of duty unless we were launched. In that event, all bets were off and anything could happen. A lot of work had gone into planning this gaggle. A like number of tankers would launch from Okinawa, and precise timing and navigation would be required to place the right tanker in front of the right bomber at the correct time and place. Once away from land, there were no navigation aids other than the sextant and tables, the same tools used by captains of sailing ships a century earlier. I felt a good deal of relief that it was not my responsibility to bring together the two huge flights of airplanes for a mass in-flight refueling.

*****

B-52 missions against South Vietnam and Laos were launched from this base and the new base at U-Tapao in Thailand. To most American airmen the target selection seemed inane. Where was the efficiency in sending a strike of thirty B-52s thousands of miles to drop more than three thousand bombs on a suspected troop concentration? A very good mission might yield a couple of trucks or a water buffalo killed. One post-strike ground inspection reported several documents destroyed. Such missions were an expensive waste of air resources. But President Johnson insisted that these raids were effective and there was no one to reveal the lie. The role of the air weapons had been strangely turned around.

Tactical aircraft were used in a strategic role and strategic aircraft were doing the tactical chores, a decision not made by military commanders but by politicians for political reasons. As sometimes happens in cases of impromptu use of military resources, an unforeseen by-product of this role reversal was the use of heavy bombardment aircraft in the role of close air support of ground troops. During the siege of Khe Sanh, B-52s were very effective in a close air support role and bombed literally along the perimeter lines of the besieged base from very high altitudes. On several occasions during RESCAPs, a flight of several B-52s was held in a standby orbit, to be called in by the FAC should he need such an enormous amount of ordinance. Such daring tactics were the result of years of practice and the consummate skill of the B-52 aircrews. Their skill, along with advancements in electronic equipment, made acceptable what would seem to be an appalling risk to friendly forces. This tactic evolved into a new use for an ancient airplane originally designed to carry a nuclear bomb to a Cold War enemy.

After the September 11th attack on the World Trade Center, the B-52 was employed in an even more sophisticated role in the war on terror. A single airplane is able to orbit for hours, miles above a battlefield, and drop a single guided bomb on a target as small as a tank or cave entrance. The target and type of bomb required is determined by ground forces and the response is immediate. One superannuated B-52 now does the work of a squadron of modern ground support aircraft. That ancient and ugly old airplane just seems to soldier on.

*****

It was just about O'dark thirty when we arrived at the hardstand far out on the southwest end of the airfield. Our tanker was parked far enough from the busy and floodlit areas of the airfield that the tropical night still had a velvet quality. I noted that the taxi route to the runway was short and direct. Should we be launched, Jim would expect me to know that. If it became necessary for me to ask him for assistance, his certain response would be, "I'm just a copilot. That is not in my job description." Unless I was about to taxi off onto the grass he would not intercede. Since our departure from the States, I had quickly learned that if I wanted to be an aircraft commander I had best act like one. The preflight went quickly. Jim sat in the copilot seat and read the checklist to me with all of the inspiration of a retarded wheel chock. He deliberately skipped items to see if I would catch them. When I did, he grunted in satisfaction, which for him truly was high praise.

. The airplane was in excellent condition, as all westbound tankers normally were. When airplanes were rotated overseas, SAC tried to send them in the best possible condition, since parts and specialized maintenance were much more readily available at home bases. The preflight completed, Jim stuffed cotton in his ears and retired to one of the bunks just aft of the galley. He was followed, in a matter of minutes, by the navigator and boom operator, and I was left alone on the dimly lit flight deck to monitor the radio, with nothing but the screech of the auxiliary power unit at the aft end of the cargo deck for company. This was a generator set, powered by a turbine engine, designed to provide electrical power on the ground when no external power was available. It was reliable but noisy. It was rumored that its purpose was to turn jet fuel into noise and that the production of electricity was an incidental by-product of this function.

I turned the cockpit lights lower and could see that the eastern horizon now had a thin line of light on it. The first bombers lumbered past on the taxiway, almost invisible in their black paint. Their taxi lights and navigation lights seem to be suspended in the darkness. Soon a long line had formed on the taxiway, each with eight idling jet engines. The combined sound of all of those engines overwhelmed the screech of our APU, and the stink of jet exhaust was intolerable. Closing the cockpit side-windows afforded some relief as I waited.

Dawn comes quickly in the tropics. The sunrise was outlining the trade wind cumulus clouds that formed, as the moist air was forced upward on its arrival over land. Soon I could see the far end of the runway where it ended abruptly and the land dropped away five hundred feet to the sea. The long line of bombers began to move. The first one started down the runway. No sooner did it drop out of sight, as it left the end of the runway and sank towards the sea, than the next one began his take-off. I watched in alarm, but presently the first bomber's navigation lights rose into view and he commenced his climb. He would be passing over the Russian spy trawler, a little over three miles off shore, by the time he had cleaned up the landing gear and flaps and reached climb speed. One after another they lumbered down the runway, using every bit of it, and then some of the free altitude that they gained when they passed over the edge of the cliff, to lift well over two hundred tons each. It took nearly forty minutes for all of them to take-off. Some wag later remarked that whenever there was a big mission launch, the entire island rose five inches from the weight reduction.

Nine hours later, numb from the high-pitched scream of the APU, we were released from strip alert. We would leave for Okinawa in two days. In the morning we would do the mission paperwork for the flight to Okinawa. It was pretty straightforward; a left turn after take-off and climb on course on a northwest heading. The weather, to use pilot's slang, was predicted to be severe clear for the entire route. Our plan was to get our flight planning chores done early and then take the shuttle bus down to Tarague Beach and spend the rest of the day there. We would have to stop by the Base Exchange and buy swimming trunks as none of us had anticipated lounging on a tropical beach under the shade of some palm trees, eating hot dogs, and sipping almost cold beer. Occasionally, there was a good day in this vagabond life.

*****

I seemed to be getting over my landing shyness after my humiliating first landing with Jim. My landing at Kadena was smooth. No one complained of spinal compression fractures and the landing gear did not collapse. Jim even grunted his approval. We taxied slowly along behind a Follow Me truck. It was warm but not as humid as Guam. I had thought that there were a lot of bombers at Anderson, but it looked as if every KC-135 in the world was parked on the ramp at Kadena. The air war seemed to be reaching a peak.

At Tanker Operations we were given our room assignments and schedule for the next several days—a schedule that consisted of nothing but a numbing round of new arrival briefings; directions telling us how to avoid being shot down or colliding with a civilian airliner; intelligence lectures filled with numbers such as sorties flown, bombs dropped and body counts; and finally, the usual rules of engagement, which prohibited any independent thought or action.

It also seemed that the president was considering another unilateral stand down. This happened whenever we got close to winning. All our forces would stand down so that the other side could meditate on the error of their ways. Of course, they spent little time in contemplation. Instead, they very wisely used any hiatus to improve and expand their air defenses, unimpeded by American air power. Such ill-considered action on our part cost us dearly. When it was apparent that the Viet

Cong and North Vietnamese were not at all remorseful and we resumed bombing, American flyers were confronted with much stronger defenses than before the stand down. Such experiments were promoted by anti-war activists. The fact that these unilateral stand downs failed time after time did not diminish their demands for this ridiculous practice. It was not the anti-war activists or their loved ones who would be sent again and again into the storm of new and increased anti-aircraft fire.

Eventually these briefings were over. It was a trial all new arriving aircrew had to endure. Jim's name appeared on the daily mission roster. Our first mission briefing was a shock. We were to lead a sixteen airplane Arc Light support mission. Because Jim was an instructor pilot, he was the designated Tanker Task Force Commander and responsible for the timing so critical to a successful mass rendezvous over the open ocean. He would make decisions involving the entire flight but would not interfere with the safety of flight decisions of individual aircraft commanders. Operational command structure in the Air Force differs from Naval command structure. The SAC units that operated in Southeast Asia were called Provisional Wings and were made up of crews from many different squadrons. Rank is considered, but is not the rigid deciding factor that it is in the Navy. In the case of a very large flight, a task force commander was designated with more consideration given to his experience than to his rank. Only in extreme situations, such as in a POW camp, did rank and date of rank become the rigid dictator of command.

I glanced sideways at him. His head was tilted back as he contemplated some speck on the ceiling and whistled softly through his teeth. In a flash he returned my glance with a smirk that said, "Not my problem. I'm just the copilot." Ron scribbled notes and looked worried. Don was busy counting his poker winnings from last night. I was not going to get to play "follow the leader" on this Arc Light mission; everyone else was.

The meteorologist spoke of a large low-pressure area over Mainland China but said it was not expected to impact our mission. The Wing Navigator then launched into a discussion of the timing triangle, the means that we would use to assure our arrival at a given point over the open ocean at a precise time. Navigation would be celestial. If this timing triangle was properly executed each tanker would find his assigned bomber a mile behind and two thousand feet below. The bombers also would use a timing triangle and the lead bomber navigator would consult with Ron by radio. The potential for a major cluster fuck seemed enormous. If I made a mess of this, Jim would bail me out, but I would most likely be returned to copilot duty.

As we left the briefing for our airplane, Jim looked innocently up at sky and said, "Sure looks like a nice night for flying."

I thought this a good time to snivel and said, "Are you sure that you want me to fly this one?"

"Hey, don't cry on my shoulder," he shot back. "You're the one who wants to be an aircraft commander."

He sure did like that line about me wanting to be an AC. The copilot's life didn't seem quite so bad at this point. Fortunately, the staff allowed plenty of time from start of engines to take-off. I was just able to keep up, as I had to do the copilot's take-off computations as well as the pilot's duties.

Night take-offs from the islands can be dangerous. The main runway at Kadena stretches nearly across the narrow neck of the island. Shortly after lift-off we were over the water. It was very dark and no horizon was visible. The sky was filled with stars that were reflected by a calm sea and gave an illusion that the stars were moving while we were suspended in the air in a nose up attitude. If one were to believe this and push the nose over he would be in the sea in seconds. I switched from visual to instrument flight. Jim raised the landing gear and did the copilot duties including raising the flaps and setting climb power. Suddenly I began to think I might get through this. My confidence came streaming back as I leveled off at altitude. My elation lasted until I reached overhead and tried to engage the autopilot. It did not engage. Several more attempts yielded the same result and a fruitless checking of circuit breakers followed. The autopilot was dead. I would have to hand fly the entire mission including the refueling, no mean task in itself.

Jim smirked, enjoying my discomfort, and on interphone said, "Better put on your oxygen mask. I'm going to the john. And don't forget to set the fuel panel for cruise." With that he disappeared.

Several minutes passed and I nervously asked, "Nav, where the hell is Jim?"

"Don't know, Art. Maybe he went back to get some shut-eye."

"Damn it all to Hell! Hey, Ron, can you help me with this fuel panel for a minute?"

"No way, Pilot. I gotta work on timing, besides I don't know shit about all that pilot stuff."

Ron knew as much about the pilot's work stations as I did, his remark about pilot stuff was a favorite expression of an old-time navigator who wanted to put a young pilot in his place. I was far too busy to waste time complaining. Soon I was so occupied that I forgot about Jim and concentrated on pacing myself. I did not know it at the time, but Jim was standing just out of sight behind me, with his headphones plugged into the spare interphone box, listening to everything that I said.

As we approached the timing triangle, Ron calculated the offset needed to correct our time. This information was passed to the rest of the flight by radio and in due course we arrived at the initial point and the flight echeloned to the left. Sure enough, to the right and below us I saw the navigation lights of the bomber formation converging with us. Unfortunately, far ahead and across our path, I also saw lightning flashes illuminating towering cumulous clouds that suggested that the weather disturbance was going to make liars out of the forecasters. The radar showed that the thunderstorms had not coalesced into a solid line yet, but were scattered. With luck we could get past that line before they got serious.

"Nav, I'm going to offset ten miles to the north and I'll offset the far-left bird ten miles to the south and spread the flight out. That'll give the formation an extra twenty miles to maneuver around the storm cells and we can still keep our base course. Check with the bomber lead, Nav, and see if they can manage that and still make their time on target."

While Ron took care of that radio call, I thought I'd better let the Tanker Task Force Commander know what I was doing in his name. "Boom, go wake the IP up and tell him I need him on the flight deck."

"Roger, Pilot, Boom checking off interphone."

Shortly, Don came back on interphone. "Pilot, this is Boom Operator. I woke the IP up, but he got mad and said to tell you, sir, to fly your own fucking airplane and not to bother him until the receiver is in the pre-contact position. His words, sir."

Of course, all of that time Jim was still standing out of sight behind me and giving the navigator the OK on my decisions. Since I was hand flying with airplanes all around me, I couldn't turn around to see what was going on. The three of them thought this was a great joke. I was beginning to enjoy this quite a bit myself. Running the show can be a lot of fun. The bomber reported one mile in trail.

"Boom Operator checking off interphone to go to the rear."

"OK, Boom," I answered. "On the way aft, wake Jim up and tell him that everything has gone to hell and I am about to crash into the sea if he doesn't come up here and run this fuel panel for me."

A minute later, Jim slid into the copilot seat and plugged in his helmet. He looked across at me and in mock surprise said, "Pilot, your flying suit is all wet. Why are you sweating? This is an easy airplane to fly. It is nothing but a four engine Piper Cub."

The secret of autopilot-off refueling is to anticipate the changes in pitch trim. The B-52 is a very large airplane and pushes a big invisible bow wave of air in front of it. That bow wave will try to push the tail of the tanker up when the bomber moves towards the contact position on the boom. It is imperative to have the airplane well trimmed before the bow wave gets anywhere near the tail. Normally the autopilot does this, but when refueling large airplanes with the autopilot off, this must be done manually. I did not rise to Jim's teasing, as that was what I was trying to do when he got in the copilot seat.

"Pilot, this is Boom, in the pod. Interphone check and refueling checklist complete. Receiver is starting to move in"

"Loud and clear, Boom. I am autopilot off, give me a call at thirty, twenty, and ten feet."

"Thirty feet."

I put in one click of back trim.

"Twenty feet."

Another click of back trim and I had to hold a little forward pressure on the yoke.

"Ten feet."

A third click of back trim and I had to hold a fair amount of pressure on the yoke.

The amber "contact made" light winked on. The receiver reported contact and Jim verified it. The bomber's bow wave was solidly under our stabilizer. The three clicks of back trim neatly compensated for that. The need for forward pressure on the yoke was gone, the airplane was in trim, and mechanically attached to the bomber while we transferred more than thirty tons of fuel. Jim's management of the off-load was so exact that I felt little need for further trim change and was able to maintain speed by small reductions in power as our weight diminished.

"Pilot, Nav. I have a thunderstorm on radar. It looks like it is about twelve miles ahead, right on track. Suggest you come right thirty degrees."

"Red One, this is Tanker lead. I am coming right thirty degrees. I'll use ten degrees of bank."

"Roger that." Our B-52 was unconcerned and stayed connected to the boom through the turn.

When we rolled out of the turn, the storm cell towered above us by a good ten thousand feet. It outlined itself with flashes of internal lightning and it seemed as if we were brushing it with the left wing tip. I prayed that it was not slinging hail out of the top, but it didn't seem that active. In another thirty minutes if it kept growing, this piece of sky would be a mean place to be. A few miles past the line of thunderstorms we finished refueling and climbed away ahead of the bombers.

Ron called, "Pilot, come right to three five zero. I suggest four twenty-five true airspeed to let the rest of the flight get in trail."

I called the turn and airspeed to the rest of the flight and we headed for Okinawa. I was getting tired. Jim took the airplane for a bit and let me catch up on paperwork. Don came back up front and passed me a paper cup of coffee. It was so hot and bitter that I wondered if it would eat through the cup before I got to drink it. Carefully, I balanced it on the footrest bar that ran below the instrument panel and let it cool a bit while I finished my paperwork. Finally the coffee was cool enough to sip. The taste was incredible. I detected no coffee flavor whatever. I wondered if the flight kitchen made a mistake and filled our coffee jugs with old hydraulic fluid. It was undrinkable. Don passed me a cup of water and I swallowed it in one gulp.

"OK, Pilot, you got the bird. I'm pretty tired after all that hard work." Jim smiled and slid out of his seat. He went to the back of the flight deck and visited with Don.

I was still hand flying but there was nothing heavy-duty going on. Except for the autopilot, the airplane was behaving very well. The other fifteen airplanes were strung out behind me in a long trail formation so I did not have to worry about station keeping; they had to keep station on me. There was no need to mess with the fuel panel until it was time for the landing checklist. It was a pretty night so I sat back and enjoyed flying the airplane. At Miyako Jima, an island about a hundred miles out from Kadena, I called approach control to check in. They had been tracking us and took over control of the flight, spreading us out to allow spacing for landing. In half an hour we were back on the ground. At debriefing, several of the other pilots thanked Jim for a smooth and uncomplicated mission. Jim glanced at me and raised one eyebrow.

*****

Captain Freddy Everett was uneasy. Rain slashed across the windscreen and the airplane trembled in the wind, even though it was sitting solidly on the ground and weighed two hundred and eighty-seven thousand pounds. He looked back over his left shoulder and saw the line of white surf spending itself in frustration on the beach where U. S. Marines had walked ashore twenty-three years ago. His airplane sat on the exact spot that had marked the end of the runway when this had been a Japanese fighter base. Now the area was paved over with concrete, and a runway more than twice the length of the former Japanese runway stretched into the distance and very nearly bisected the island. By looking forty-five degrees to his right he could look down the length of the runway until the driving rain blurred the lights and it faded into darkness. Water ran everywhere, driven by the gusting wind as it tried to find its way to the sea. In just a matter of minutes, Captain Everett was expected to advance the throttles and, with his left hand on the nose-wheel steering, guide the heavily loaded tanker onto the runway and take off into the darkness. His crew sensed his uneasiness and was quiet.

Two miles away Major Tracy Eagan, the duty controller, sat at a console in the command post and eyed the clock. Seven minutes to go and this kid would be on his way. No more launches for almost six hours. Things should quiet down. Flight crews annoyed him. They were frequently short tempered and constantly calling on the radio complaining about one thing or another, disturbing his peace and quiet. Major Eagan was very good with sarcasm. With the flight schedule in front of him he knew who was on each airplane, and as long as the pilot was of lesser rank, he felt free to make full use of his sarcasm. When he got off a particularly clever remark, both he and his overweight sergeant would yuck it up. Twice in the past month he had been overheard and rebuked by his immediate supervisor, the Deputy Commander for Operations. Several years earlier, he had clipped a light pole with a wing tip while taxiing. A pilot may bend a bird in flight and just might get off with that, but there is no acceptable excuse for a taxi accident. As a result, Eagan had been removed from crew duty and sent to the command post. He knew that the pilot sitting in the tanker out in the rain was a youngster and that it was very unlikely that any brass would be monitoring his radio frequency at this hour of the night.

The copilot scribbled the winds he had just received from the tower onto his kneeboard. It was just two minutes to their scheduled take-off time. He pulled his green covered binder of performance charts out of his briefcase and worked out the crosswind component.

"Boss, we got a steady crosswind component of thirty-six, but the gusts put us well over our limit of forty knots."

Captain Everett keyed his mike, "Control, this is Dora Two Seven. The gusts are exceeding my maximum crosswind component by at least five knots." He fully expected the Command Post to at least delay his take-off.

In the Command Post, closed off from the outside weather, Major Tracy Eagan could not feel the slashing rain or hear the powerful wind gusts. He shook his head and grinned at his Sergeant.

In a voice heavily laced with his best sarcasm he answered Dora Two Seven's radio call, "Well, take off between the gusts," he said shaking with the cleverness of his own wit.

In Dora Two Seven, the two pilots looked at each other in stunned disbelief. "Copilot, call the tower and tell them that we are ready to roll and to call the peak of the next gust."

"Kadena Tower, this is Dora Two Seven ready for take-off and please call the peak of the next gust."

"Say again, Two Seven," came the startled reply from the tower.

"I want take-off clearance and I want you to call the peak of the next gust. We intend to make our take-off between gusts."

"OK, Dora Two Seven. You are cleared for take-off at pilot's discretion. Wind is a direct right crosswind at thirty-eight knots increasing, now forty-two, forty-six knots, now dropping to forty..."

"Dora Two Seven rolling."

The engine sounds rose abruptly and the airplane skidded slightly as the tires rode up on a cushion of water. The copilot followed the throttles with his left hand. The engine sound abruptly increased as the water injection took effect. He took over control of the throttles and set two point eight three across the board on the EPR gauges. Rain streamed across the windscreen unaffected by the blast of high-pressure bleed air that was supposed to provide clear vision. Captain Everett held in full right aileron and a foot full of left rudder as the crosswind acted on the tall vertical fin and tried to weathervane the airplane into the wind. The nose wheels juddered in its effort to steer the airplane. It was rapidly becoming more difficult to keep the airplane tracking down the runway centerline, even with full control deflection. He felt the right wing start to lift. I've got to abort, flashed through his mind. The copilot held the throttles firmly in take-off position. He would not pull them back until ordered to do so. In the fraction of a second that Captain Everett could not scream abort and could not free his right hand to snatch the throttles back himself, the left outboard engine struck the ground. The right wing rapidly rose higher as the airplane slued to the left and then cart wheeled. In the tower, the Airman on duty saw the fireball, diffused by the rain, and pushed the crash alarm. None of the four crewmembers survived one of three tanker losses on a mission in direct support of the Vietnam War.

*****

Jim and I sat in the Officers' Club at Anderson Air Force Base. The view northeast over the Pacific was beautiful. The tradewinds made little whitecaps that marched across the sea until the rocks arrested their progress five hundred feet below us. We were about four days out on round-robin duty. This was a chore that was rotated among the crews and served to move parts and personnel between the area bases. It originated at Kadena and the usual route was from there to CCK, a base with an unpronounceable name on Formosa, then to U-Tapao in Thailand, and finally on to Guam by way of Clark Field in the Philippines. Sometimes we would then reverse ourselves and fly the whole trip the other way around or, if there were no cargo or passengers that rated priority transportation, we would return directly to Okinawa. It was a pleasant change from the highly charged Arc Light Missions and got us away from direct supervision for a spell.

We had flown the leg from Formosa to U-Tapao at night. Our route had taken us south of Hainan Island and across the coast of Vietnam sixty miles or so north of Danang. It had been a very dark night. The air seemed thick and we could smell the land even in the pressurized cabin. Beneath our path, dozens of orange colored flares hung in the sky. The night silently pulsed with the evil flashes of a great battle. We were looking through the keyhole of hell as the siege of Khe Sanh raged beneath us. This contest would last for six months. Our forces would withdraw and our leaders would claim a victory. I was beginning to think that we could bomb, using these tactics, until the end of time and not change a thing in Asia.

The conversation came around to the recent crash at Kadena. Jim was pretty steamed over it, but the crew had come from another base in the States and he had not known them. It didn't matter now; they were all dead.

"What do you think caused that crash?" Jim asked.

"Trying to take off with too much crosswind," I answered.

"That's obvious. Don't be obtuse. What really caused that accident?"

I thought a moment trying to see what he was getting at. Sometimes his lessons occurred at odd times and places. "That shit head in the command post badgered him with his remark about taking off between the gusts."

"Well, at least you're in the ballpark," he said, "but that was just a contributing factor. That accident happened because the Aircraft Commander didn't realize that he was in command of the airplane. That's what the word 'commander' means. Most of those jerks in the command post are there because they can't cut it on a crew. Their job is to answer the phone; they have no direct control over the pilot in command. They can pass operational orders from our commanders but they can only relay those messages. No one, not even CINCSAC can overrule a safety of flight decision the pilot in command makes. If he makes a poor one, then you can bet he will be standing in front of The Man the next day, but the decision will stand. If a pilot makes a bad one, then he probably will be dead. Never let someone sitting at a desk badger you into a situation that puts you and your airplane in an untenable position. They'll try like hell to do that, but if things go bad they will disappear or claim that they have never even heard of you. The only reason that jerk Eagan got found out was that the strip alert crew heard his remark over the radio. They couldn't believe it when that kid started his take-off roll. If I don't teach you anything else, learn that."

I think that I did learn that lesson. Several times in later years, I had to take a stand against some pretty heavy pressure, but I am here to write about it. For this reason I fear to fly on airlines that boast of their on-time departures and arrivals. I suspect that management is making too many decisions that should be made by the man in the left front seat.

TWELVE

◆ ◆ ◆ ◆ ◆ ◆ ◆ ◆ ◆ ◆ ◆ ◆

Resolve to be thyself; and know that he,
who finds himself, loses his misery!
-Mathew Arnold

The military pilot is subjected to constant testing and examination. In the Strategic Air Command, the very minimum of check flights in a twelve-month period was two. That was mandated. More were very common. One check flight each year was called the formal standardization check. It involved seemingly endless written examinations and flight testing of every aspect of one's duties. A flight check could be made on a single crewmember or, as was usual in the annual standardization check, the entire crew would be evaluated.

When we ask for regular examination of professionals such as teachers and those in health care professions, these same specialized practitioners, empowered by their unions, furiously resist such testing or recurring examination, for it is the nature of humans to exempt themselves from rules or qualifications that they will eagerly apply to others. Should a professional aviator suffer an accident, these same people would be the first to question the frequency of examination of his skill and credentials.

A B-47 copilot had to demonstrate proficiency in gunnery, electronic countermeasures, bombing, and high and low level navigation, in addition to all of the skills of a pilot. It was not unusual to require as many as three separate flights to complete a full flight check. A formal standardization check could easily keep a crew involved for more than a week.

When all of this was completed, the crew was allowed to stew for a few more days while the flight examiners completed their paperwork. Unless the flight check was an obvious failure, the examiners wanted time to review their many notes before committing to a grade. Then a time was set when all would meet in the Wing Commander's office. If the door was left open, smiles would prevail. If the door was shut, things got ugly. A failure on the part of any crewmember would remove the crew from combat ready status and place them in training status. The Wing Commander had to report this to SAC headquarters. Combat ready status was a level of training required for a crew to stand alert on a war sortie. Should a crew fail to maintain that status, then there was one less crew available for alert or war duty, and other crews would have to fill the void. The SAC Commander would not be pleased with the Wing Commander. This psychological tsunami traveled from the highest levels of command, collected all kinds of debris, and then crashed down on the heads of the unhappy crew. The black smear on their records occasioned significant loss of professional pride and did nothing to enhance their careers. Planned leaves and backyard barbecues were forgotten until the crew or individual was retrained, re-tested, and returned to combat ready status. In the interim, they slunk about the squadron feeling like pariahs under the gaze of those who had to stand extra alert or reflex duty while they retrained.

In SAC, two additional flight checks were critical to a pilot's career. The first was his upgrade check to Aircraft Commander. The second was an Aircraft Commander's upgrade to Instructor Pilot. The latter could only be taken if his Squadron Commander nominated a pilot for instructor duty.

In the hair-trigger days of the Cold War we worked constantly with nuclear weapons. An international incident was a distinct possibility whenever one left the U. S. to fly missions in sensitive areas of the world. Failure in any duty area was not tolerated. Most of us would fly into the mouth of hell if that would excuse us from a formal check flight. This was our Sword of Damocles. As each flight passed I knew that my day to fly an upgrade check was drawing closer. With the fortitude of the condemned, I pretended the day would never come.

We had been back several weeks from our latest paid vacation to beautiful Southeast Asia. Jim's wife, Jan, had called Carolyn and invited us to a backyard barbecue the coming Saturday. During the six months we had been overseas, they had become good friends. Our kids were about the same ages and they, too, got along very well. It was shaping up to be a pleasant Saturday and I intended to make the most of it. I didn't get to see much of either my wife or children between the so-called Cold War and the much hotter war in Southeast Asia. I intended to take advantage of the few opportunities that arose.

Jim dumped half a bag of charcoal into his grill. The two youngest kids, their son Alan and our Bob, came immediately up to the grill and tried to peer over the edge, their small boy incendiary instincts fully aroused. Jim shooed them away and started to squirt some sort of unidentified flammable fluid onto the charcoal.

"Art, you know we are scheduled for alert next Friday?"

"Yeah, I do. If you put much more of whatever that is on that grill we might not make it."

Jim looked at the can in surprise. He capped it and set it aside. "I've talked to the ground training folks and had you taken off of all ground training for that week."

The two little boys watched Jim furtively from the other side of the yard, wanting to see the flame when he lit the grill.

Alarm bells rang in my mind and I had a sinking feeling. "Why'd you do that?" I asked.

He took the near empty glass from my hand and walked over to the picnic table. With a toss he threw the dregs of my drink on the grass. The dog waddled over and sniffed hopefully. Jim mixed me a fresh martini and stood holding it.

"Because you are going to be studying the first four days and then taking your written exams before we get off alert on Friday. The following Tuesday, you will take your check ride with Les Terrell."

I stared at him for a moment. I knew this was coming but didn't expect it to happen quite so soon. "Are you going to give me that martini or are you going to drink it yourself?"

"Oh, yeah, sure," he handed me the drink and said, "I had to argue my head off to get you scheduled with Les."

"What the hell did you do that for? Les and I are not exactly what one would call friends!"

Les Terrell was the Chief of the Standardization Division and called by most crewmembers Terrell the Terrible. I had flown with him once or twice in the past and had come away badly shaken by the experience. He made me feel like the most incompetent pilot that ever got in an airplane. I had hoped for any one of the other check pilots when it came time for my flight.

"Hey, you should thank me," Jim said. "If Lester passes you, you will have earned it. Besides, my ass is on the line, too. If I put a student up for an AC check and he fails, it doesn't say much for me as an instructor."

He struck a match and threw it onto the soaking charcoal. With a small whoosh, a ball of flame rose up. Bob and Alan squealed with delight; I felt like throwing up. Carolyn and Jan talked happily away about some topic important to them. Our daughter was steadfastly pursuing Jim's second boy, Michael. She was just eight years old and had suddenly decided that some boys were "cute." Jim gave me an innocent look and started to season the steaks.

An upgrade check to aircraft commander is a full formal standardization check or, in the slang of the era, the whole Mary Anne. The written portion covers everything that could possibly have anything to do with flying. Much of it is open book and is designed to make the pilot root out or locate information that he may not use every day, such as international procedures and HF radio wave propagation. It is intended mainly as a refresher and includes complex performance and weight and balance problems. Since it is open book, a minimum-passing grade of ninety percent is expected. Meteorology, engineering, and aircraft systems are also part of the testing. The emergency procedure portion is closed book and no errors are allowed. The pilot is expected to be able to recite all emergency procedures without reference to the tech order or checklist.

During the flight phase, the candidate for aircraft commander usually flies with the crew that he trained with. He must direct all the mission planning and, during the flight, demonstrate proficiency in any maneuver common to the airplane, as well as instrument and emergency procedures. The more dangerous emergencies are checked in the flight simulator. Normally, the instrument check portion is flown at the home base, giving the advantage of familiarity to the candidate. To simulate instrument flight conditions, this portion of the check flight is performed with the candidate's vision restricted to the instrument panel by means of a long visor. The pilot must fly at least three different instrument approaches and missed approaches, an instrument departure, and a jet penetration, which is the transition from high-altitude cruise flight to the low-altitude instrument approach to the runway. He must also demonstrate his ability to recover from unusual airplane attitudes on instruments and to navigate to various points using radio aids to navigation. These demonstrations must be performed without the copilot or navigator offering any solutions, such as which heading to fly. Other than this restriction, they perform their normal crew duties.

The copilot seat may be occupied by any available pilot, since the flight examiner usually sits in the jump seat. From this position he can more closely monitor the candidate. This is the most nerve-wracking part of the check. One cannot help but wonder what awful errors or omissions are being recorded. He will tell the candidate what maneuver to perform but can offer no instruction. Should the examiner intercede in any way, the check-flight is over and the hapless pilot has failed. In theory, the evaluation is intended to be objective but, as in any field, palace intrigues occasionally intrude. Should this be the case, the examiner is in a position to be unreasonably critical and the unfortunate candidate has little recourse. This had happened to me several times and I survived only by the greatest good fortune.

In the following ten days I was filled with worry and the dread of failure. I had forgotten the adage that what is hard by yards is easy by inches. Had I been asked to perform any one of the many tasks involved in this check ride, I would have thought nothing of it. Instead of thinking of the flight check as a series of tasks that are just a part of my job, I saw it as a massive obstacle. This disabling state of mind is referred to as "check-itis" and many suffer from it. It is a common malady among younger pilots. In later times, when I was giving check flights, I saw this frequently and would do my best to reduce the intimidation factor.

During mission planning the crew was thorough and professional. Ron and Jim both took the time to revue the entire flight with me, carefully pointing out areas where things might get a little busy. This helped me to plan the pacing of the flight and not fall into the trap of getting behind the airplane. Their very business-like attitude impressed me with the seriousness of this flight check. My career literally was at stake. Jim knew I was nervous and did his best to reassure me.

Weather on a check flight is simply the luck of the draw. If the gods of aviation smile upon you, beautiful weather will prevail on the day of the scheduled flight check, but should you be in disfavor with the mysterious deities of the sky, then fog, rain, wind, scattered tornadoes, and occasional hurricanes will be the order of the day. As long as the weather does not exceed the flight limitations of the airplane, the flight is expected to proceed. Luck was with me. On the day of the flight the weather was beautiful. Seven hours and twenty minutes after take-off, I taxied the airplane back into its parking place.

A flight check very much mirrors the activities of a normal training mission. With the exception of a navigation leg, when the airplane is flown essentially in a straight line and the autopilot does the flying, the pilot is very busy. My apprehension and fear of failure were overcome by the concentration required by the various tasks I had to demonstrate. Les Terrell sat in the jump seat and quietly made his notes. He said nothing to intimidate me. The copilot, assigned for the flight, was experienced and competent. He observed the activities and made mental notes with an eye towards his future. As we deplaned Les looked at the yellow, taxi guideline painted on the pavement. It should pass between the dual nose gear tires. It was a good foot to one side. Les made a big deal out of measuring this distance using a plotter as a ruler. After some muttered, pseudo-scientific conversation with the crew chief, he looked at me and shook his head.

"You just barely passed," he said and got onto the crew bus.

I had anticipated having to wait several days for results. Les could have strung me out by saying nothing. The relief was immense.

At the Squadron, Jim was waiting for us to get back. As we trooped inside he asked, "How'd it go? I suppose I've got to fly the next six months with you clearing corrective action?"

Les answered, "Against my better judgment, he squeaked by, but I'll be watching him. We'll hold the informal critique in my office about two tomorrow afternoon, if that's OK with everyone? I'll have my secretary set up the formal critique with the Wing Commander."

I couldn't believe it was over.

Jim groaned, "Damn, now I'll have to start all over with some other ten-thumbed, retarded copilot. But anyone should be an easier job than you were, Art." With that left-handed compliment he slapped me on the back and said, "Come on, let's go to the Club. You owe me a drink."

Pay-off finally arrived. I found my name on the sixty dash nine flying schedule. An aircraft commander had taken a week's leave while his wife was busy providing him with another tax exemption. Since I had not yet been assigned a crew of my own, scheduling plugged me into the vacant spot. It was an ideal first flight for a new aircraft commander. Take-off time was about sunset and the mission was a PACCS, or Post Attack Command and Control Squadron flight, an eight hour mission with nothing to do but orbit over a given geographical point with a dozen radio operators, missile officers, and assorted electronic wizards doing their thing in the back of the airplane. The PACCS squadrons were established, in the days before satellite communications, to lift all military communications off the surface in the event of a nuclear attack. When a full link was established, an airplane was in orbit every two hundred miles, in a line that stretched from the east coast to the Hawaiian Islands. Most PACCS airplanes also were able to perform the launch of an intercontinental ballistic missile squadron that might have lost its launch facility in a nuclear attack.

In any other circumstance, I would have groaned with boredom at the thought of one of these missions, but this would be my first time out. I didn't want to dive right in but preferred to ease my way into the pilot-in-command situation I had lusted for so long. I knew the crew very well and the copilot was an old-timer about to start upgrading himself. It looked like a piece of cake.

At the appointed hour the crew bus pulled up in front of the airplane. Together with all of the electronic types, we made quite a crowd. A van escorted by two armed Air Police vehicles arrived simultaneously. The van contained the "black boxes" that gave the missile crew the ability to launch Minute Man missiles from the airplane, should that awful event be necessary. We were performing a drill of this procedure. The black boxes were dummies in this case, but the practice of the security procedures was impressive.

I talked with the Missile Crew Commander for a moment or two and made the usual agreement that he should be responsible for all personnel aft of the cockpit door. Then, in full view of this huge audience, I strutted about the airplane performing the exterior inspection while I whistled the theme to "The High and the Mighty." Pretty heady stuff this being the main man. Of course, I strove to appear as the wise and ancient aviator when in reality a railroad steam engineer, complete with bib overalls and oil can, would have been more believable. But everyone knew that I was a virgin facing initiation and were all very tolerant and allowed me my moment to strut. The harsh truth of reality would arrive soon enough.

The pavement still reflected the warmth of the sun, now sinking behind the Black Hills, as we taxied to the northwest end of the airport. The copilot copied our clearance, handled the radios, and rechecked the take-off data. As he worked, I am sure that he reflected that soon it would be his turn. I was having fun. The agony of the last several weeks was forgotten. For the first time since my last flight in a T-33 I felt like a pilot. The copilot acknowledged the take-off clearance as I armed the water injection system. I took a quick look around as the airplane lined up with the runway centerline, throttles standing up; I could feel the copilot's hand behind mine.

"Your throttles, set two point eight three." I moved my right hand to the yoke and the airplane accelerated smoothly. At seventy knots the navigator started his stopwatch for the check timing.

"S-one," the copilot said over the interphone.

No turning back now!

"Rotate," he said calmly.

I pulled back on the yoke, the nose came up smoothly and the airplane soared off of the runway. What a rush! I ordered the gear and flaps up and leveled off at five hundred feet to accelerate to two hundred and eighty-five knots. As the water ran out, the copilot set climb thrust and I turned onto the first heading for the Linden One departure. To keep up the appearance of the wise old pilot, I turned the airplane over to the copilot to fly on the pretext of drinking a cup of coffee and lighting my pipe. I put both feet up on the bar that runs below the instrument panel and sat back to enjoy the scenery. The boom operator handed me a cup of coffee that was perfectly drinkable at this stage of the flight and I fished my pipe out of my pocket and lit up.

The departure route brought us back over the field at about eighteen thousand feet. It was just about dark on the ground, although still quite light at altitude. Looking down to the left I could see the empty spot on the parking ramp that we had vacated a few minutes earlier. The runway and taxiway lights outlined the airfield. A cold breath of doubt swept over me and was gone in a second. I was expected to return this airplane and all of these people to that very same parking spot in a little over eight hours, and I also was expected to return all in as good a condition as they enjoyed when we left. Quickly, I pushed such sober thoughts out of my mind. A left turn was coming up shortly and I could make out the loom of the Black Hills ahead in the growing darkness. I settled back to enjoy the flight.

"Pilot, this is Missile One," came a slightly urgent voice over the interphone.

"Go ahead," I answered laconically.

"Sir, we're on fire back here! Can you send back some help?"

No one moved. The copilot continued to concentrate on flying the published departure. The airplane climbed serenely into the growing darkness. I am sure that my lack of an instant and commanding response was due to a sudden cardiac arrest. Fortunately, the acrid stink of whatever brand of tobacco that I was smoking must have revived me. I puffed once on my pipe and the horrible significance of that last message penetrated my numbed senses. Those silly bastards had built a bloody bonfire on the plywood deck immediately above the biggest portion of some one hundred and eighty thousand pounds of fuel and now they wanted help to put it out! I was losing my virginity, not in a pleasant interlude in the back seat of an old Chevy, but in a violent back alley rape.

The training that I had grumbled so much about came to my rescue. There was a checklist for just such an event as this. It wasn't a very long one, but it was the crutch that I needed. I reviewed it in my mind: 1. Crew on one hundred percent oxygen. 2. Extinguish the fire. This seemed a capital solution.

"OK, everybody, this is the pilot. Go on one hundred percent oxygen. Missile One, check on your people. Boom, you go aft, find out what is burning and see if you can put the damn fire out."

The Navigator stood up behind the copilot, lifted off his headset, put on his helmet, and attached oxygen mask while he continued to fly the airplane. The boom operator checked off interphone, hooked up to a walk around oxygen bottle, and went aft. The Navigator reported on oxygen and went back to his normal duties. I sat with my feet up on the bar and tried to think of what else I should do. I would have to wait until I heard from the boom operator. My pipe had gone cold, so I sipped my coffee and looked out the window, not because I was brave but because I could not think of any other useful thing that I could do. They would either put the fire out or we all were destined for a ride on the nylon elevator. I did reflect upon how long it would take to get that many people out of the airplane, and upon the grim fact that I would get to go last. What happened to all the privileges of command?

Parachuting from a tanker is a bit tricky. The airplane is not equipped with ejection seats. Leaving by way of the over-wing hatches poses a high risk of striking the airplane. The entrance hatch behind the pilot seat is the recommended route for bailout. The pressure door is released and falls away. Immediately after that a spoiler, or flat piece of metal, extends downward from the forward edge of the opening and breaks the smooth airflow past the opening, so that a person is not held against the airplane by the slipstream. Each person then jumps feet first through the opening, hopefully missing any parts of the airplane. Should he be unconscious for some reason, his parachute is designed to open automatically as soon as he falls below fourteen thousand feet. I began to mentally run through the various steps that it would take to bail this crowd out. I considered dumping the cabin pressure but was reluctant to do that until I knew what was going on. Everyone was supposed to be on oxygen but I did not know that for sure, and we were high enough that oxygen would be necessary if the cabin lost its pressure. I was frightened enough myself and it would be best if I did not show it. This seemed to be one of those times that Jim had cautioned me about. I could hear his voice telling me to fly the airplane first, don't do anything sudden, and think the problem through. The copilot seemed to be doing very well with the flying part of Jim's advice, so I pretended to be doing the thinking part. It seemed that the boom operator had been gone a long time when I heard the cockpit door slam.

"Pilot, this is Boom." He sounded pretty exasperated. "The only thing they had going on was an overheated converter. It made a shit load of smoke and no one knew where the circuit breaker was for it. It's all secured back there and that converter won't interfere with the mission. In fact, they don't even know what it's for."

"Thanks, Boom. Crew, this is the pilot. Go back to normal operations and we'll continue the mission."

I had seven more hours to reflect on this incident. The joy had gone out of that first flight in command. This was serious. People could get hurt, including me! I didn't mind having to look after myself, but I still wonder; if that had been a serious fire, could I have gotten all those people out? In-flight fire and structural failure are the two terrors that haunt pilot's dreams.

Two days later I talked to Jim about the incident. I still was unsure of my actions. He laughed.

"There wasn't much else you could have done without knowing what was going on. The departure route simply boxes the field, so you were staying close to the flagpole, and if you had called the Command Post and said you were on fire, there would have been all hell to pay. Especially when it turned out that the problem was nothing but a little smoke. I've talked myself silly telling you that when you have a problem in the air, don't do anything sudden. If you do, you will fuck up for sure. Figure out what is wrong, then make your decision on what you are going to do. It seems that's pretty much what you did, but I suspect it was more by luck than intent. Once you have made a decision, call the Command Post and tell them what you are going to do. Do not ask them what to do. That will get you into trouble every time. By the way, you should have gone on oxygen yourself instead of sitting there drinking coffee like some tourist!"

A strange follow-up to this incident happened a couple of weeks later just before alert briefing. Copilots are terrible gossips. I know. I was one for what seemed like forever. I walked into the back of the day room with a cup of coffee in my hand. A group of three or four copilots hadn't seen me and were chattering away about some hero of theirs.

"He must have ice in his veins. He just sat there drinking his coffee while the whole ass end of his airplane was on fire. The Boom put it out and..."

So that is how legends are born. Never believe a legend. I slipped out the door I had come in and went quietly to the briefing room.

THIRTEEN

◆◆◆◆◆◆◆◆◆◆◆◆◆◆◆◆

And the skies of night were alive with light,
with a throbbing, thrilling flame;
-Robert W. Service

Those who make their way in life by spending much of their time far above the earth, enclosed in what truly is a fragile machine, must endure long years of seasoning. This period of growth is fraught with dangerous obstacles, both physical and professional. Should the fledgling military aviator be excessively timid and suffer from indecision or choose to abdicate his command by allowing others to seize it psychologically, his death may well be professional. If his nature is at the other extreme then, in all probability, he will die a violent death in a single moment of either incompetence or very bad luck. In battle, either extreme can be fatal. Operational commanders who have traversed the minefield of experience know this. They much prefer men endowed with common sense over those who are excessively skilled aviators, for it is the overconfident and very skillful man who will exceed either his or his airplane's limits simply because he does not know where these frontiers lie. The timid must be dismissed for incompetence. The arrogant are often much more difficult to eliminate. Aggression and self-confidence are essential attributes of military airmen, especially the fighter pilot. Without these characteristics, he cannot survive. Neither can he endure with an overabundance of these qualifications. This seasoning is gained by observation, experience, and luck.

*****

"Goat Four Four, Ellsworth Approach, turn right now to heading two one zero. Descend to four thousand five hundred feet."

"Roger Approach, Goat Four Four." Captain Frank Welsh rolled the B-52 into a ponderous right turn and throttled back slightly to start the descent. Numbers seven and eight engines were shut down for a problem that had arisen earlier in the flight, but with six good engines left, he felt no particular concern about getting the big bird safely on the ground. With most of the fuel burned off he had more than enough power available. Lieutenant Colonel Murray, a staff pilot from Wing Headquarters, sat in the jump seat. He was on board simply to fly the monthly time that would earn him his flying pay. He had hoped to be able to fly a couple of approaches just to keep his hand in, but with two dead engines on the right outboard pod, that was pretty much out of the question. He vented his frustration by making snide remarks about Captain Welsh's decisions and flying ability and by this point in the flight, Captain Welsh was thoroughly rattled. Colonel Murray was causing a distraction. It would be more helpful if he saved his remarks until the airplane was on the ground. The young pilot's lack of assertiveness prevented him from saying this and as a result he was getting behind the airplane and it was out of trim. His short stature dictated that he fly with the seat in the full up position. In this position, his legs were not long enough to apply full rudder deflection. So far in his career, that had never been necessary, hence he did not consider it a problem.

"Goat Four Four, turn further right now to heading two five five to intercept the ILS localizer. You are cleared ILS approach to runway three zero, contact Tower two nine one point four at the outer marker."

"Roger Approach." Captain Welsh had his hands full and could manage only the minimum radio responses. The copilot completed the before-landing checklist and advised Welsh of the stopping distance. The localizer needle came off the left side of the instrument case and seemed to race to the other side. Welsh started his turn too late and overcorrected. Colonel Murray sneered at the young pilot's struggle. The glide slope needle came off of the top of the instrument case as the glide path was intercepted and the airplane was still out of trim. He was not prepared to begin the descent to the runway. The approach was going to hell rapidly. As the B-52 approached the field boundary, it was well right of the runway centerline. Welsh knew he would have to go around and take the necessary time to calm himself down and make the approach in the steps that he had been taught and with the airplane in proper trim. He advanced the six available throttles part way and reached for the rudder trim knob. Murray's exasperation exploded.

"Dammit to hell. If you're going to go around, then go around!" He reached from the jump seat and slammed the six throttles forward. This was an outrageous breach of etiquette. Colonel Murray's status on the airplane was that of a guest. Since Captain Welsh had already stood the throttles part way up, the six J-57 engines immediately spooled up to full thrust. Far out in the right outboard engine, pod numbers seven and eight engines remained inert. The asymmetrical thrust rolled the airplane sharply into those silent engines. Welsh tried to stuff in enough left rudder to stop the roll but he physically did not have the leg length to apply sufficient rudder to overcome the unexpected roll. The airplane stalled and crashed flat, with wings level, onto the refueling pits that lined the east side of the ramp. A huge fireball erupted and rolled upward.

From my home fourteen miles away, I glanced out the front window and saw the towering cloud of smoke over the intervening hills. I had no doubt as to the source of that smoke. In just five hours I had a crew report time for a flight that night. I went back to the bedroom and lay down, but I could not rest.

At the base hospital, Carolyn was visiting a clinic for routine shots for the kids. When she attempted to leave, the entire hospital was locked down. No one was allowed to leave or enter. Whenever an unexpected event of a disastrous nature occurs on a military installation, the response is always as if the base were under some sort of an attack. Until the commander was convinced that no attack was underway, his command assumed a defensive status. Emergency equipment and armed security people responded. No one else could move about the base and the gates were blocked.

From the front door of the hospital, Carolyn could see the tower of flame and smoke. The wail of sirens made a terrible soundtrack to the scene. She had no doubt that there had been a crash. Over the years, the frequency of crashes had made her excessively sensitive to aircraft accidents. She asked a corpsman if she could wait with the children in a different part of the hospital. He looked at her and immediately surmised that she was the wife of an aircrewmember. He escorted her and the children to a waiting area away from the emergency room and on the far side of the hospital.

On the flight line, the Captain assigned Supervisor of Flying duty for the day was at the take-off end of the field checking a tanker that was ready to leave. He saw Goat Four Four wobble overhead well right of the approach path. Suddenly smoke came from six of the engines as they tried to accept the sudden throttle demand. He saw the airplane roll to the right, start back left, then stall and crash onto the pits. He spun the staff car around and started towards the scene.

"SOF, this is Goat control." The Command Post was calling him already.

"Go, Goat. This is SOF," he answered.

"Are you at the scene yet?"

"I'm heading there on the taxiway. About a half mile to go."

"Do you have any estimate on the possibility of survivors?"

"Not a chance, Goat Control. No one could survive that fire. The entire plane is engulfed in the fire ball."

"Roger, SOF. Keep us advised. Goat Control clear."

The base fire department was housed in a building on the flight line, just southeast of the control tower. In just over a minute after the crash, every piece of equipment was charging towards the fire. Two of the crash trucks closed on the nose of the aircraft and poured foam from the cannons on top of their cabs onto the fire. Several firemen in asbestos suits climbed ladders to the top of the cockpit, opened the escape hatch, and dragged out the four men on the upper deck. The crash trucks poured a fine water mist over the area to keep the unprotected men cool. None were seriously hurt.

The navigator and bombardier were trapped in the lower compartment. Since the landing gear had retracted as the missed approach began, the airplane rested on its belly on the ground. The fire department attacked the side of the bomber with crash axes and cut into the lower compartment. Again, a fine water mist was used to protect the men. One crewmember was extracted, stunned but alive, from the lower deck area. The other man did not respond or come to the opening. The young fireman, trying to force his way into the lower compartment, could not get through the opening with his asbestos suit on. He started to peel off his protective clothing. The roar of the fire made communicating by shouting impossible. The Fire Chief, seeing his man stripping off his protection, ordered more water sprayed over him. Horrified, he watched the young airman squeeze through the opening that had been hacked in the side of the bomber. The roar of flames was undiminished by the massive amount of foam being used. It seemed an incredibly long time before the Fireman reappeared and ran to the Fire Chief followed by the drenching spray. His clothes were smoking, yet less than a minute had past since he had entered the burning bomber. The Fire Chief sagged with relief.

"Sir, he's conscious but trapped by some equipment. One leg is jammed and I can't move it. He says to cut it off. He doesn't want to burn alive!"

"Can you get in there with a pry bar?" The Chief asked.

"No chance, sir. Everything is pushed back against the aft bulkhead."

In a quick huddle, the Chief made a decision. He would get a man in there and using a shaped charge would blow enough of the aft bulkhead out to work a pry bar. It had to be fast. They were not getting ahead of this fire. The airplane was sitting right on top of the refueling pits. They still had the gunner trapped in the tail turret to think about. Three minutes later the injured navigator was extracted and on his way to the hospital. His leg was badly lacerated and the femoral artery torn, but this was his lucky day; a vascular surgeon was visiting the base hospital for a conference and in minutes the injured man was in surgery.

Fate also passed the gunner by that day. The crash crew could not get close enough to cut him out of the tail compartment so they used a crash truck as a battering ram. They simply backed off far enough to get a good run and charged the side of the bomber just forward of the tail plane. The huge tail section broke away and moved to the airplane's left. The gunner wasted no time scrambling out of the opening under a drenching spray of water.

In what I believe is the most spectacular rescue by an Air Force crash crew, everyone aboard the crashed B-52 was saved.

Later that evening I taxied by the crash scene in a tanker. Only the eight engines, the huge main landing trucks, and the severed tail section remained. The guys in the Ellsworth crash crew were the darlings of anyone who flew an airplane. The Commander in Chief of SAC arrived several days later and hung medals on the lot of them.

It took several days for the details of the accident to reach the flight crews. Captain Welsh was transferred to an aircraft more suitable to his stature. The trapped navigator survived the surgery, but with a permanent limp that ended his active flying career; at least he was not burned alive. A minimum height was imposed for B-52 pilots. I do not know what became of Colonel Murray, but I did promise myself never to tolerate interference of that kind in the cockpit

*****

Several of us had evolved from humble copilot to aircraft commander in a time span of two months. Henry Miller kept us busy. He knew that we would be deploying to Southeast Asia in a few months and wanted us as experienced and confident as possible. He knew that the only way to increase our experience level was to put us in situations that would force us to make our own decisions. We spent more time flying short TDYs, or trips away from home, than we did on alert. We flew constantly and were sent off on every errand that involved at least one night away from home. The Squadron was enjoying a hiatus from duty in Southeast Asia. We needed time to re-acquaint with our families, rest from the charged environment overseas, and catch up on training items. New people were coming into the squadron and others, such as myself, were moving into new jobs and needed time to get comfortable with their new responsibilities. The word was out via the Officers' Wives Club, a group that always knew what was going on long before the flight crews did, that we would not deploy until early summer and that the entire squadron would go this time.

One afternoon as I was passing the door to the commander's office, Henry called me in.

"Art," he began. "I got a little TDY for you. Now don't get your bowels in an uproar. It's only for a couple of weeks and I want you to have a little time out on your own before we deploy again."

I nodded, wondering were I'd be going.

"Your crew can mission plan on Tuesday and leave on Wednesday. Take the rest of today and Monday off. Have a good trip and be careful." With that he handed me the TDY orders and returned his attention to his desk. Obviously dismissed, I saluted and left.

The temporary duty orders were sending us to Alaska for two weeks. Our destination was Eielson Air Force Base, a few miles from Fairbanks. The base is at approximately fifty-five degrees north latitude, or a little over a hundred miles south of the Arctic Circle. Winter was well established in Alaska by this time of year. I suppose that if one is going to visit Alaska, he might as well see the original stereotype of ice and snow. I had been there several times before as a copilot, but this would be my first real winter visit and first time on my own.

The weather wasn't awfully warm as we pre-flighted our airplane the following Wednesday morning. The wind blew briskly out of the northwest and the dregs of several inches of snow that had fallen over the weekend hid among the wheel chocks and tires. The sky was bright blue.

A little more than an hour later we leveled off at our cruising altitude. The interior of the airplane was comfortably warm. All four of us were happy to be away from the constant supervision that prevailed at our home base. Our route was very nearly a great circle route. We passed over Montana and crossed the Canadian border into Alberta. Our northwesterly course carried us within sight of Edmonton, but the undercast was beginning to thicken as we crossed the corner of British Columbia and on into the Yukon Territory. What land we could see through the broken clouds below us was white. Soon the Canadian border lay behind us, and the VOR pointed ahead to the Big Delta omni. This radio navigation aid was the final checkpoint for aircraft arriving at Fairbanks from the south.

Cap Witzler stirred in his seat and called the command post to report our imminent arrival. They advised us that the runway was covered with three feet of packed snow and that the centerline was marked with orange dye marker, also to use caution as they had been having a problem with moose wandering out onto the runway. Cap was my copilot. A tall man of medium build, he was quiet and very competent. I fully expected him to advance in minimum time to aircraft commander, but he left the service shortly before he was due to start his upgrade training. I talked to him several times from the air after he had left the Air Force, for he had become an air traffic controller at Denver Center.

As a teenager, I had been fascinated with the stories of the early days of aviation in the far north and had read everything that I could lay my hands on about the subject. There had been a number of improvements in aviation in the past four decades, but I could still see the four of us as a band of daring adventurers.

As we approached our destination, all was covered with a thick blanket of snow. The tops of buildings poked through the snow, but without visible roads to give them some sort of a pattern, they appeared to have been dropped haphazardly into a white field in which they partially sank. The trees of the surrounding forests all were of the same height and formed a field of hopeful green striving to see above the deep snow. Happy with our unfolding adventure, we made the descent and landing without incident or the use of skis on the landing gear. There were no moose on the runway today. I did find that the unbroken expanse of white made judging the flare, or point where the descent of the airplane is reduced and the airplane placed in the proper pitch attitude for landing, a bit difficult. I mentioned to Cap that I should remember to flare just a little higher than I usually do, especially in poor visibility. He rudely remarked that I already flare too high so why should I compound the problem. I silently vowed to let him make the next landing and find out for himself. Of course, he slid the bird in like a feather several days later and I had to eat a large plate of crow. Cap didn't have a lot to say but when he did, it flew like a bolt from a crossbow. Fortunately for him, we didn't practice keelhauling in the Air Force.

A Follow Me led us to the fuel pits. The taxiways were lined with huge piles of snow. I worried about hitting a wing tip or outboard engine pod but all went well. At Operations we found that, after a short mission briefing, we were free for the following day but would fly the day after. Mission planning was simplified here. In most cases our flights were pre-planned or "canned" missions that were made on a regular basis. Operations was located on the ground floor of a building of about four stories called Ptarmigan Hall. It appeared to be the largest building on the base, barring the hangars, and it contained all of the services we would need, including mess hall and quarters. The sleeping quarters all had heavy shades over the windows that could completely darken the room owing to the long daylight hours of the arctic summer. In the summer there was little or no darkness and flight crews would be trying to sleep at the odd hours dictated by their flying schedules. This was not a problem at this time of year as daylight lasted but a few hours.

The Officers' Club, however, was located separately and required a trip out into the weather. Lanny Andres, the navigator on my crew, opted to check out the Officers' Club for dinner. Cap decided on a nap; he liked naps. Billy Brown, the boom operator, had disappeared with some friends of his. I elected to accompany Lanny.

Any outdoor activity, however mild, required careful preparation. We wore our military parkas over our civilian clothes, the only legal mixing of civilian and military dress that I was aware of and this only in deference to the intense cold. I guess that the powers that be had decided to ignore tradition, preferring to have folks available for duty rather than on the sick list because of frostbite. Security and maintenance people suffered from this problem in the Alaskan winter when the temperature could, and often did, reach minus fifty degrees. This happened most often when high pressure sat over the area. The air was very still and the temperature would fall. The stillness of the air often tricked people. The air seemed much warmer than it actually was. If a person grew careless, it did not take long for exposed skin to freeze. An airplane taking off in these conditions would often leave a contrail that started with the take-off roll and would lie on the runway for a quarter of an hour or more, reducing runway visibility to below take-off minimums. We were forbidden to run when these conditions existed, even when responding to an alert, for fear of frosting our lungs.

We walked to the Officers' Club in the waning minutes of daylight, through trenches dug in the snow. In many places, the tops of the trench were six feet above the bottom. I had no idea how far below that the ground was. We wore issue mukluks on our feet. These are canvas boots that come about half way up the calf and have soft leather soles. A thick felt liner is inside. Heavy wool socks over cotton street socks make up the rest of the protection. I found no better way of keeping my feet warm, especially on long flights. The area around the rudder pedals gets very cold, no matter where the cabin temperature is set. Mukluks were comfortable, much like slippers, and were the only hope of avoiding frozen feet should it be necessary to abandon the airplane over the Arctic. Preparing for the short walk to the Club was a lot of work for an indifferent meal. Perhaps the mess in Ptarmagin Hall would have been a better choice.

*****

Far below us solid clouds roiled in the light shed by the Aurora Borealis, or Northern Lights. The weather on the surface must be awful. Flying at high altitudes could lull a pilot into a trap. Not all that long ago, when all aircraft were propeller driven, few airplanes had the ability to climb above severe weather. A pilot flew through the weather and was very much aware of conditions. At over thirty thousand feet the air was smooth, the Northern Lights spectacular, and the stars bright. It was easy to give little thought to the turmoil far below. But any airplane aloft must sooner or later descend and land. The pilot must either fly beyond the bad weather or descend and land through it.

The storm below us, far out over the polar ice cap, had been an unknown, and thus, was not reported during our weather briefing before this mission. It occurred to me that it might be moving over Alaska. I was concerned by the restriction placed on our timing for some exercise that NORAD was carrying out. It was their job to watch for missiles or bombers attacking from over the pole. Our schedule required that we be at Prudhoe Bay on Alaska's north coast at a very specific time. Amber One One, the RC-135 that we were to refuel, had arrived nearly an hour early and much farther south than we had expected. The refueling had been conducted in radio silence. The reconnaissance Hog Nose 135, named for the strange radome on its nose, had appeared out of the darkness, flashed its lights, and dropped back to the pre-contact position. Once refueled it had silently disconnected and dropped away into the darkness to continue on its mysterious duties. I would now have to loiter for more than an hour over the ice cap north of Prudhoe Bay to make good my timing. I had a bad feeling that the weather in Alaska was going to hell in a hand basket.

"Cap, see if you can raise Anchorage on HF and find out what's going on with the weather."

Cap tried working the high frequency radio. I turned on the HF switch on my radio-mixing box so that I could listen. Nothing but crashing static rewarded his attempts. Once I thought I could hear Anchorage trying to answer, but it was unreadable.

"Never mind, Cap. These northern lights are raising hell with the radios. Lanny, give me a heading for Prudhoe Bay and we'll try them on UHF."

I hoped that the ultra-high-frequency radio would not be affected by the radio disturbance that the Lights caused. Prudhoe Bay was a radar site and a part of the Distant Early Warning system built in the fifties to give warning of an over-the-pole missile strike from Russia.

"Two twenty grid to Prudhoe Bay, pilot. You should be in UHF range in about twenty-five minutes," Lanny answered. It seemed that he always had the heading and distance to anywhere I wanted to go at least two minutes before I asked for it.

Prudhoe Bay answered loud and clear from one hundred and twenty miles out. I asked them if they could get me some weather information for the next two hours, especially for the Fairbanks area. It took him less than five minutes to call back.

"Actor Four Five, I have your met. for you. Ready to copy?"

Cap had a pencil poised over his kneepad. "Roger, go ahead," he answered.

"Four Five, there is a fast moving storm system moving in over Alaska. We have blizzard conditions here on the surface at Prudhoe Bay, and both Eielson and Anchorage are expected to go below IFR minimums within the next two or three hours. Eielson present weather is two thousand overcast, two miles in light snow, wind northwest at fifteen, altimeter two nine eight six and falling. How copy?"

"Loud and clear," I answered. "Can you land-line Anchorage Airways and NORAD and advise them that I am coming in early due to weather? My ETA to your station is two seven and I'll give you an ETA for high station at Eielson when I'm overhead."

"Roger, Actor Four Five. I'll pass the information. Give me a call overhead and I'll confirm it for you."

"Pilot, Nav. Forty-two minutes time en route from Prudhoe Bay to the fix at Eielson. They were pretty insistent about timing at the mission briefing."

Lanny was correct. The briefing officer had been adamant on that point. We were to cross the Alaskan coast at Prudhoe Bay within a five-minute time block. I sensed a trap forming. The mission profile provided enough fuel to reach Anchorage should I not be able to land at Fairbanks, but beyond that there were no reasonable choices. I recalled the stories that I had read about early flying in the Arctic. Accounts of enormous storms that roared in from the pole and covered vast areas in an incredibly short time came to mind. No bad weather had been forecast for tonight but the report from Prudhoe Bay now made that forecast worthless. I made up my mind.

"Thanks, Lanny. I think we better get on the ground before we have to fly all the way to California to find a place to land."

Cap piped up with one of his rare comments. "I don't want to go to California tonight. I'm not dressed for it. Besides, we'll run out of fuel somewhere over Canada."

"OK, Cap," I answered. "Eielson it is. NORAD will probably raise hell about our not sticking to their timing, but the Air Force will be a lot madder if I lose this airplane and crew. When you can reach Approach Control, ask for an en route descent with vectors to an ILS final."

Cap looked sidewise at me. "I like that choice, boss."

"Pilot, Nav. We're just about over Prudhoe Bay. ETA to Eielson one zero past the hour."

Cap immediately passed this to Prudhoe Bay.

"Actor Four Five, Anchorage wants to confirm that you are at flight level three three zero."

"Copilot, ask him if he has advised NORAD that we are coming in early," I interrupted.

Cap nodded. "That is affirmative. We are at flight level three three zero. And have you advised NORAD that we are coming home early?"

"Yes, I have," Prudhoe Bay answered. "I will also advise your Command Post of your ETA."

"Thanks much for your help. We'll talk to you next trip."

A hundred miles north of Eielson, Cap made contact with Approach Control and we started descending for an instrument approach. The weather was now at minimums for an instrument approach, the field was expected to close at any time, and the weather at Anchorage was also going sour. My nearest useable alternate now was in Washington State. I did not have the fuel to go there. To add to our troubles the RCR or runway condition reading was six. This meant that the runway and taxiways would be slick enough for ice-skating. There must have been a little melting during the day and it now had frozen.

"Approach, this is Actor Four Five. Be advised I do not have fuel to reach an alternate."

"Roger, Actor Four Five, understand."

This was my way of telling Approach Control that I had to land. This controller sounded like an old head and would not call the field closed until I had made at least one attempt to land. I had hoped to use the automatic ILS, a way of connecting the autopilot to the instrument landing system, which would have done much of the work of flying the approach. All I would have had to do was control the airspeed until it was time to flare for landing. Of course it would not engage, so it was necessary to fly manually. I guess that gadgets like that work only in clear weather. Their function is definitely within the control of gremlins.

The outer marker sounded in our headsets and the panel light blinked. We started down the glide slope. I had Cap flick the landing lights on, but he immediately turned them off. There was nothing to be seen but a swirling white glare.

"Actor Four Five, Eielson Approach. Tower clears you to land. Wind three four zero at twenty gusting to twenty-eight. Altimeter two nine eight zero. Remain this frequency."

Cap acknowledged and called out five hundred feet above the ground, echoed by Lanny who was cross checking the approach on his own altimeter and radar. Billy Brown was in the jump seat straining to see ahead for any sign of the runway.

"Copilot, we'll use forty flaps for landing."

"Roger. Three hundred feet. Nothing in sight. Two hundred feet, minimums. I see a glow. Do you want landing lights?"

"No!"

"Runway lights in sight, you are on the centerline."

I raised the nose slightly to reduce the rate of descent and looked up from the instruments. The threshold of a big beautiful wide runway was spreading out in front of us. Forward visibility wasn't more than a quarter of a mile. The thought flashed through my mind that I hoped the local moose were all tucked in somewhere to wait out the storm and not out wandering around on the runway. Throttles idle, we landed with a solid thump. The speed brakes came up and the airplane started slowing. The gusty wind tried to weathervane the airplane on the slippery runway. I was having second thoughts about the adventures of flying in the Arctic winter. The runway at Eielson is almost fifteen thousand feet long and I used it all slowing the tanker to a walk. Carefully, we turned off and started slowly along the parallel taxiway. Cap contacted Ground Control and the Command Post.

"Actor Four Five, this is Actor Control."

"Go ahead, Control. This is Four Five," Cap answered.

"I got a light colonel on the line from NORAD and he's pretty angry. Do you want me to patch him through to you?"

Cap looked at me questioningly. I took my right hand off of the throttles and made a rude gesture with the middle finger of my right hand. Cap grinned.

"Actor Control, this is Four Five," he answered. "We've got our hands full with this airplane and the storm. Tell him the pilot will call back later by landline."

Eielson closed immediately after we touched down. Anchorage, as well as all of Alaska and much of northern Canada, was closed by the fast moving winter storm that had come roaring in unannounced from the Polar Regions. We finished our maintenance debriefing and trudged up to our rooms in Ptarmigan Hall. It wasn't until I was just falling asleep that I remembered the unhappy lieutenant colonel waiting for my call at NORAD. I started to get up with the idea of dressing and going downstairs to the command post to soothe the irate desk jockey. Then I remembered the day I sat in the Officers' Club on Guam with Jim Loosley after the crash at Kadena. He had warned me never to let someone on the ground talk me into a dangerous situation. My airplane was down safely and my crew was warm and dry. That guy sitting at a desk under a mountain in Colorado would just have to figure it out for himself. If I had been trapped above the storm and run out of fuel, it wouldn't have been his problem. I lay back and went to sleep. I never did hear anything about the incident.

Open ocean and Arctic navigation can be difficult. When flying over the landmasses of Europe and North America, there are abundant aids to navigation. Most of the radio ranges and direction finding stations had been eliminated by the middle sixties and replaced by VOR and TACAN, which operated on radio frequencies less vulnerable to interference from weather. However, once out of range of these aids, which were limited to line of sight, SAC aircraft were dependent on radar navigation over land or celestial navigation over oceans. SAC aircraft were not provided with inertial navigation systems like the airplanes of Military Airlift Command, and satellite navigation still lay in the future. The reasoning behind the determined use of celestial navigation on SAC aircraft was that, in the event of general war, all aids to navigation would be shut down so the navigators needed to continuously practice celestial and radar navigation.

Celestial navigation in jet aircraft is complicated by the fact that the airplane is moving at more than five hundred miles per hour. By the time a three-star fix had been shot and calculated, the airplane would have traveled hundreds of miles. To solve this problem, the navigator pre-computed the azimuth (direction) and the elevation (height above the horizon) of the stars to be observed. He based his computations on where he expected to be when the observation was completed. That position was referred to as the assumed position. By comparing the difference between the actual observation and the pre-computed numbers, the navigator was able to arrive at a range and bearing from the assumed position. Navigators and most copilots of B-47s became quite adept at this, but the margin for error was large and if a man once got behind, it was very difficult to catch up. Radar was useful in the area directly north of Canada's Northwest Territories because of the large number of islands. In this method of navigation we looked at the ground using the radar set. We identified the area by comparing prominent land shapes to a chart and determined our position by measuring the bearing and distance from that landmark. Of course, one had to correctly identify the land he was looking at, which was difficult in the winter because the water was frozen, everything was buried with snow, and the outlines of the islands were distorted on radar. In some cases the land-water contrast was reversed. Getting horribly lost was not all that difficult. Smart crew commanders place great value on a competent navigator and would go to unusual if not downright sneaky and underhanded means to recruit a hotshot navigator to his crew. I was very lucky to have Lanny Andres on my crew. Several aircraft commanders, who maintained lesser ethical standards, had made questionable attempts to have him assigned to their crews.

One mission flown frequently from Eielson was the Ghost Cabin Mission. I loved to fly this one with its romantic sounding name. Its route was from Eielson out over the Barents Sea and eastward at about seventy-five degrees north latitude to the area of Thule Greenland. There we refueled an orbiting B-52, called the Thule monitor, and then returned to Alaska. The Thule monitor was established several years earlier when all radio contact with the base at Thule Greenland was lost for several days. SAC bombers were positioned at the end of runways, with engines running, and remained so until an aircraft could be dispatched to fly to Thule and report that the base had not been obliterated by a Russian attack. The radio blackout was the result of solar storms, but an armed B-52 was kept in orbit in sight of Thule for years after that.

It took about twelve hours to complete the flight. The navigator had his hands full with the demands of exacting navigation and the copilot had an enormous amount of work to do on the high frequency radio. The pilot sat in sovereign splendor and ate his flight lunch while the automatic pilot flew the airplane.

However, bad weather could rear its ugly head at any time. This happened to one crew flying the Ghost Cabin route. They became lost over the ice cap above bad weather and did not find themselves until they finally wandered over Montana. Canadian Air Traffic Control was upset by this unscheduled intrusion and diplomatic notes were exchanged. I do not know what became of the pilot, but I do know that I was very happy that it was not my crew that had gone astray, and grateful for Lanny's consummate skill as a navigator.

Eventually our tour in Alaska was up. We spent a few hours flight planning for our trip home the following day and went shopping in the afternoon for some King Crab. We bought ten-pound boxes of crab legs and stored them in the mess hall freezer until we were ready to leave. For the flight home, we would pack the crab in the keel bay area where it would stay safely frozen.

The next day came and went. We were postponed twenty-four hours because of bad weather in the Dakotas. Ellsworth was closed due to blizzard conditions. Twice more we were delayed twenty-four hours. Finally, we headed home after a delay of three days.

Arrival at Ellsworth was an eerie experience. We circled the base at low altitude and all that could be seen were the tops of buildings sticking out of snowdrifts. The runway had been cleared and looked like a black slash in an enormous white desert. Snow had drifted so high on the northwest side of the old B-36 hangar that it created a slope all the way to the roof. The tail of a B-36 is as tall as a five-story building and required a very large hangar. Someone had driven a pick-up to the very top of that hangar. I could see him standing beside it watching us. The base housing area was a scene of desolation. Many houses had snow drifted against them right up to their roofs. The crews that flew the PACCS missions stood their alert in mobile homes installed at the northwest end of the field. They had been trapped there and had to be supplied by helicopter, but for the three days that the storm raged, no one had been able to reach them. They subsisted on what snacks they had hoarded in their quarters.

It is not necessary to go all the way to Alaska to experience Arctic weather. Because the military draws people from all parts of the country, many stationed at northern bases have no concept of how severe the weather can be until they have spent a winter or two at a northern base. A few people are trapped each winter. Usually, they are caught in a stalled car and freeze to death. Two maintenance men who were driving on the flight line at Ellsworth became lost one winter in a blizzard. Unfortunately, they were both dead of hypothermia when they finally were found.

The folks in town had their problems, as well. The local population was accustomed to these conditions and able to move about more readily in their four-wheel-drive pick-ups. Neighbors had kept Carolyn and the kids supplied in my absence. Our youngest still was having trouble with respiratory illness and had come down with another bout of pneumonia. Carolyn was unable to get him to the emergency room, and medical help was unable to get to the house. She followed the physician's instructions by telephone. Eventually, a doctor was able to reach our house in a National Guard half-track. The boy did well. Military wives learned to be very independent and resourceful in this strange Cold War.

I had been home for several weeks when Henry called me into his office and handed me the orders for another trip. This trip was a choice plum. The Squadron had been tasked to escort two F-4s to Hickam Field in Hawaii and I got the job. We were to fly to March Air Force Base in California, top off with fuel, then depart in formation with the two fighters for the trip across. We would refuel the F-4s en route, provide navigation support, and when we got to Hawaii, we would lay over for thirty-six hours before returning home, escorting any fighters that might be making the eastbound crossing.

Two days later a happy crew departed Ellsworth at about eight in the morning and headed for California. The weather was pleasant. Winter was getting tired and thinking about a vacation in the far north. Three hours later, we landed at March AFB. Our plans began to go sour.

We were informed that there would be a delay and that was our first indication of a problem. No one seemed to know why. We had a flight plan partially completed and could go no further with it until we knew just when we would be departing. The four of us idled time away in the coffee shop. After an hour of that, we wandered into the crew lounge to read six-month-old Newsweek magazines. I began to suspect that our excursion to Hawaii was falling apart. Finally, a rumpled major hurried into the crew lounge at Base Operations and told us that our airplane was fueled and to get the paperwork done for a flight to Westover Air Force Base.

"Westover!" I exclaimed. "That's in Massachusetts. We're supposed to be going the other way."

"I don't know what's going on," he answered. "SAC called and said to send you guys to Westover as soon as possible."

In the planning room, Lanny asked, "What route do you want to take?"

I looked at the latest weather FAX pinned to the wall. "Doesn't seem to be much in the way of weather. Just draw a line on the chart and we'll go direct. Plan on thirty-seven thousand feet."

Six hours after we had left South Dakota on our great adventure, we passed over that state eastbound. From our perch at flight level three seven zero, the state looked flat and brown, mottled here and there with patches of old snow. The Black Hills made a slightly darker smudge that marked the western extreme of the state. It was late afternoon and growing dark when we landed at Westover in central Massachusetts. I could not imagine another flight today. We were at the peacetime limit for flying hours allowed in a single twenty-four hour period and regulations required that we rest for a twelve-hour period before our next take-off time. I expected the crew bus to take us to maintenance debriefing and then to the BOQ. That did not happen. It took us straight to Base Operations where two staff officers waited for us. As we trooped into the crew lounge and dropped our bags in a heap, confident that our day's work was finished, one of the staff officers pushed several charts into my hands and said, "SAC wants you to figure fuel for a maximum gross-weight take-off, go to Bermuda, join with a flight of F-4s, and escort them to Torrejon at Madrid. You won't be landing at Bermuda and you'll have to hurry to make the rendezvous time. We had one of our navigators do a wind flight plan for you." He beamed happily at his own foresight and looked at his watch. It must be getting close to his cocktail hour at the Club.

It took me a few seconds to digest this news. "Sorry, pal. We are out of crew rest. This crew gets fed and rested before we can do your little four thousand mile flight."

The second of the pair spoke up. "We've already taken care of that. We told SAC that you would probably be pushing your crew rest limit and they have waived that regulation. Exigencies of the service, you know."

"Pushing it!" I exclaimed. "We'll exceed it by a hundred percent. We have flown over four thousand miles today and you want us to do another four. Don't you guys have any tankers here on the east coast? I saw about a dozen of them parked out on the ramp."

The first of the two staff officers started getting red in the face. "This order came from Strategic Air Command Headquarters. I suggest that you calculate your fuel load. I will expedite it for you, and while the airplane is being fueled you can grab a burger or a bowl of chili in the snack bar. Then get your airplane to hell off the ground and fly the mission you are assigned."

I could see that my protests were going nowhere. Cap, non-confrontational by nature, buried himself in the performance charts and began the calculations necessary to determine the very maximum amount of fuel that we could safely take-off with. He gave the information to the two staff officers who immediately fled. I don't know if this was to avoid further protests from me or if they were very late for their cocktail hour. At any rate, they would be sound asleep while we would be wandering around over the Atlantic. They also would be up and back at their desks after a night's sleep about the time that we landed in Spain.

Less than an hour later I pulled back on the yoke, after a take-off run of more than seventy seconds, and we lifted off into the darkness. The airplane climbed reluctantly, burdened with its heavy load of fuel. We turned southeast and crossed the New England coast just south of Cape Cod. It is about eight hundred miles to Bermuda and we could make our rendezvous time comfortably. I was about to get another lesson in decision making.

Cap had been busy trying to establish the HF radio contact necessary for the ocean crossing for longer than usual when he said, "Pilot, I think the HF is tits up."

"What? Are you sure? If we turn back now, those people at Westover will figure we're dogging it." I knew in my heart that the radio in question would work just fine as soon as we landed.

Cap fiddled with the thing for another ten minutes. We soon would be out of range of Boston Center and would not be able to proceed if we had not established HF contact.

"Boom, this is the pilot. Would you get me a cup of coffee, and while you are back at the galley, give that radio cabinet a damn good kick."

"Boom operator checking off interphone to perform brogan maintenance," Brown replied.

A half minute later there was a loud thump from the area of the equipment cabinet and the HF radio came alive.

Billy Brown handed me a cup of coffee and said, "This airplane couldn't get off of the ground if it weren't for my hi-tech boots."

Cap closed out with Boston Center and we were on our way. Less than two hours later we were established in a lazy left hand racetrack pattern over Bermuda. Our rendezvous time passed. We rechecked the assigned radio frequency for the join up with the fighters. All was silent.

"Cap, does it occur to you that we are wandering around in the dark of night, over the Bermuda Triangle, and haven't a clue as to what the hell we are doing here?" I was tired and my exasperation was showing.

"Pilot, this is Nav. We are fifteen minutes past our control time. We need to think about how long we can wait and still continue our crossing if the fighters do show up."

Cap answered, "I'm checking it now, Nav. Maybe another half hour at the most. After that, fuel will be a problem if we take both fighters across. We may have to make a fuel stop in the Azores."

I thought about this for a minute or so. I couldn't imagine what the wild hurry was to get a couple of F-4s to Spain. As far as I knew, the Middle East was as quiet as it ever gets. It was time for some guidance from the people who sent us out here.

"Lanny, I'll hold this orbit. Encode a message to SAC. Tell them the fighters are a no show and ask them what they want us to do."

Five minutes later I listened as Lanny made contact with SAC headquarters on the HF radio and recited a long series of four letter code groups telling SAC of our situation. Twenty minutes passed. I heard our call sign on the radio. Lanny answered and copied another long string of four-letter code groups. The radio went silent as he rapidly decoded the message.

"Pilot, this is Nav. The message decodes to "continue mission." There are no other instructions and the authentication is correct."

I sat there puzzled. What the hell did that mean? Were the fighters late or were they not coming? Did they want me to go to Spain without the fighters? I was out of time. If the fighters were to show up now, I would have just enough fuel to take them across the Atlantic. Any further delay would require a stop at the Azores for fuel. Without the fighters I had more than enough fuel to go to Spain or even back to South Dakota. No point in second-guessing. My frag-order said, "Go to Torrejon Air Base." It made no provision for fighters not showing up. I turned east.

"Lanny, encode another message and call SAC back and tell them I have departed the ARCP and give them an ETA for Torrejon. If they want us to do something else I'm sure they will let me know."

Twenty minutes later, with Bermuda well over a hundred miles behind us, Lanny received the last of these coded messages. He called me on interphone as soon as he had decoded it.

"Pilot, Nav. They simply acknowledged receipt of our last message."

I was getting a lesson in the unwillingness of some of my superiors to make a decision. Whoever was running this operation was not available for one reason or another and nobody else was willing to speak in his place. If someone became unhappy over my wandering all over the western hemisphere, the onus would fall on me.

"OK, Lanny. Save a copy of the messages and log the times."

Our track took us south of the Azores. Just as the sun cleared the horizon and blazed in our faces Cap announced, in his usual unemotional voice, that the right hydraulic gauge was at zero. That meant that some of our important systems were not working. Included were the flaps, the powered rudder, the nose-wheel steering, and the copilot's brakes, along with a few other odds and ends. Boeing engineers had thought of such an unhappy event when they designed the 707 series of airplanes and had made provisions for switching the more vital components from one hydraulic system to the other. Crossover of hydraulic components was a simple operation accomplished by moving a lever above the copilot's head. As long as one hydraulic system was operating, all of the more important airplane components could be operated. For some reason, staff officers did not want crews to use this crossover system. It may have been that they feared a total loss of hydraulics. My faith lay more with the designers of the airplane and my own knowledge of the aircraft's systems than with the opinion of someone who had no responsibility for the outcome of his decision. This was lesson number one from my instructor, Jim Loosley.

Presently, we crossed the coast of Portugal and headed inland towards Madrid. It had been more than twenty hours since our take-off from South Dakota. As soon as we were in UHF radio range of Torrejon, Cap called and got our landing weather. The ceiling was unlimited and the visibility ten miles, but a strong gusty crosswind complicated things. I would need that powered rudder and, although we could put down some flaps manually, I might need to be able to raise them in the event of go-around.

"Should I tell the Command Post that we have lost the right hydraulic system? They'll be wanting the maintenance status as soon as they know we are in the area." Cap asked.

"Not yet," I said. "We'll cross over the hydraulics first and then tell them. Otherwise, they'll tell us not to."

"I'll bet they would," he answered. "They're not the ones that have to land in a crosswind without a rudder."

We had checked with the auxiliary pump and knew that the system would hold pressure. That told us that we could cross over safely.

"De-pressurize both systems, Cap. Read the label on the crossover valve so that you go in the correct direction and then cross the flaps and powered rudder to the left system."

As soon as Cap had done this, he pressurized the left system again and we were in business.

"OK, Cap, now you can call the Command Post and let them know we have lost the right hydraulic system," I said. "Don't tell them we have crossed over, I want to see what they say."

Less than five minutes after Cap made radio contact with the Command Post they called back. "The Deputy Commander for Operations says do not cross over."

I grinned at Cap.

Twenty minutes later we landed. I stopped on the runway and asked for a tug. The nose-wheel steering is not one of the systems that can be switched to the other hydraulic supply.

I have no idea what was behind this journey. No one offered any information about this flight or why we had traveled so far. Perhaps the plan to move two F-4s across the Pacific fell apart. Because we were committed for several days, another task was assigned to us and that too disintegrated. We had spent almost nineteen hours in the air and used ninety-five tons of jet fuel. Two days later the hydraulic problem was repaired and we flew back to South Dakota.

As to my anticipation of the instructions not to use the crossover valve, I never did understand the reason that staff people were loath to recommend its use. That attitude existed for as long as I remained in the Air Force. The valve was there for a purpose and it seemed much safer to me to have both flaps and powered rudder available when a landing had to be made with a strong wind blowing across the runway. Jim had taught me that such decisions belong to the aircraft commander, for it is he who is responsible for the outcome. I was growing very suspicious of technical instruction that came from men who flew once every month or so, and then only for flight pay.

FOURTEEN

◆◆◆◆◆◆◆◆◆◆◆◆◆◆◆◆◆◆

*Behold, a pale horse: and his
name that sat on him was Death.
-Revelation, 6:8*

When the squadron deployed, luck sent my crew and me to U-Tapao, a base built to accommodate B-52s and KC-135s for support of the Vietnam conflict. This had been a huge undertaking and the base was easily the size of most bases in the U.S. I seriously doubt if the General Accounting Office could come up with a number reflecting its incredible cost. It was one of many bases built just for this conflict and lay near the town of Sattahip, about eighty miles south of Bangkok on the Gulf of Siam.

We started using the base as soon as the runway could accept aircraft. This is a lot like moving into the house you are building as soon as the floors are down. Living conditions were awful and sleep nearly impossible with the constant roar of construction equipment and the sound of blasting. Construction would continue until the end of the war, when the base and all its equipment would be turned over to the Thai Air Force, along with all the other bases we had built in Thailand. The many bases built in Vietnam were lost when the North Vietnamese overran the south after our withdrawal.

Thai Marines provided much of the security for U-Tapao. I suspect that, at times, they were less than assiduous in their discharge of security duty. Those of the local population with a penchant for dishonest activity saw the enormous piles of equipment and material as a giant shopping center where no cash was required. Once the stolen material was off of the base it simply disappeared and was beyond recovery. This implies an organization of some sophistication. The acquisition department of this organized thievery was known as the "stealy boys." This was a general term common throughout the Asian theater of operations. Some of their heists were truly spectacular and elicited grudging admiration.

Clark Field in the Philippines lost a large and very expensive fire-and-rescue truck. The stealy boys simply boarded it in broad daylight, while it was parked outside the fire station, started it up and, with sirens and lights going, raced towards the main gate. Guards at the gate stopped all traffic for the emergency and waved the speeding firetruck through. Eventually, the stolen crash truck surfaced at the Manila International Airport, with a new paint job and new lettering. Because of the convolutions of Philippine law concerning stolen vehicles, the Air Force could not legally recover it. Exasperated officials bundled up the operating and service manuals and delivered them to the new owners.

Thai stealy boys were no less resourceful. They managed to get away with a large bulldozer, complete with the flatbed trailer truck that it was sitting on. This little item was removed from a fenced and guarded motor pool located within the confines of the base. Protection surrounding the base was a chain link fence, eight feet high and topped with barbed wire. It was not uncommon to see a stealy boy scaling this perimeter fence in broad daylight, with a bundle tied to his back that seemed to weigh as much as the thief did.

Thai Police had little effect on this drain of material, but were zealous in their protection of American service people. One GI had the misfortune of being robbed and seriously stabbed not far from the base. Within a matter of several days, the culprit was marched up to the main gate by Thai authorities and executed in front of the startled American gate guards. Americans had very little trouble with violence after that demonstration of swift justice.

*****

The tan water of the Mekong River passed below us. A flight of four Thuds finished their post-strike refueling and sped out ahead of us on a heading for Takhli. The early afternoon sky was bright blue, with fair weather cumulous scattered about our altitude of fourteen thousand feet. We looked forward to landing and a frosty gin and tonic, together with the hot salty peanuts that would help to replace the salts that now stained our flight suits. Cap guided the airplane with the autopilot. Lanny followed our progress on his plotting board and I dug my pipe from my pocket and contemplated packing and lighting it.

"Orange Anchor Three One, this is Brigham." The radio voice from the GCI sight at Udorn was quiet and unhurried.

"Go, Brigham, this is Three One," I answered.

"Orange Anchor Three One, we have a report of a beeper on the ground about fifty east of Invert. Looks like a RESCAP forming. If you have any fuel to spare, can you head over that way and lend a hand?"

"Heading zero nine five, Pilot," Lanny interrupted before I could answer. Cap was already turning the airplane to the east.

"Roger, Brigham, Three One is on the way. We are angels base plus nine."

"Thank you, Three One. Contact Invert on two eight five point seven. Brigham clear."

Invert was the GCI sight at Nakhon Phanom, called NKP for short, on the Mekong River in northeast Thailand. The unexpected duration of the war had earned them a new facility. They had just moved their operations from a temporary tin-roofed shack into a more permanent steel and aluminum building. As we came up on their frequency, things were beginning to get busy. The operator at the search radarscope in the darkroom had acquired our airplane a few minutes earlier. At the front of the room, on the backside of the Lexan wall, plotters using fluorescent china markers recorded our turn to the southeast. They also began to track the OV-10 that, with the call sign of Nail One Four, had just taken off from NKP. The FAC, or forward air controller, was checking in on the radio.

Nail One Four soon arrived at the general area of the downed pilot and was organizing the aircraft that were swarming to the area. An RF-101 had been hit by a burst of thirty-seven-millimeter anti-aircraft fire while making a low-altitude photo run along the Ho Chi Minh Trail. The pilot had ejected from the dying airplane and it was his beeper that had been heard. Ford and Dodge flight, each a flight of four F-4s en route to their strike area, were diverted by Brigham and were put into orbit just north of the scene of action by Nail One Four, who now had become the on-scene commander. In a RESCAP, he could commandeer any air assets in the area. A gaggle of Thuds from the 355th at Takhli converged and were given holding orbits by Nail One Four. A huge armada was forming. When one of our own was down, all other duties were secondary to his recovery. If captured, the airman could look forward at best to torture and exploitation for propaganda purposes, at worst to a savage and immediate death. All of these aircraft, encumbered as they were with ordinance, were going to need a lot of fuel. Cap handed me scrap of paper. On it he had scribbled 50K.

"Invert, this is Orange Anchor Three One. Advise Nail One Four that we have fifty thousand pounds available. It's not going to be much if this show drags out. Suggest that you round up the pre-strike tankers for Ford and Dodge flight and tell them that their receivers are over here and to come on over and join the party. We're going to need their fuel unless this guy gets real lucky."

"Roger, Three One, they're both at the White Anchor ARCP. I'll give them a call and see if they'll divert."

The observer in Nail One Four was talking to the downed pilot. "Cable Zero Five Alpha, are you able to read me on guard?"

Two clicks answered Nail One Four. The downed pilot was unable to talk on the radio. There must be enemy troops very close to him.

Captain Ted Learner banked Nail One Four sharply. He had spotted part of the parachute canopy in the trees and did not want to linger over the spot for fear of giving away the position of the downed pilot. He continuously skidded and jinked his airplane. Whatever had knocked down the recon bird was around here somewhere. As he looked down, he caught glimpses of activity through rare breaks in the jungle canopy. This was going to be a tight rescue. There was only one possible LZ, or landing zone, just west of the downed airman and that was surely well covered by the Viet Cong. The Jolly Green would have to use a jungle penetrator and it would have to be quick.

"Cable Zero Five Alpha, are you under the chute?"

Two clicks answered.

"OK, I'm going to hose down the countryside around you and see if I can take a little of the pressure off."

Again two clicks answered.

Learner called one of the F-105 flights. "Crane flight, Nail One Four. What have you got for me this afternoon?"

"Nail, this is Crane lead. We have four chicks with CBUs and some willy pete." He was telling the FAC that he was a flight of four and they were carrying cluster bomb units and white phosphorous rockets.

"Outstanding! Crane flight, position yourselves due south of me.

I'm going in to mark. I'd like the willy pete laid down first and then come back over with the CBUs."

Learner lined up south of the tiny rag of parachute canopy that he could see and aimed just east of it. The rocket tore into the trees and a ball of white smoke soared up. Just as Nail One Four streaked over the spot, the hair on the back of Learner's neck stood up. He didn't know what, but something was wrong. Instinctively, he stamped on the right rudder pedal. The Bronco skidded violently as he rolled hard right and pulled back stick. The propellers roared in protest at the sudden change of airflow over them. Both men sank in their seats from the abrupt G force as a burst of anti-aircraft fire tore through the sky they had so recently occupied.

"Crane Flight, make your run south to north. Do not hit west of my smoke. There is a thirty-seven-millimeter gun a half click beyond my smoke. I want him gone! Make your break to the west and circle back. Nearest safe area is west of the river. You are cleared in hot."

From our perch at fourteen thousand feet, a couple of miles west of the scene, we could see the trails of the rockets and the brilliant white shower of phosphorus that burst from each impact. The Thuds circled in a racetrack and repeated their runs, dropping the cluster bombs along the same track that they had sown their phosphorous rockets. As the third F-105 made his run, a huge secondary explosion erupted out of the jungle.

Cap grunted, "Looks like the lads are onto something."

Ted Learner's voice blanked out guard channel, "They got Cable Zero Five! They just dragged him out in that little open area west of his 'chute! The fuckers are waving at me! Dear Christ, they just cut his throat! They're hacking at him with machetes!" Nail One Four zoomed low over the killing field. He could see the decapitated body of the American pilot.

"Banjo Flight, set up for a run north to south. I'm rolling in to mark." The excitement was gone from his voice and its tone was flat.

Banjo flight was carrying napalm. He streaked towards the little clearing and put a smoke rocket into the center of it. "Banjo Flight, Nail One Four. Make your run north to south. Box my smoke. Break west. Safe territory is across the river. Cleared in hot."

For the next half-hour, Nail One Four directed the strikes of fast movers along the section of the Ho Chi Minh Trail. Several violent secondary explosions indicated that Nail One Four had found a truck convoy on the trail. One after the other, the Thuds and F-4s curved in behind us or one of the White Anchor tankers for fuel.

Cap checked the fuel remaining. "Time for us to go, Pilot. We'll have less than seven thousand by the time we get to U-Tapao."

"OK, Cap. Tell Invert we're bingo fuel and are RTB."

"Heading two three zero, Pilot," Lanny said over interphone.

Cap told Invert we were returning to base. This had looked as if it would be a sure thing RESCAP. Instead of bringing our man home, we were left with a depressing sense of anger and loss.

The loss of Cable Zero Five had a dismal effect on us. Joking and game playing was forgotten. All of us were more serious about our job. One of our favorite games during flight took place during landings. Cap and I would alternate making the landing. We would stand a Zippo cigarette lighter on the glare shield above the instrument panel when we were a mile or so out on final. The object was to touch down and roll out to the point where brakes were first applied without the lighter falling over. Should the lighter fall over, the pilot making the landing bought beer for the crew at debriefing. This was a free ride for the navigator and boom operator, as they didn't make landings and both would be quick to remind us if it appeared that we might overlook this contest. Since we flew at least once each day for months on end, our proficiency was high. Yet somehow, no matter how gently I would touch down, that damn lighter would topple over. Cap seldom had to buy the beer. I think he was just smoother on the rudder after touchdown. Neither of us had even suggested this contest since the loss of Cable Zero Five.

Several weeks later, we took off from U-Tapao as White Anchor Four One. The White Anchor control point was one of the more active ones and was situated east of Vientiane on the Mekong River. We all were on the tired side from our unremitting schedule, but the flight up was routine. Our tour was a hundred and eighty days long and we didn't see much sign of a let up before it would be time for us to rotate back to Ellsworth.

The day before the flight, I received a telephone call from the flight commander that would be leading the flight of F-4s we would refuel. He wanted to know the tail number of the tanker I would be flying on this mission. I thought this a bit unusual, but he had called me on a secure military line and I saw no reason not to tell him that I would be flying aircraft number two three five six seven unless maintenance made a change before take-off. He seemed quite pleased with this information, thanked me, and hung up. I gave the matter no further thought and had forgotten the incident until Buick Flight checked in on refueling frequency the next day.

"Buick lead on freq."

"Two."

"Three."

"Fo'."

In rapid succession the flight of F-4s reported in on the frequency change from the GCI sight to refueling frequency.

"White Anchor Four One, Buick flight up on freq."

"Roger, Buick flight. White Anchor Four One is three five south of the ARCP," Lanny answered as he took over the rendezvous.

"Lead, this is Fo'. I got radar contact, eleven thirty-fo' six five nautical."

"That checks, Four. Lead has radar contact, also."

I recognized Buick lead's voice from the telephone call the night before. I still hadn't figured out what he was up to. Shortly after they called, ten miles out to our right, Buick Two reported visual contact. He had seen the sun flash on some part of the tanker. A couple of minutes later, Buick lead stunned his flight.

"Roger, Buick Flight, lead has visual, also."

"Pappy, you can't see that airplane," One of his young pilots teased. "You can barely see across the bar at happy hour."

In feigned indignation the flight leader responded, "I damn sure can see that airplane, I can even read the tail number. It's...it's two eight, no make that two three five six seven."

"Son of a bitch!" Lanny exclaimed, "They're still two miles out."

Cap looked across the cockpit. "Sounds like the old graybeard is teaching the kids some respect."

Buick flight quickly formed up on us. They were still squabbling about lead reading the tail number from so far out, but settled down to business and topped off their tanks. Once refueled, the arguing resumed as they switched to their tactical frequency and, trailing the typical brown smoke that was the trademark of an F-4, pulled out ahead of us and headed northeast. We were not scheduled as the post-strike tanker for Buick flight. I looked at the fuel totalizer and decided to hang around for a bit and see if anything exciting turned up.

"Nav, this is pilot. We got some extra fuel. I'm going to wander up the road apiece and see if anything is going on. Follow along on the tracking board and keep an eye on the back door in case we have to get out of town real quick."

"OK, boss, but that's Indian country out there."

Ahead of us a small range of mountains rose. They were incredibly green and just to their northwest the Plain of Jars stretched out covered with dust and haze. The radios were quiet except for Brigham occasionally talking to someone. There was no evidence of activity below us. To the east, the dark green hills of North Vietnam lay shrouded in damp mystery. Well north of the Mekong River, I had just about decided it was time to head back south when the radio erupted on GCI frequency.

"Brigham! Brigham! This is Cash Three. May Day, May Day! I need a tanker! Pigeons to the nearest tanker."

Cash Three had apparently found himself separated from his flight and low on fuel. From the sound of his voice he was very low on fuel.

"Roger, Cash Three, tanker is at your eleven o'clock for three miles. White Anchor Four One, Brigham. You have a 105 that's mayday for fuel three miles north of you.

"Roger that, Brigham. Cash Three, I'm turning left and will roll out on one eight zero." I answered. The boom operator checked off interphone and raced to the rear of the airplane. Cap set the panel for refueling. We had no time to run formal checklists.

"I'm moving in position now. I've only got a minute or two of fuel left. I don't know where the hell you came from, but I sure am glad to see you!"

The "contact made" light came on while we still were in a thirty-degree bank and were accelerating to refueling speed. No pilot is more proficient at in-flight refueling than one who is just about out of fuel and over hostile territory. Two minutes after we rolled out of the turn Cash Three disconnected, now fat on fuel for his flight home.

"White Anchor, I'd sure like to buy you guys a round. I got mixed up in a bit of a fur ball and had to use a lot of afterburner. I'd have been afoot by now and the best I could have hoped for would have been the Hanoi Hilton."

"Glad to help," Cap answered. "Sorry we didn't have time to clean the windshield."

The happy Thud sped away ahead of us. I kept the speed up until we were back across the river and over Thailand, then throttled back to cruise. The pall was lifted. My crew was all smiles and the interphone chatter terrible as they speculated on the reason for his low fuel. He had mentioned being in a fur ball which was slang for a dogfight, so he might have been in an encounter with MIGs and been separated from the others in his flight. Two miles out on final at U-Tapao, Cap stood his lighter up on the glare shield and looked over at me. It was my turn to make the landing. The touchdown was a whisper. I slowly lowered the nose. The lighter wobbled, then stood solid as a post. I started to grin at Cap and the damn thing fell over with a clink. I still had to buy their bloody beer.

Our life consisted of flying and sleeping. Each afternoon the schedule for the next day's flights was posted on the bulletin board. We were on the schedule every day, and on some days we were scheduled for two flights. One afternoon we were surprised to find ourselves free for the following day. We decided that a visit to Sattahip was in order. Rumor was that a single visit usually was enough to satisfy one's curiosity. Of course, we had to find out why. The next morning the four of us boarded a wildly painted Thai bus for the short ride to Sattahip.

The town was small with a sewer system that consisted of open ditches, lending a stunning aroma to the place. There also was a large, open marketplace. Everything imaginable was sold here in open stalls. There was no refrigeration, so meat was butchered on the spot and the carcasses hung on hooks in the open air. Offal and blood covered the ground. Flies gave everything a writhing black coating. I will never forget the overwhelming smell of that marketplace. It was so powerful that I am sure that it could be bottled and shipped as a simple form of chemical warfare. After returning to the base, I saw no further reason for expeditions to Sattahip and stifled any further complaints about the unremitting flying schedule.

Shortly after our trip to town, our crew was scheduled for a night flight. This was a little unusual and provided a break in routine. At mission briefing, we learned that we would be using the Cherry Anchor ARCP and the call sign Cherry Anchor Four Three. Our receivers were two F-4s with the call signs Night Owl Five and Night Owl Seven. These were not familiar call signs to me, so I asked the intelligence officer who they were. The Night Owl call sign belonged to the 497th Tactical Fighter Squadron, a part of the 8th Tactical Fighter Wing. It seems that Night Owl flights operate in pairs. One tools about at low altitude to see if anyone will shoot at him while the other watches for gun flashes. When an antiaircraft site is located, the two F-4s make a determined effort to put that gun out of business.

Contemplating the hazards of such aggressive behavior left me happy to be a tanker pilot. Manning fast and heavy airplanes loaded with explosives, and zipping around in the dark amidst a strange landscape covered with towering jungle-clad cliffs was hazardous in the extreme. Adding to this difficulty was the fact that the cliffs were full of caves, and the caves were full of anti-aircraft artillery. At this time in the war, the anti-aircraft artillery this far south was aimed manually rather than by radar. The gunner had to see his target and to lead it a sufficient amount to compensate for the target's speed and distance. To compensate for the lack of both radar and gunnery skills, the enemy used barrage fire. If the gunners had a reasonable idea of where the target aircraft would pass, they would aim all their guns at that specific area of the sky. When the aircraft approached that area and was committed on its course, all the guns would fire together. This was a deadly trap to blunder into and very effective. One of these flak traps would cost the life of my friend, Bob Morrissey, just months before the end of the war.

It was full dark when we loaded all our gear on the crew bus and rattled out to the flight line. We had rested most of the day, as this was our only scheduled flight, and were feeling boisterous. It was still hot, but the direct heat of the sun was gone. The Cherry Anchor ARCP was south of Nakhon Phanom on the Mekong River so we did not anticipate a long flight. A pair of floodlights powered by a small generator illuminated the forward area of the airplane. The rest of the airplane, from the leading edge of the wing aft faded in the darkness. The MD3 power cart produced its continuous uproar and would continue to do so until the engines were started and external power was no longer needed. The crew chief handed me the aircraft forms and I checked the maintenance status and began the walk around preflight inspection accompanied by him, while the rest of the crew lugged our gear up the steps of the aerostand.

We taxied with the cockpit windows and the over-wing hatches open. Ten minutes later we were climbing out to the northeast. Our route passed well east of Bangkok and skirted the northwest border of Cambodia. At fourteen thousand feet we leveled off and throttled back to cruise. We were on time and it was not a long way to the Cherry

Anchor ARCP. With the cabin temperature turned very low, the pressurization system provided a modest amount of cool air, even at this low altitude. We did not anticipate either a long flight or the need to leave the relative safety of Thailand. Our parachutes and survival vests were stored on a rack in the cargo compartment. We would put on this equipment just before refueling. Below we could see occasional lights from the scattered villages. It was as peaceful as a ferry flight back in the States.

"Pilot, we're coming up on the ARCP. Expect a left turn to two seven zero in one minute." Lanny logged the time and checked his radarscope for our receivers.

"Holy shit, Cap! Look at that!" Ahead of us a tremendous anti-aircraft barrage lit up the sky. I had never seen so much Flak.

Cap looked up from his paperwork wide-eyed. The flashes from the shell bursts made strange shadows on his face. Lanny came half out of his seat to look over Cap's shoulder.

"How far out do you think that is?" I asked him.

"I don't know, but I Goddamned sure don't want to go there!" He had dropped back into his seat to try and plot the approximate position of the barrage when the whooping klaxon sound of distress beacons swamped guard channel. Cap read the bearing to him from the ARA-25.

"Pilot, turn ninety left. Hold it one minute and then return to heading zero nine zero. I'll try to get a fix on the beacons, sounds like two of them." The turns would allow Lanny to plot several radio lines of position.

"OK, Pilot, disregard turning back to zero nine zero, continue on around to the left another two hundred and thirty degrees. Roll out on heading one five zero. That should put us back over the ARCP and will give me a shot at another line of position. I think I've got their position nailed. They're both on the ground now, not far apart. Looks like about thirty-five west of Mhu Ghia pass. Not a good place to be." Lanny was earning his keep.

"One five zero, it is," I answered. "Any idea where that barrage came from?"

"Just about where they are," he answered.

"Beautiful. Just fucking beautiful. It's going to be a pisser getting them out." I had bad memories of the RESCAP several weeks ago of Cable Zero Five that went so terribly wrong.

The barrage had looked like a giant fireworks display. It had lasted perhaps half a minute, but now all was quiet. I hoped that it did not involve the Night Owl Flight that we were supposed to refuel.

"Pilot, left turn now to heading zero nine zero. That will put you over the ARCP one minute after roll out." Lanny was both tracking the downed airmen and maneuvering us on our primary mission. I no sooner rolled out on a heading of east when I heard Owl Seven calling.

"Cherry Anchor Four Three, this is Owl Seven I'm off your right wing in a right turn to roll out behind you."

Cap sensed the urgency in his voice and started running the refueling checklist. He routinely turned on the refueling lights. This bathed the underside of the airplane with floodlights. Under-wing lights were lit and the pilot-director lights that ran the length of the underside of the airplane added their red and green lights to the display. All this was intended to aid a receiver pilot refueling at night. Unfortunately, it was a bit more than the anti-aircraft people on the ground could resist. They patiently waited for us to fly into their allotted box of sky. The boom operator had gone aft and reported ready in the boom pod.

"Cherry Anchor, Owl Seven is in position. Owl Five is down. Give me fuel and take me east."

"Roger, Owl Seven. We have his position fixed. Has Invert been notified that we need a RESCAP?"

"That's affirmative."

"Pilot, this is Boom. There's a shitload of Flak going off back here."

With a startled look at each other, both Cap and I checked outside. The sky was dark and silent.

"Boom, what the hell are you talking about? We don't see anything up here." I answered.

"Its behind us and it's starting to get too dammed close!" His voice had risen several octaves.

I craned around in my seat to look as far aft as I could. Fourth of July was on again. Cap was looking back on his side.

"Holy Shit! That stuff is walking right up our ass!"

Cap didn't usually get excited, but the flak was overtaking us. Apparently, the gunners had started their barrage late for our altitude but were rapidly correcting their error.

"Owl Seven, this is Cherry Anchor. You can have all the fuel that you want but you will have to get it in the dark!" I nodded to Cap and he switched the outside lights off...all of them, including navigation lights.

"Thanks, Cherry Anchor. I thought you'd never turn off all those fucking lights."

The gunners lost us and the firing stopped. Owl Seven, with his fuel tanks full, disconnected from the boom and dropped away in the darkness. We could hear him calling Owl Five Alpha and Owl Five Bravo on guard channel. When a crewmember makes it to the ground and needs rescue, his call sign becomes the call sign of his aircraft plus a phonetic letter starting with alpha for the pilot and working through the alphabet with a different phonetic letter for each additional crewmember. I once heard the letter kilo used after a call sign when a crewmember fell out of the back of a C-130 while dropping flares. That would have made him the eleventh crewmember on that airplane. He created an awful fuss and demanded to be rescued forthwith. I don't think he anticipated finding himself afoot that night. It now occurred to me that we were milling around at a fairly low altitude over a bit of ground occupied by men who did not like us at all and were prepared to act upon their feelings of hostility. They had just proved that they were well able to shoot down aircraft at our altitude.

"Nav, Pilot. Go back and get our 'chutes and survival vests. The way things are going, anything can happen."

Lanny clicked the interphone twice and was off the flight deck and back with our emergency gear in a matter of seconds. Normally, we would have at least put on the parachutes before refueling. Owl Seven had joined on us before we had a chance. The boom operator had put his gear on when he went aft to the boom pod. I set up an orbit at the point that Owl Seven had left us. He and other airplanes would have no trouble finding us with their radar. We had no idea how long this would go on and this short lull might be our only chance to get our survival gear on. It was just after two thirty in the morning. A FAC, Nail Two Seven, had taken over the RESCAP and other aircraft were arriving. The all-too-familiar effort to get our guys out before they could be captured had begun.

The guns on the ground were wisely silent. The area was blanketed with tactical air power just itching for a target. From the radio talk we learned that one man was unhurt, the other had an injured leg that probably was fractured. A Jolly Green Giant, or rescue helicopter, was standing by but would have to wait until first light before trying to snatch the two men from the ground. A couple of Sandys, or A-1 Skyraiders, were on scene. These huge, single-engine, propeller-driven aircraft had the endurance to loiter for most of the pilot's tour in Vietnam and could absorb a lot of damage with little effect. They also had enormous firepower; a salvo from one of them had about the same punch as a broadside from a World War II cruiser.

"Owl Five Alpha, Nail Two Seven, can you see Bravo?"

"Negative." The answer was whispered and muffled as if the pilot was talking with his radio stuffed inside his flight suit to muffle sound. "I think he's about a hundred yards above me in the karst."

"Owl Five Bravo, does that sound about right to you?"

Two clicks answered Nail Two Seven.

"OK, you two. Lay low for now. I'll stay in the area and I'll keep the Sandys and F-4s here in case anyone gets close. The troops at Udorn are getting a party together for a first-light pick up. Nail Two Seven listening-out."

The radio chatter died out. The quiet masked the tension that anticipated the morning light. At Udorn, the Combat Reporting Center had gone into high gear and was marshaling resources for the coming rescue. The rescue of downed airmen had progressed from the haphazard scramble of the war's early years to an organized and determined activity. On the opposing side, the capture of these airmen now took priority over simply killing them. The North Vietnamese leadership found POWs a valuable asset in their determination to reinforce anti-war sentiment in the United States and embarrass American political leaders. They had refined their skills, learned after the fall of the French at Dien Bien Phu, and developed a complex system to exploit those captured. The American government seemed to counter this by ignoring the plight of those who became prisoners of war. The strange attitude of ignoring the POW situation would not change until the wives of the POWs organized and created public pressure at the Paris Peace talks. Such attitudes intensified a powerful determination on the part of aircrew not to allow downed airmen to fall into enemy hands.

Through the several hours before dawn we loitered at endurance speed over the area. From occasional talk on the radio, it was apparent that frequent sweeps along the nearby Ho Chi Min trail were made to keep the area from being reinforced.

"What do you think their chances are?" Lanny asked.

"I don't know," I replied. "This is a little too similar to the Cable Zero Five RESCAP." I had not considered that this rescue had several hours of darkness to get organized and at first light the area would be smothered with air cover.

"Cherry Anchor Four Three, Owl Seven."

"Go, Night Owl. What's up?" Cap answered.

"I'm moving into pre-contact position. I'd better top off. It's about half an hour now to first light and things are going to get busy."

"You don't seem to have any trouble finding me," I answered. "Haven't seen any more triple A activity have you?"

"I've got a better radar. You're easy to find. The bad guys don't want to give up their position with those Sandys milling around down there. One pass from those big bastards would ruin their whole day."

"You got nine thousand," Cap said.

"Thanks, Bud," Owl seven answered. "It's about showtime." With that he disconnected and dropped away into the night, now showing gray off to the east.

Another FAC, Nail Two Four, had relieved Nail Two Seven. From the growing uproar on the radios, we knew that the cavalry was coming. Light comes fast in the tropics and the landscape below us was materializing. I had the unhappy feeling that gunners on the ground could surely see us now, but they remained silent.

"Owl Five Alpha, this is Nail Two Four. I'm your new nanny. Pop your smoke."

Two minutes later a thin wisp of smoke from the pencil flare drifted up out of the jungle canopy. Nail Two Four ordered in the Sandys. They sanitized the area around the two downed airmen with a storm of fire. Jolly Green One Zero came whop-whopping in at tree top level. He hovered over the wounded man while a PJ rode the penetrator down to him, splinted his leg and tied him to the penetrator. In minutes, both the injured man and the parajumper were back in the Jolly Green. I think that the PJs are tall-walking dudes. They will risk all for a chance to save a downed airman. My bowels would turn to water were I ever required to perform their duty, for when they are riding the penetrator they are simply suspended targets that are shot at by all of the bad guys with every kind of a gun.

The airwaves were now in an uproar. Nail Two Four was directing strikes. Jolly Green One Zero was talking to the second man on the ground; F-4s and Sandys were pounding the whole area. The big helicopter shifted its position a few yards to the north and again dropped the penetrator. There was no need for the PJ this time as the remaining man on the ground was uninjured. Another two minutes and he was inside the Jolly Green. Suddenly, it was over. Nail Two Four called off his dogs and we all headed west out of the area.

Shortly after crossing the Mekong River, we leveled off at twenty-two thousand feet. An F-4 pulled alongside just off the left wing tip, and the pilot gave a casual wave.

"Hey, Cherry Anchor, this is Owl Seven. How about landing with us? We owe you guys a round or two and it just might turn into one hell of a party."

I guess life in Tactical Air Command was a little less rigid than in SAC. "Sorry, Night Owl. I wish we could, but this bird is up for another sortie today and I'm already late."

"Sorry 'bout that," he answered. "I'll make sure that the SAC Commander knows what you did for us."

"Please don't do that!" I answered. "If it gets out where I took this bird, I'll be hanging from the flagpole in the morning. As far as anyone is concerned, I never went east of the ARCP."

Owl Seven was silent for a moment. Then he said, "You guys sure work for a strange outfit. You should transfer to TAC. See you another day." With that he banked away and soon was out of sight.

I never learned the names of the two men that had been recovered. I hope they both made it through the war and are safely retired, tormented only by a herd of grandchildren.

Our crew continued flying daily missions. Although we frequently flew the busy Orange and White Anchor missions, with an occasional trip over the Gulf of Tonkin, our flights fell into a period of routine. Some of the airplanes we refueled took on their own personality and were like old friends. There was a Thud named after the actress Goldie Hawn, with "Goldie" emblazoned in huge letters on its nose section. I wonder if she ever knew that she had an airplane named after her. Another was the "Frito Bandito," which had a cartoon character on its nose—a little Mexican bandit wearing a big sombrero and firing a six-gun in each hand. Seeing these airplanes day after day gave them a personality. We did everything that we could to see that they were topped off with fuel as close to their target area as we dared go. If we were scheduled for their post-strike refueling, we worried like a she-bear over her cubs until they were all out of Indian country and on their way safely home.

One sunny morning we met a flight of four at the Orange Anchor ARCP. Frito Bandito was in the flight. They were loaded with ordinance and topped their tanks as we took them towards their target area. That day we also were tasked to provide their post-strike refueling. After they left us for their targets, we idled back south at best endurance speed. Our plan was to return to the point where we had dropped them off and meet them as they exited the strike area. If things got hot for them, they would need extra fuel. At the estimated time, we were orbiting in the area where we had last seen them.

The appointed time came and went. The radios were silent. Anxiously we checked and rechecked the refueling frequency set in the command radio. Minutes passed. We edged a little further to the northeast.

"Orange Anchor Five Four, Sturgeon Flight up on frequency. Radar contact."

Yes! They made it and were on their way out. "Roger, Sturgeon Flight, at twenty-one miles we will start a left turn to a heading of two two zero." On that heading we would be making a B-line out of the area.

In minutes, three Thuds formed up on us. Their racks were empty; the undersides of their wings were clean.

"Where's the Bandito?" I asked.

"He had a little trouble and we got separated," Sturgeon Lead answered. "Any chance you guys can wait for him? He'll be hurting for fuel by the time he gets this far south."

"You bet. As soon as you three are fueled we'll wander back up track for him."

Less than ten minutes later, we heard Sturgeon Three calling us. Frito Bandito was on his way home. Again we turned to the southwest while the nearly empty Bandito gulped JP-4. After he had taken on his fuel he pulled alongside our left wing and flew in formation with us until we were back across the river into Thailand. That was the last time I saw the Frito Bandito. We never did find out what the little bit of trouble was. Two days later we left U-Tapao for Kadena. It was time for us to rotate back to the World.

FIFTEEN

◆ ◆ ◆ ◆ ◆ ◆ ◆ ◆ ◆ ◆ ◆ ◆ ◆

'Tis all a chequer-board of Nights and Days
Where destiny with men for pieces plays;
Hither and thither moves, and mates, and slays,
And one by one back in the closet lays.
-Omar Khayyam

In the world of airline flying, a man's security and status with a company is determined by a number system. His seniority is simply established by his hire date. His advancement, choice of routes, and equipment, as well as his job security, are determined by this seniority. Should he change employers and sign on with another airline, then he must start over again at the bottom of the roster.

In contrast, the military aviator's status is skill dependent. It is not unusual for the aircraft commander to be a rank lower than the copilot or navigator. This occurs most frequently when a man is substituted on a crew for some administrative reason. A pilot may advance to senior or even command pilot while falling behind in the promotion race. The advancement of rank will determine how long he stays in the military and whether or not he will be allowed to stay long enough to reach retirement. In most cases, an officer must reach the rank of major to accumulate enough active-duty time to retire. The company grade ranks, those from second lieutenant through captain, are a matter of time, and promotions arrive pretty much on schedule if the individual has kept out of serious trouble. Field-grade rank, major through full colonel, is another matter. Promotion boards meet annually and the chosen few are identified. Each step up in rank thins out the force as the higher grade has far fewer positions than the number of eligible candidates. You must make promotion or you are out of a job. You are allowed to meet the promotion board on a second consecutive year if you are passed over the first time. Few advance on the second attempt. I suspect that the second try is to allow the candidate time to start seeking other employment. This is known as the "Up or Out" system.

At least once a year every officer has an effectiveness report, or ER, written by his immediate superior. In most cases, the reporting officer wants to assure that his boy will be promoted. Over time, the check marks in effectiveness reports have crept to the far right column and the narrative portions have grown more and more colorful in some strange contest of looking out for ones own protégé. Eventually, this desire to reward one's subordinates progressed to the point where every officer had become an unbelievable model of leadership, honor, and dedication to duty. The term "water walker" came to be applied to an otherwise average officer.

It was imperative that a man be considered a water walker, if only to stay on active duty. One's future could easily depend on the literary skills of the reporting officer and a man could quickly be damned by receiving only the barest hint of praise. A realistic and fair effectiveness report would mark the immediate end of any chance for promotion and probably would result in that officer being shunted off to some obscure corner of the world where he would spend his few remaining military days counting paper clips.

There were any number of calls from senior officers to stop inflating ERs, but no one was willing to be first. Should a reporting officer be gullible enough to heed this call, he most certainly would condemn his subordinates to obscurity, unless every other reporting officer simultaneously reverted to the intended way of writing ERs, a highly unlikely event. I know of several fine officers whose careers ended early because their reporting officer wrote a fair ER. The Air Force struggled mightily with this problem but it was not solved during my years in the service. As a result, many talented people were terminated while at the same time the Air Force bemoaned the loss of skilled pilots, navigators, and highly trained technicians. This pleased the growing airline industry as they were provided with a large pool of skilled people to draw from and were spared the cost of training their own flight and maintenance crews.

A couple ways that one could skew the odds for promotion in his favor were to accumulate impressive academic credentials or find a way into staff duty. For those on crew duty during the Cold War and the war in Vietnam, either could be a daunting accomplishment. The attempt to go to any elective military school in residence was hampered by the reluctance of most commanders to release any of their crew force to other duty. All of my applications to Squadron Officer's School, the first of several military schools one must attend in order to advance, were rejected. I finally took the course by correspondence only to find out that this method was not weighted in the same manner as actual attendance. It was a no-win situation. Night school in community colleges was out of the question. More than half of our time was spent on alert or overseas on temporary duty, which absented us from the classroom. The balance of our time was spent flying or preparing for a mission. Time studies in the sixties revealed that SAC crews were averaging well over ninety hours of duty per week. Air Force Officers not on crew duty did not have to contend with these obstacles. This seemed to give an unfair advantage to those who did not carry the burden of crew duty.

The other option, staff duty, was often attained by the back door. It was the practice to place a crewmember who was unable to maintain the standards of flight duty in some entry-level job on the wing or group staff. This job might be chief pencil-sharpener or coffee go-for but that individual now had high visibility. He could make it to cocktail hour at the Club every evening and exert all of his charm in the proper places. If he could make himself useful and keep his nose clean, he would do well and provide credence to the adage that it is better to be despised than unknown.

From this practice arose the somewhat disgruntled expression used by flight crews of "fuck up and move up." This also accounted for the very cynical attitude of crews towards staff and the unflattering epitaph of "staff weenie." Rewarding an individual unable to perform his assigned duty with a nine-to-five job, all his weekends and holidays free, and a better chance in the promotion lottery, as well as no loss in income, was not well received by those with years of crew duty. Unfortunately, the flight crews branded all staff with the same iron, and this included some very talented people.

During my visit with the Royal Air Force in the early sixties, I discussed this subject with several field grade officers. The RAF approach to the problem was effective. Early in an officer's career, those with talent for organization and command were identified and groomed specifically for staff duty. In other words, they chose their brightest early on and trained them for staff and command positions. The RAF has the same problem as far as promotions are concerned. They, too, have only so many positions in each grade that they can fill. However, they are unwilling to cut adrift skilled flight crew simply because there is no room to promote them. The British are far too provident with training resources to embrace such a wasteful practice. The individual is allowed to remain on flying duty, but his rank is frozen, he is no longer considered for promotion, and he is not counted as holding a space in his present rank. This prevents a plug or roadblock at any particular rank. The number of officers allowed to take this status is regulated by projected demands for aircrew or other specialty positions. As for aircrew who are unable or unwilling to maintain the standards of their flight position, they are removed from flying status altogether and either transferred to some other field of endeavor or separated from the service. Their inadequacy is not rewarded. I dutifully reported this information when I was debriefed after my visit with the RAF but it excited no interest in our Air Force.

Many of the organizational practices of the Royal Air Force and the U. S. Air Force are similar. This certainly is the result of their very close association during the Second World War. Promotion is difficult to carry out with total fairness. Ideally, the best person would always receive the advancement, but this is difficult to achieve in practice. I do believe that the military comes closer to this goal than does private industry.

For these many reasons, I was astounded when notified that I had been named on the newly released major's list. I still believe that this was either the result of a clerical error or a single rather spectacular flight over the Gulf of Tonkin a year or so earlier as Dave Huff's copilot. My obnoxious ways and penchant for identifying a horse's ass when I encountered one were not endearing. I loathed palace intrigues and avoided military social functions, especially above the squadron level, preferring to spend what little time I found available with my family.

All officers on crew status had what were called additional duties. These usually were jobs such as assistant safety officer or assistant electronic countermeasures officer. These additional duties were sometimes used, to the detriment of the officer's primary duty, by the politically inclined in order to maneuver into a more permanent staff position and out of crew duty. I did my additional duties thoroughly but without enthusiasm. I wanted to fly airplanes and had little interest in other aspects of military life. Thus, that all-important promotion to major was a stunning event, surprising not only for me but for a lot of other people, as well. At least I wouldn't have to start job-hunting in the near future, a fortunate situation as our three children were rapidly growing into the most expensive years of childhood.

SIXTEEN

◆◆◆◆◆◆◆◆◆◆◆◆◆

When one door is shut, another opens.
-Cervantes, in Don Quixote

In the rigid caste system of the military, the contributions of enlisted men are seldom recognized. Few civilians comprehend the enormous effort necessary to operate a single warplane, to say nothing of the energy expended to operate something as massive and complex as an aircraft carrier or a bomb wing. Most enlisted men work long hours at tasks that are difficult, unpleasant, sometimes boring, and often dangerous. They seldom are justly rewarded and, unfortunately, frequently taken for granted. There is a hierarchy in the military that is difficult for a democratic society to understand, even though the caste system is every bit as rigid in most civilian organizations. The basis of the military system of rank grew out of the ugly necessity in battle of having to order soldiers to perform dangerous tasks which they, very wisely, might refuse to perform. The Air Force is the youngest of the armed forces and the majority of the combatants are officers. The trappings of rank, especially among aviators, are often ignored during combat operations. Saluting and the wearing of hats are dispensed with on most flight lines. It is unreasonable to expect a sergeant, up to both elbows in an electronics bay or engine, to salute simply because some young lieutenant wandered up to see what he was doing. Hats are great to keep the sun off your head, especially if you have a bald spot, but have the bad habit of getting sucked into jet engines with disastrous results to an engine that can easily cost more than a million dollars. It takes a year or two for both the young officer and young enlisted man to learn when this casual attitude is appropriate. In both officer and enlisted training, the courtesies of rank are rigidly enforced. Although fraternizing between officer and enlisted is officially proscribed, this restriction frequently is ignored among aircrew.

It was about a week before Christmas, one year late in the war, when we left Okinawa for South Dakota. The KC-135 was limited to a maximum of one hundred passengers, at that time. Any aircraft bound from Asia to the United States that close to Christmas would have every seat filled before it left its departure base. As soon as we were within radio range of Guam, our first stop, the command post was calling us and asking if we had any passenger seats available. Of course, we were full and the odds of someone getting a space-available hop eastbound out of Guam were about as good as a tourist drawing four of a kind in a crooked poker game.

We planned a two-hour stop. I wanted to refuel to the maximum. The Pacific is a big ocean and fuel that was not on the airplane was of little use should circumstances turn unpleasant. Cap had already calculated the maximum weight we could take off with and had radioed ahead our fuel requirements. We had no maintenance problems so all we needed, aside from fuel, was to replenish water and coffee and empty the chemical toilets. In Base Operations, Lanny was busy updating his wind flight plan and Cap had the rest of our clearance paperwork under control. I started for the coffee shop leaving them to their tasks.

"Sir! Sir!"

Someone was tugging at my elbow. I turned to see a young Airman about nineteen years old. He couldn't have been a year out of boot camp and was obviously struggling to muster the courage to approach someone as untouchable as a field grade aircraft commander. It was difficult not to smile at his discomfort. He obviously was unsure of whether to salute or genuflect.

"What can I do for you?" I asked, hoping that he would not call me "your majesty." He seemed awfully nervous. The kid must work at some job where even second lieutenants are gods.

He swallowed and pointed at the arrival board behind the dispatch counter, "Is that your airplane, sir?"

I looked up at the board and saw my name next to the tail number of the airplane. It also said under destination "South Dakota" and under seats available "zero."

"Well, it's not really mine. It belongs to the Air Force and they are sort of letting me use it."

He now decided that in for a penny, in for a pound and said, "I know it says no seats available, but is there any way you can squeeze me in? I won't take up much space."

"Sorry, son, I'd get in a lot of trouble if I exceeded my passenger limit."

"Sir, I've been waiting here three days and every time I get a seat some officer bumps me. Sorry, sir."

He looked like he'd been here three days. He was rumpled, tired, and discouraged. I had a strong feeling that this was his first Christmas away from home. I started to move away but his pleading look stopped me. I tried to think of some way to take him.

"Airman, where is it that you are trying to get to in the States?"

"Home, sir. Sioux Falls, South Dakota."

Shit! How the hell could I enjoy my Christmas if I left this kid here on Guam? It suddenly struck me that my passenger list was limited, but I didn't know of any limit on my crew size. I also was pretty sure that I didn't have the authority to change my crew list.

"Let me see your ID card," I said.

Sensing a solution he eagerly handed it to me. I walked over to the dispatch desk and the NCO looked up questioningly.

"Sergeant, put this man on my flight orders as an Observer."

The Sergeant glanced at the smiling Airman. He knew the kid had been hanging around for several days and finally had won a seat. Not a passenger seat, he would ride home on the flight deck sitting on the jump seat between the two pilots and he could not be bumped.

An hour later we lifted off with a delighted young Airman in the jump seat. Luck was with us. At altitude we caught the jet stream much farther south than usual. Our ground speed was close to seven hundred knots. The wind held. We made such good time that we overflew Hawaii and went directly in to Ellsworth. This was convenient since it saved me having to answer any embarrassing questions in Hawaii about a non-rated name on my flight orders. Two hours after we landed, the young man was at the bus station with just a few hundred miles between him and his home and I had paid just a fraction of the debt that we all owe to the enlisted force.

SEVENTEEN

◆◆◆◆◆◆◆◆◆◆◆◆◆◆◆◆◆◆

He is in the way of life that keepeth instruction:
but he that refuseth reproof erreth.
-Proverbs, 10:17

Man's relationship with most machines is usually indifferent, but when the man and the machine are associated in a close and possibly dangerous relationship, a man may ascribe life-like qualities to his machine. On occasion he may be moved to speak to it with praise. Sometimes he will refer to it using a feminine name or endearing term. This is the exception. In most cases, when a man wishes to ascribe anthropomorphic qualities to some machine, he addresses it with vitriol and rage induced by his own incompetence. Frequently, the offending machine is not only reviled but is physically assaulted, and the more clumsy and inept the operator, then the more violent the attack. Some men have been known to completely destroy an offending machine in a fit of rage.

There are other men, though small in number, who hold a genuine affection for the machines they operate. Usually, they are quiet men and are easily embarrassed when caught speaking softly to their machines as if they were living entities. In terms of repair, lubrication, and cleanliness, these men are always attentive to the needs of the machines in their care. The controls are manipulated with a soft touch, and perhaps, the man may be heard quietly coaxing the machine through some particularly difficult task. This odd relationship often manifests itself between ships or airplanes and those who spend a lifetime operating them. The machines are very much capable of killing the men and these men are calmly aware of this.

I was one of a small group of men that approached the large tanker parked in the sun. Something of this synergistic relationship seemed to pass between Gordon Phillips and the airplane. The airplane seemed assured by Gordon's calm demeanor and allowed us to perform our ministration without interference. Not once was it spoken to with profanity and its various parts were not struck or kicked. In short order, we performed the rituals and incantations that brought the four mighty engines to life. A terrified cottontail that had been hiding amongst the huge tires of the left truck broke its cover and fled the vicinity in a wild zigzag pattern. The auxiliary power cart was disconnected, its heavy black umbilical cords were coiled on top of it, and it was removed to a spot a dozen feet beyond the left wing tip. The attending acolytes dragged away the huge, wooden chocks that blocked the wheels. One of them took position a hundred feet in front of the airplane and held his hands above his head and waved the airplane forward. The low whine of the engines increased slightly and the airplane moved gently out of its parking spot. The man pointed with his right arm held straight out from his side and continued waving forward with his left. The airplane turned with minimum fuss and moved down the taxiway, the yellow, center stripe passing exactly between the twin, nose tires.

Several months earlier, I had been designated as an instructor pilot and had taken the flight check. SAC required that any new instructor attend the Central Flight Instructor course at the earliest opportunity. One other new instructor and I were under the tutelage of Gordon Phillips, a CFIC instructor and one of the most accomplished aviators I had encountered.

Gordon talked continuously to both of us. "You can get away with anything when dealing with both airplanes and women. All you have to do is be gentle and smooth. Don't bully or get rough with either one. If you do, you are going to get smacked hard. On our flights in this course, I'll show you what I mean. This airplane has abilities that are not in any book. They are not things that you will teach to your students, but when you fly this lady to her limit, you will gain a confidence that will save your hide and your airplane one day."

While Gordon chattered away, the two of us kept our own counsel. A quick glance between us confirmed our wait-and-see attitude. Forty minutes after we had lifted off the ground we joined with a B-52, also on a CFIC or Central Flight Instructor Course flight. Both airplanes were heavy this soon after take-off, but that didn't seem to concern either Gordon or the CFIC instructor in the B-52. What followed was a continuous, air-refueling hook-up, with the autopilots in both airplanes off and various throttles being retarded and returned to function, all the while both airplanes rolling in and out of sixty degree bank turns, which under normal circumstances was twice the acceptable angle of bank even for flights not involving air refueling. Both CFIC instructors performed these demonstrations as a matter of course and with a level of competence that I could only envy. The wait-and-see glance that I had exchanged with the other student instructor pilot was replaced with a heavy dose of self-doubt. We were flying with the big boys, and I had a hell of a lot left to learn about flying.

For the next several weeks we flew every other day. Our non-flying days were filled with instruction in the art of teaching, aerodynamics, and the incredible detail of the systems in the 707 family of aircraft. The military had not yet adopted the limited training concept of "teach only the minimum that a crewmember needs to know." We were still expected to know how everything worked on any airplane we flew; and what might make it fail. I think that a serious mistake was made when flight training dropped the concept of in-depth instruction, but that event was still a few years down the road. One of our ground sessions was devoted to the causes of accidents and the best way to dodge that bullet.

"Instructing in an airplane can be truly hazardous," Gordon said. "The problem is that someone other than yourself is primary on the controls. Things can happen very fast. If a student makes a mistake at a critical time of flight, you have to correct it before it becomes a disaster, but you can't be grabbing the controls away from your student for every little mistake. If you do that, he will never learn a damn thing. The trick is not to let him take you beyond your own abilities, but sooner or later both of you will have a student get away from you. If you are not fast enough and good enough, that will be the day that you die. Don't ever take another pilot of unknown abilities for granted. This is the reason for all of this "gee whiz" flying that we have been doing. You need to know both your own limits and the airplane's limits."

On another ground session Gordon got on the topic of accident causes. He was merciless on the pilot-error factor. "I can think of very few accidents that do not have some component of pilot error," was the statement he made to start the argument.

"Come on, Gordon. What about that tanker that blew up over Spain a while back?" I asked.

Gordon smiled. "That airplane had an explosion in the center wing tank. I'll bet you a month's pay that there had been some sort of write-up on the override pumps in the previous week or so, and they had been signed off. Either that or the tanks had been run dry. A combination of an overheated pump or the insulation on wiring breaking down, along with the right combination of air and fumes in the empty tank turned it into a bomb. I know that those pumps are not supposed to overheat if run dry, but safety systems do not always work. You cannot count on them. There will be very few occasions of system problems that don't give some kind of warning, and it almost never will be a *single* item that fails and does you in. It is the nature of fate that several small things happen in sequence to build a trap. Your only protection is knowledge. You must know everything about your bird and be able to anticipate these traps."

Some years after this class, TWA flight 800 exploded in flight off the Long Island coast. The 800 was a Boeing built 747 with a very similar fuel system. Suspicion fell on the center wing tank. Several years earlier, the KC-135 that I had referred to had exploded over Spain. The wreckage, much easier to recover since the incident happened over land, pointed directly to an electrical problem in the center wing tank.

In the flights that followed, Gordon taught us how to fly the 135 to limits that were beyond any that we had imagined. Landings and missed approaches with two engines inoperative were routine. We learned how to make an approach and missed approach with three engines inoperative and carrying over twenty tons of fuel. This was all a great deal of fun and impressed the hell out of me. I did not anticipate how soon the skills that I was learning from Gordon would become deadly urgent and snatch me from the edge of darkness.

*****

Captain Harry English was assigned as my copilot for upgrade training to aircraft commander. He was of medium build and height, with a relaxed and friendly personality. Prior to his Air Force career he had played baseball in the minor leagues. He now spent his off-duty time coaching Little League and was very popular with the young ballplayers.

Just a little after six on an early June morning I met Harry, our navigator and boom operator, at Base Operations. We were scheduled for a crew flight, which meant that no students would be along. The flight was intended for our use to maintain our own proficiency and to complete quarterly training items. At mission planning the day before, I had told Harry that he would perform the entire flight in the left seat and carry out his duties as first pilot. As an instructor, I could log my quarterly training items, such as instrument approaches, from either pilot's seat. Harry was delighted as we also were scheduled for a minimum interval take-off or MITO, an item that Harry would have to demonstrate proficiency in to become an Aircraft Commander. MITOs could become hairy because the airplanes took off at fifteen-second intervals. Under normal circumstances, the take-off interval for heavy airplanes in civil aviation was two minutes. A surprise missile attack would not allow this luxury. It would be necessary to get as many airplanes off the ground as possible, so every pilot had to make at least one MITO take-off each training quarter. Wake turbulence became increasingly intense at lift off for the planes farther back in the line, so training MITOs were usually limited to two or three airplanes. It was one of the few times that a pilot hoped for a good stiff cross-wind to carry the turbulence downwind and out of his path during take-off. We were number two, a good position for a student making his first MITO. Harry worked hard during the mission planning and had prepared himself well for the flight.

It was a soft, early, summer morning at Ellsworth. We were in a good mood, joking with each other and looking forward to the flight. I had just picked up our mission package at the counter in Base Operations when a captain in flying clothes approached me. I had seen him a few times at the squadron but did not know him, a not unusual situation, as crews were constantly being sent to Southeast Asia. A year could easily pass without my seeing people in the squadron who were on an opposite rotation.

"I'm Captain Shields," he said confidently. "Scheduling put me on the flight for the MITO in the left seat. I'm getting ready for my upgrade check and need to get that done."

I could see the disappointment on Harry's face. "Well, Captain Shields, if you were assigned to this flight, where were you when we were mission planning yesterday?"

"Uh, I was off yesterday," he stammered.

He had given himself away. He knew he was to be on the flight and had dodged mission planning, leaving the work to Harry. He had to be someone's pet, as anyone else in the upgrade program would split a gut for any chance to get left-seat time and that meant doing the grunt stuff, too.

"OK, Captain," I said as I handed him the mission package. "Go put yourself on the flight orders, check the paperwork over, and be ready to brief the crew for the MITO in ten minutes."

"You mean I have to do the take-off data, too? That's the copilot's duty."

This guy had more brass than a Thai gift shop! "Captain English is my copilot, not yours. If you're going to fly with us, you pull your weight. See you in ten minutes, and after you have demonstrated a crew briefing, I'll explain what I expect during the MITO." I was mildly irritated, but things like this happened all of the time, even on our training flights. I would make it up to Harry. Shields would get the MITO but that was all. Once we were on the climb-out, I planned to put Harry in the left seat for the rest of the flight.

A quarter of an hour later we met in the planning room. Major Andrews, the flight leader, gave the general MITO briefing.

"We have a slight, right cross-wind," he began. "After lift off I'll drift a little to the left and you guys can keep upwind a bit."

He would do this to minimize the wake turbulence and to give us a break on visibility. During water injection, the engines make a lot of smoke.

"If I have to abort the take-off, I will call abort three times over the radio and try to take the left side of the runway. I'll hold off on braking as much as I can, depending on how much runway I have left. You guys take the right side of the runway. If you are going to over-run me, take the airplane off of the runway to the right. That will take you away from the fuel pits. Since there are only two of us in the MITO, if you have to abort the take-off, just do it and don't call it on the radio. Let me know after you get the airplane stopped. Any questions?"

I nodded to Andrews that we had none and the crews split up to finish their paperwork. Captain Shields gave a textbook crew briefing, putting me a little more at ease. I took him aside to let the Navigator finish his work.

"This is how I want this MITO done," I explained. "When lead crosses the hold line, you follow fifteen seconds behind him. Try to taxi at or a little less than his taxi speed. The trick will be to advance your throttles so that water injection kicks in fifteen seconds after you see his start. Since this is your first MITO, I'd rather you be a little behind than too close. It takes a little practice, so don't try to crowd him. Once the water injection starts, we can't pull back on the throttles or we'll lose water and have to abort. As soon as the water starts, I'll take the throttles and set take-off thrust for you. You concentrate on the take-off, and fly the airplane just as you would on any take-off. I'll make any decision to abort. You'll know when the power comes back. I'll raise the speed brakes. I don't have anti-skid on my side so you'll do the braking. If we have to go off of the runway, I'll tell you and you steer to miss lead and to leave the runway with as gentle a turn as possible. If that happens, we will abandon the airplane as soon as it is stopped and assemble upwind, in this case to the west. Once we are off the ground, I'll raise the gear and flaps on your call. If I want to take over control I will say, 'I have it.' You will immediately release control of the airplane to me and we will talk about it later. Any questions?"

Shields paid close attention and seemed to have lost some of his arrogance. His attitude change did much to increase my confidence in a man I had never flown with. He would be controlling the airplane during a maneuver that could suddenly go to hell in a handbasket. I signed for the flight, and the crew bus took us out to the airplane. We had almost forty-five minutes to take-off, plenty of time to preflight and taxi out behind the lead airplane to the northwest end of the airfield.

The base fire station was on the opposite side of the tower from Base Operations. Master Sergeant Nolen looked up at the wall clock and decided that he had time for another cup of coffee before they would have to position a fire truck at the mid-field taxiway for the MITO.

"Hey, Sarge, we gonna have any action this morning?" one of his crew called from the parked crash truck.

Things had been quiet ever since the B-52 had crashed on top of the fuel pits over a year ago. Nolen grinned at his Italian friend, "Not likely, you bloodthirsty little Wop. This is just a two ship MITO and both pilots are instructors."

At twenty minutes after seven Nolen called to his crew, "OK, guys, let's saddle up. They roll at seven thirty."

It was only a few hundred yards from the fire station to the mid-field taxiway where they would wait until both airplanes were safely in the air. The crash crew was relaxed. They did not expect a problem and thought that they would be back in the station for their daily routine in ten minutes. In the cab of the control tower, the man on duty picked up his binoculars and watched the Supervisor of Flying circle the two airplanes in his staff car. The SOF was making a last minute check of the airplanes for leaks or hanging red streamers that would indicate some ground lock pin or cover had been missed in the preflight, and that the flaps were in the take-off position. The tower controller saw a coyote, disturbed by the engine noise and activity, sprint across the taxiway behind the airplanes and disappear into the brush at the side of the taxiway. The SOF gave a casual wave to the cockpit of the lead airplane, sped away down the taxiway and pulled over to the edge of the ramp to wait until the flight had departed.

I sat in the copilot seat of the number two airplane and listened to the clearance for the flight. When we finished with Clearance Delivery, I switched command radio two to departure control frequency. We closed the sliding cockpit windows and completed the Before Take-off Checklist. Captain Shields had been all business and seemed to know what he was doing. The tower cleared us for take-off.

I heard Major Andrew's voice on tower frequency, "Lead rolling." Shields brought the power up and followed the lead airplane onto the runway.

"Easy on the power," I said. He was eating up the space between the lead airplane and us. "OK, watch the sweep hand on the panel clock. He's crossing the hold line. You want to cross fifteen seconds from now......Dammit! Go easy on the power!"

The main trucks squealed and the nose gear juddered as he made the turn onto the runway too sharply. The tail of the lead airplane loomed above us. A cloud of black smoke poured from the lead airplane's engines as his water injection cut in. I followed the throttles with my left hand. Suddenly, Shields shoved the power up hard. With a roar, the water injection cut in. I could see the rudder of the lead airplane sticking up out of the smoke. We were tight behind him.

"Shit! We are close! You must be seven seconds behind

him," I said.

For an instant I thought of pulling the throttles back and aborting the take-off, but instead I set power for take-off thrust.

Sergeant Nolen watched the lead tanker pass in front of him. Seven seconds later the number two tanker flashed past.

"Damn, they're close." He sat up abruptly in his seat, his attention locked onto the speeding airplanes. He watched critically as the first one lifted off, drifted slightly to the east and folded its wheels into its belly.

I saw the lead rise out of the smoke. The airspeed indicator passed S-2. I called, "Rotate!"

Shields lifted the airplane off and called for gear up. I leaned forward and raised the gear handle. The left wing dropped in the boiling air of the wake turbulence. Shields had the control wheel hard over to the right. He was making basic stick-and-rudder errors. I'd have to take the airplane away from him if he didn't get it together in the next second.

"You need right rudder, dummy! Right fucking rudder!"

The rudder on a tanker has more area than the entire wing of a small Cessna and is powered by three thousand pounds of hydraulic pressure. Piqued by my rebuke, Shields stomped hard with his right foot and shoved in every bit of right rudder that there was. The result was instantaneous and spectacular. The nose slued hard right, the airplane pitched up violently, and we rolled to the right.

"I have it!" I screamed. The jolt of the control yolk hitting the forward stop as I slammed the nose downward jarred my right arm. The airplane buffeted violently as the stall spread outward from the wing root area. I saw that the landing gear was not yet fully retracted, and the flight director command bars were sulking in the bottom of the instrument case with a full fly down command. Beyond that I remember nothing except an impression of trees and buildings flashing past and a sense of ground above me to the left. I was holding the hand of darkness and it was a merciful amnesiac.

It took Nolen almost a full second to react. He stared in horror as the second tanker in the flight pitched up and began to tail-walk in its death throes so violently that he could see clouds of fuel spewing from the vents on the wings. In a single movement, he switched on the red, rotating beacon on the roof, put the crash truck in drive, and stuffed his foot down on the accelerator. His crew grabbed for handholds as the powerful diesel belched a cloud of black smoke from the exhaust and the crash truck jumped forward. Speeding down the runway in pursuit, he lost sight of the tanker as it sank behind the base flight hangar. A second crash truck came howling out of the fire station and joined the chase, launched by the crash alarm from the control tower.

The Supervisor of Flying watched in disbelief. He grabbed for his microphone, dropped it, fumbled on the floor of his staff car, found it, and said into it, "Control, this is the SOF. I think number two just went in." He followed the crash trucks.

Nolen was doing nearly seventy when the crash truck reached the runway overrun. He could see the lead tanker climbing out serenely. Number two had disappeared. It was nowhere to be seen and there was no fireball. The perimeter fence loomed. He took his foot off of the accelerator, went through the fence and coasted to a stop in the open field beyond. Puzzled, Nolen looked down into the depressed valley that lies southeast of the base and saw the number two tanker rise up from the area of the town of Box Elder. It was this falling away of the terrain that gave the airplane the blessed few hundred feet that it needed to recover.

When the airplane was established on the published departure route I said to Captain Shields, "Maintain this climb speed until Captain English is in the seat, then he will fly the airplane." Over interphone I said to the crew, "IP checking off of interphone. Harry, take over for a bit."

I slid the seat back, unplugged my headphones, and left the flight deck. I closed the door to the flight deck behind me, grabbed hold of the galley, and struggled to keep from spewing my breakfast all over the galley floor. Waves of nausea washed over me and I was shaking uncontrollably. A minute or two passed and I composed myself enough to drink a little water. I had been reminded of my own ineptness and mortality with terrible clarity. But with the foolish arrogance of the vain, I soon was able to dismiss the incident and return to the flight deck. Unaware of the consternation that I had caused on the ground, we continued with our scheduled flight. Only after we landed, parked the airplane, and saw the Supervisor of Flying stop his staff car in front of us did I realize that my unusual take-off had not gone unnoticed.

"The boss wants to see you," he said.

He drove me to wing headquarters in ominous silence. Upon presenting myself to the Wing Commander's secretary, she cheerfully told me to go right on in.

"The Colonel is expecting you," she said in a motherly way that she employed on all who were going to their professional execution.

The movies make a great deal of military folk reporting to their superiors. They generally have the reporting officer standing at an exaggerated position of attention and holding a salute that goes unanswered for an agonizing period of time while the senior officer pretends to be engrossed in some very important paperwork. This makes great drama for those who haven't been there. In reality, commanders do not have the luxury of the time it takes to carry out such a charade and few flight crews would be impressed by it in any event. The Colonel came right to the point.

"Major, I was fortunate enough not to have witnessed your take-off this morning but certain information has come to my attention. There is an eighty-foot-long hole in the perimeter fence. The front of one of my crash trucks looks as if it engaged a battle tank. There is jet fuel all over hell; the base swimming pool is contaminated with that fuel. The town of Box Elder wants to declare independence and secede from the Union. Some of the more vocal citizens are muttering about reparations or a declaration of war. I just got a call from maintenance. They think that they will need to change all four engines on that plane because they have no idea how long the engines were in over-boost or how high the exhaust-gas temperatures went. And the crowning blow is that one of my very best NCOs, Sergeant Nolen, is up at personnel putting in his retirement papers. Perhaps you might tell me what the hell happened."

I told him of the too close MITO and how I'd let the student get away from me and added that I thought Captain Shields most certainly required further training in minimum interval take-offs, preferably with any instructor other than myself.

"Hmm, you probably should have aborted the take-off if you were that close. But I'm not going to second guess that decision. I don't think that I've ever heard of anyone kicking in full rudder like that." He paused a second. "When do you fly again?" he asked?"

"Tomorrow, sir. It's a re-qualification flight for a Major Chalmers."

"Oh, yes," he answered. "I know Dick Chalmers. He's coming back to tankers from a tour in Vietnam. You won't have any problems with him. He's an old multi-engine pilot. By the way, aren't you transferring out to the school at Castle soon?"

"Yes, sir, the end of this month."

"Have you already gone out there for an interview?" he asked.

"Yes, sir, I got back the week before last."

"How did you talk your way into a sweet job like that? No alert, no Southeast Asia tours. Who vouched for you?"

Instructor duty at the Crew Training School at Castle was considered important enough to require an interview by the wing commander and a recommendation from one of the Central Flight Instructors Course IPs.

"Major Phillips vouched for me," I answered,

"Gordon spoke up for you? I know him. I wonder what the hell weird brand of whiskey he's been drinking."

He paused. I stood nervously for a moment. The mention of whiskey had reminded my shattered nervous system that such a ministration might be a very good idea. I wanted very much to remove myself from his calculating gaze and swiftly scanned the carpet in front of his desk for a convenient dime to disappear under. He must have read my mind.

"Major," he began. "I want very much to be a general one day. If you make a huge smoking hole in the ground with one of my airplanes and kill your silly ass, not only will the Chaplain and I have to make an unpleasant visit to your wife and the wives of your crew, but I will not get to be a general. In fact, I will be very lucky if I am allowed to be in charge of laundry and recreation at some distant arctic outpost. Now, go away. Be careful, and if you want to leave early for Castle, let my secretary know. I'm sure that I can arrange for you to be on your way to California in less than an hour." With that thinly veiled rebuke, I saluted and left.

At seven thirty the following morning, Major Chalmers and I began our take-off roll. Somewhere just short of take-off speed, the oil pressure on the right outboard engine dropped to zero.

"Do you want to pull back number four?" He asked.

Since I placed a great value on altitude and airspeed, my answer was succinct. "No fucking way!"

As he rotated the airplane to the take-off attitude the number four engine seized with a rumble and vomited parts and oil out of the tail pipe, but in its dying it had provided thrust until we could safely fly. The climb-out was uneventful. We dumped enough of our fuel to get down to a safe weight for a three-engine landing. When the airplane was parked, I leaned out of the cockpit window to see if the chocks were in. The Supervisor of Flying drove his staff car under the nose and leaned out the driver's window.

"The Boss says you are off the flying schedule. He says you are snake-bit and he's going to hide you on alert until it's time for you to sign off of his base for Castle." With that information delivered he put the car in gear and sped away. I had flown my last flight for the 28th Air Refueling Squadron. I still have my coffee mug with the squadron emblem on it.

EIGHTEEN

◆◆◆◆◆◆◆◆◆◆◆◆◆◆◆◆

But to stand an' be still to the Birken'ead drill
is a damn tough bullet to chew,
-Rudyard Kipling

ommunist China, a nation that had tried so hard to lure Brown
Anchor Two Six over Hainan Island, was admitted to the United
Nations. President Nixon was struggling to disengage from the
Southeast Asian conflict and save face. The anti-war movement had so
emasculated our government that a war that should have ended years
ago kept grinding on and led to a dark and covert war financed by the
poppy. For years, the meddling of the Johnson administration in the
military's tactical prosecution of the war, along with the increasing
activity of the anti-war movement, produced a giant, black hole that,
like it's celestial counterpart, swallowed all that came near. North
Vietnam was winning the propaganda war. In March of 1972, North
Vietnam launched a massive offensive from Cambodia that came
within sixty miles of Saigon.

*****

Bob Morrissey lay naked on his bunk; a towel draped across his
middle was still damp from his recent shower. He had a little over
twenty minutes before the crew bus would pick him and his pilot, Bob
Brown, up for their flight to the north. This was his second tour of the
war and the Aardvark, or F-111, had been having problems in the
Southeast Asian Theater. It had returned to active service just a little
over six weeks ago, and since then there had been two combat losses.

Jim Hockridge and Allen Graham had gone missing in Coach-33 during a single plane raid on Phuc Yen Airfield. That was just over three weeks ago. Just a couple of weeks before that, in late September, Bill Coltman and Lefty Brett were lost in Ranger-23 in Route Pack One in the very southern part of North Vietnam, considered the safest area if one had to fly over North Vietnam. Bob stretched and stood up. Idly he wondered about the four men missing in the two recent F-111 losses. It seemed odd that the Search and Rescue people could not bring back a higher percentage of the crews shot down while flying the airplane equipped with the most sophisticated escape and survival equipment in the war. At this loss rate, we were about due to drop another.

He threw the damp towel on the foot of the bed and started to dress. He was off for a couple of days after this flight and planned to finish his Christmas shopping and get his packages to his family in the mail.

"Are you up and about?" He called through to the adjoining room to his pilot, Robert Mack Brown.

"Yes, old-timer, I'm way ahead of you." Brown was three years younger than his Weapons System Operator. Of medium build, he weighed one hundred and sixty-five pounds and stood just over five feet, eight inches tall. He walked with the bearing that he had learned in Colorado at the Air Force Academy.

Bob grunted and finished dressing. His friend and roommate, Ken Harten, was still at the Officers' Club, now much improved since the early days of the war. He toyed with the idea of sabotaging Ken's bed somehow, since he wasn't flying tonight, but gave the idea up when he heard the crew bus squeal to a stop outside of their quarters.

The lights of the briefing room seemed harsh, perhaps because it was after midnight and having to prepare for a flight at that hour always seemed harsh. Brown and Morrissey were the only crew in the large room, which gave a hollow sound to their voices. They were scheduled for a solo mission, one of a series of similar sorties code named "Constant Guard." A captain from the weather office began the mission briefing. He seemed distracted. His shirt was rumpled and his eyes tired. He would be working through the small hours of the morning preparing briefings for the morning strikes. His weather briefing was short: severe clear en route with a few scattered thunderstorms in the target area. As soon as he had finished, he gathered his acetate transparencies from the overhead projector and left.

Bob checked his notes as the Operations Officer continued the mission briefing. Tail number 67-0063, call sign Whaler Five Seven, take-off time 0220, time on target 0311, and the estimated time to climb out off the target 0319. Their target was the Luat Son highway ferry in western North Vietnam. They would carry twelve Mark 82SE high-explosive incendiary bombs. The mission appeared routine and very similar to others that he had recently flown with Brown. It was not the route he would have chosen. He felt rising resentment at the unknown person who had usurped the prerogative of the local commanders to make use of their local knowledge to plan the route of attack. No other airplanes were involved. Surprise was essential, as they had only their great speed and ability to operate at very low altitudes to protect them.

Bob looked at the route and said, "Why the hell are we using the same route over and over again? We're going to do that one time too often and get bushwhacked in a flack trap or catch the golden BB"

The Ops Officer shook his head. "I know it's dumb, but that's what the strike order says we do, and ours is not to reason why... That's probably what happened to Hockridge and Graham last month."

They gathered up their gear and headed next door to the intelligence office to pick up side arms, blood chits, and code tables. The room was brightly lit, but appeared empty. Their equipment was piled on a table behind the counter. Brown hit the little call bell on the counter with the palm of his hand and glanced at the Playboy centerfold displayed under the Plexiglas countertop. It was the same one that had been there for the past two months. One of the assistant intelligence officers appeared from behind the storage shelves where he had been dozing in a tired, office, swivel chair. He was a junior captain three months into his first tour. The boss did not stand night shifts.

Morrissey did not make mistakes. He carefully checked the serial number on the short barreled Smith and Wesson and inventoried every scrap of classified material that he signed for. The captain yawned, scratched at his crotch where his ill-fitting undershorts had bunched up, and gathered up the receipts. Ten minutes later, Brown and Morrissey arrived at the revetment where Whaler Five Seven poked its long nose out and waited for them.

Less than three hundred and fifty miles to the northeast, the 359th Provincial Local Forces Company lay waiting. Their intelligence had learned that a radio call was usually intercepted to someone called

Moonbeam shortly before the sonic boom of an American bomber shook their hut. Just under a minute later, the bomber would roar through the notch in the hills where the 359th troops were bivouacked.

The F-111s depended on their great speed and low altitude to take any defenders by surprise, but more of these airplanes had been lost than could be explained by mechanical mishaps. Equipment failure is seldom catastrophic; it almost always gives some warning. We had excellent airplanes, and our maintenance personnel were proficient and dedicated. Single plane strikes were sent out on what should have been a straightforward sortie, and simply did not return. The crews and staff at the operational level suspected that their nemesis was nothing more than a simple flak-trap. Missions that flew repetitive routes were easy game, especially if they flew at low altitudes.

A set of portable floodlights lit the revetment where the Aardvark waited stoically. The air smelled heavy and damp. An MD3 powercart roared away, sounding as if it would fly to pieces at any moment in its effort to provide power to the inert airplane. Brown and Morrissey completed their preflight. Brown glanced at his watch and looked across the cockpit at Morrissey and nodded. With the practice often repeated and with little conversation, the two men brought the two Pratt & Whitney turbofan engines to life. The various systems were started and checked, while the ground crew moved steadily through their ritual. In short order the Aardvark moved its near fifty tons out of the revetment, and with a bob of its long snout, as the nose-gear strut compressed and extended, turned down the taxiway. Ten minutes later Sergeant Donavan watched from the control tower as twin horizontal pillars of flame pushed Whaler Five Seven into the night sky. He logged the take-off at 0219 local time 7 November 1972.

At the GCI sight called Invert on the Thai-Laotian border, Willy came back from the latrine into the darkened operations room, still buttoning the fly of his fatigue pants, and sat down at the scope for the L band search radar. His position was in the front and lowest level of the darkened theater-like operations room. In front of him, beyond the radar screen, was a lexan wall. On it were concentric rings drawn to a scale of twenty-five mile intervals ranging out to three hundred miles. Invert was the center of these circles. As his eyes adjusted to the sweep of the search radar, a return was starting to show at the two-hundred-and-fifty-mile ring. That would be Whaler Five Seven, right on time. Willy talked to the plotter on interphone. Presently, Whaler Five

Seven's track began to appear on the lexan, drawn on the backside by the plotter using a fluorescent china marker. Invert would follow Whaler Five Seven to within a hundred miles of the target before losing contact. Willy sipped at his bitter, almost cold, coffee. As the radar showed Five Seven almost overhead and approaching, the Mekong River the radio came alive.

"Invert, this is Whaler Five Seven, approaching the fence and descending." It was Brown's voice.

"Roger, Whaler Five Seven, contact Moonbeam on three one nine point four."

"Three one nine point four, Whaler Five Seven clear."

The Aardvark dropped rapidly towards the dark ground. Haze obscured the horizon. Brown could see nothing below the airplane.

Morrissey was concentrating on the radarscope in front of him. "Terrain following radar looks good for a change," Morrissey commented to his pilot.

Brown felt a slight easing of tension and pushed up the throttles. With the wings fully swept back, the bomber went supersonic. The terrain-following radar maintained a constant height of two hundred feet above the ground, climbing and diving the airplane to follow the contours of the land. It was a hair-raising experience in the dark, but the navigation computer tracked perfectly to each preset way-point. Should the terrain-following radar so much as hiccough, the airplane would automatically climb. Both men concentrated intently on their tasks. In just minutes they would be at the initial point for the bomb run.

"Moonbeam, this is Whaler Five Seven, switching to tactical freq." Browns voice was laconic. The time was six minutes after three in the morning.

"Roger, Five Seven. Call back on climb out. Moonbeam listening out."

"Four minutes, thirty seconds to target," Morrissey said on interphone. He was busy with his final checks.

Twelve miles away the 359th local forces received a radio message from a ground observer monitoring American tactical frequencies. "The American just called Moonbeam. He just passed over me"

Every available weapon of the 359th was aimed at a single spot in the sky. It was in the center of the notch in the hills that previous bombers had used. Tensely, the commander watched the second hand on his watch. He could not hear the oncoming airplane; it was traveling well ahead of its own sound. His carbine was pointed at the sky. If he fired too soon, the American might see tracers and be able to avoid his guns,; and if he fired too late, he would miss. He squeezed the trigger on his carbine. Instantly, the whole area erupted with small arms fire. The double crack of a sonic boom jarred them and he ordered cease-fire. They had only been firing for a couple of seconds. The American was already through the notch.

Whaler Five Seven pitched up abruptly. The airplane rumbled with the sound every pilot fears, as both engines tore themselves to junk and vomited a huge gout of flame out of the twin tailpipes. At the speed and power setting that they were running, the engines sucked in a huge amount of air every second. They had managed to ingest enough of the little pieces of metal shot into the air by the 359th troops to kill both of their Pratt & Whitney engines.

"Shit," Brown swore. " Bailout!" At so low an altitude, there was little time. In the tension of the moment he had used the older order from his pre-F-111 days rather than the order, "Eject," but Morrissey had no doubt what he meant.

It flashed through Morrissey's mind that once, long ago near Lincoln, Nebraska, he thought that he would have to eject from a crippled bomber, trailing smoke and spraying fuel all over the crew cabin. They had limped home that day and had not had to bail out over the friendly Nebraska farm country. He knew that *this* bird would not make it to friendly territory.

Morrissey squeezed the D handle of the initiator on his side of the center console and pulled. The harness-inertia reels for both men retracted and locked as explosive-powered guillotines severed wiring and control cables. Rocket motors fired, and an explosive cord severed the capsule, which consisted of the entire cockpit, from the airplane. The rocket pushed the capsule far from the crippled airplane. A catapult deployed the seventy-foot recovery parachute, reefed to diminish opening shock. As the capsule slowed and the shroud lines reached their full length, a line cutter sliced the reefing line and allowed the parachute to fully deploy. Airbags on the bottom of the capsule inflated to act as shock absorbers. This sequence was complete before Brown and Morrissey were fully aware that they and the aircraft were going their separate ways. The capsule landed in brush and trees. A little more than a mile away seventy-five million dollars worth of airplane destroyed itself against the high side of a jungle-covered hill. Whaler Five Seven was scattered and smoldering junk. Troops of the 359th

Provincial Local Forces Company moved rapidly to locate and surround the capsule.

The C-130, call sign Moonbeam, droned around its racetrack orbit with sedulous application to its duties. No off-target report was received from Whaler Five Seven. Precious minutes slipped away. The first hour, as vital as that golden hour in battlefield trauma centers, fast ran out. Fifty-four minutes after Whaler Five Seven had last spoken to the Airborne Command and Control Center, Moonbeam tried to raise them on the radio and began a communication search of all possible radio frequencies. Not until a full hour after the start of a communication search, at the first sign of coming daylight, was SAR, or Search and Rescue efforts, initiated. By that time, Whaler Five Seven had been down for almost two hours.

By the very nature of the Constant Guard missions, SAR was difficult. These missions were flown at night by single aircraft. They flew very low and very fast. No wingman or tanker was assigned to them. Should it be necessary to leave the airplane, the only option open to men who might make it to the ground alive was to hide until daylight and then try to contact friendly forces with their survival radios.

With the arrival of daylight, a visual search by air was made for ten miles either side of the intended flight path. Nothing was found. Thirteen days after it had begun at dark on 20 November 1972, the search was discontinued.

*****

The loss of Whaler Five Seven was investigated and documented up to the last radio call just after three AM local time. Evidence suggests strongly that it was a victim of a flak trap. The 359th Provincial Local Forces claimed to have shot down an F-111 on the seventh of November at about that time. No other American aircraft were lost on that date.

At the time that the F-111 was used in Southeast Asia, both China and Russia were immensely interested in its technology. Recovery of wreckage and live crew was an intelligence coup that just was too good to pass up. Of the eight F-111 combat losses in the Vietnam conflict, sixteen United States crewmembers were involved. Two men were returned alive. They were Captains Bill Wilson and Bob Sponeybarger, shot down in Jackal Three Three. It took a few days for the North Vietnamese to capture them, and they were very nearly rescued. Perhaps it was the fact that they were known to be alive and captured that saved them from an airplane ride to Russia. The remains of another F-111 crew, Captain Hockridge and Lieutenant Graham, were handed over by the North Vietnamese on September 30, 1977. The North Vietnamese claimed that they were found dead in the capsule, but gave no reason for holding the bodies for five years.

Too many of these airplanes, equipped with the most advanced survival system of its time, simply vanished to be believable, unless one wishes to embrace theories of extra-terrestrials or some such phenomena as the Bermuda Triangle lurking in the jungles of Indochina. Burger Five Four with Captains Donald Stafford and Charles Cafferrelli and Snug Forty with Lieutenant Colonel Ronald Ward and Major James McElvain crossed into that twilight zone in November and December of 1972

Neither Brown nor Morrissey were returned after the war. Department of Defense investigators reported that the data plate from Whaler Five Seven along with Robert Brown's identification card and a photo of an F-111 handbook were displayed in Quang Binh Provincial Museum. Morrissey's son David testified to this before the National Security Subcommittee on December 14, 1995. Two years earlier, in December of 1993 David Morrissey had addressed the Senate Select Committee. Prior to his testimony he had been told by a government official that hardware was probably not transferred to Russia and that personnel were definitely not transferred to Russia. Several weeks later he learned, through unofficial channels, that a crew module from an F-111 had been discovered in a Moscow museum. The government knew this before David had been told that nothing had been transferred to Russia. There is an even chance that this module is from his father's plane.

*****

I tried to put the war behind me. We lived in a small town in central California, and I went to work every morning teaching people how to fly the tanker. Most days I was home by five. The kids were into sports and Boy Scouts, and Carolyn spent much of her time driving youngsters all over the San Joaquin Valley to swim meets. But still, the war muttered and nagged in the background of my mind.

The Pentagon papers became public, the Watergate scandal broke, and the war officially ended. Some of the POWs came home, many did not. We went merrily on with the good life and abandoned those who had done the most to earn that good life. Our soldiers suffered the same fate as the French defenders had after the fall of Dien Bien Phu. Where were the brave Rangers who stormed the POW camp on Baatan in World War II, and brought out over five hundred American prisoners of war in a hailstorm of gunfire?

The veracity of statements from our government became suspect, and soon these statements fell more and more into the category of outright lies. Monika Jensen-Stevenson and William Stevenson, co-authors of *Kiss the Boys Goodbye*, wrote that former POW, Bobby Garwood, stated in an interview that Henry Kissinger's remark, "There are no more live POWs in Vietnam," was played over and over again on loudspeakers to many of the eleven hundred and seventy Americans yet unaccounted for. Many we know were captured and some, including Robert Brown and Robert Morrissey, almost certainly were taken to Russia. One can only imagine their fate.

The last sentence of Article Six of the Code of Conduct states, "I will trust in my God and in the United States of America." We had memorized that code. It was The Faith, and the fighting men had kept that faith. But a covert war, operated by a shadow government accountable to no one, raged on long after 1973. It was not in the best interest of this shadow government to bring home those left behind. The covert war would be exposed. Men who abused their stolen power would be revealed, and they would finally be held accountable. But if there were no men to return and the families were left in limbo, these men of hidden power would be safe. The men who went to war for us were denied. We can only imagine what the Americans that were left behind must think of us.

NINETEEN

◆ ◆ ◆ ◆ ◆ ◆ ◆ ◆ ◆ ◆ ◆ ◆ ◆ ◆ ◆

There is an evil which I have seen under the sun,
As an error which proceedeth from the ruler:
-Ecclesiastes 10:5

It was the fall of the year. Though still warm, the air was hazy. Smoke from the burning stubble of California's rice fields obscured the Sierras, and frequently made an instrument approach necessary on days that otherwise were suitable for visual-flight rules. I needed to get the cobwebs out of my head. At nine in the morning, the burning of the fields had just gotten started and there was enough of a breeze to carry the smoke south towards Fresno. Visibility was about five miles and above the haze and smoke it was clear.

I walked down to the hangar where Jim Wilkerson kept his Pitts. It is a two-place model and, in exchange for aerobatics lessons, I was allowed to fly it to maintain my own proficiency. That was just another way of saying that Jim shared his all-time favorite toy with me.

I slid the hangar door open. The perky little Pitts sat amidst two or three humdrum Spam Cans, the slang term for ordinary light planes. November One Seven Delta Mike was a tiny two-place biplane with open cockpits, and built for nothing but aerobatics. Its taut, fabric covering was painted blue and white, and the entire airplane was sparkling clean. In-flight it was feather light on the controls, and a pilot had more of a sensation of wearing the airplane than of flying it. I pushed it out from amongst its everyday sisters into the sunlight. Slowly I did the preflight, savoring the moment. The engine rumbled into life promptly and I sat for a few seconds watching the engine instruments stabilize.

"Merced Tower, Pitts One Seven Delta Mike, taxi for take-off, VFR local." My voice had a distant quality as it was fed back through the headphones in my leather helmet.

"Delta Mike, taxi runway three zero, wind three two zero at five, altimeter two nine nine eight."

It took little throttle for the Lycoming engine to move the Pitts. Making a sinuous path in order to see past the long nose, I taxied north on the ramp and turned on to the taxiway just past Captain Billy's restaurant. It seemed that every small airport had a Captain Billy's. At the end of the taxiway, the engine run-up was perfect. Jim took very good care of this airplane.

"Merced Tower, Delta Mike ready for take-off. I'd like a straight-out departure, if traffic permits."

"Pitts One Seven Delta Mike is cleared for take-off. Straight-out departure approved, no reported traffic northwest. Be advised Castle has military traffic in their radar pattern to their east at thirty-two hundred and below."

"Delta Mike."

With a quick check of final approach, I steered the skittish little airplane onto the runway and brought the power up. The tail wheel came off of the ground and the airplane immediately became more manageable. All business, the little bird rapidly accelerated. As it lifted from the ground, I held it just a few feet above the pavement and rolled in nose-down trim as it gathered speed. Runway markers flashed past on either side and the grass was a green blur to the sides. When the runway overrun disappeared under the nose, I let the nose come up and Delta Mike went for the sky. In half a minute it popped out of the haze into clear blue sky. Off to the right I saw three or four heavies lumbering around the traffic pattern at the Air Force Base. Switching to their frequency, I called Castle Tower and said I would be operating above their Airport Traffic Area and directly overhead. The air over the San Joaquin valley is always very busy, and small aircraft liked to follow highway Ninety-Nine. They would swing wide either to the east or west of the base. Military traffic from the base would be departing to the northwest and arriving from the southeast. On a day when visual flight rules prevailed, the base's airspace went from the ground to three thousand feet above and outward for a radius of five miles. The safest place of all would be more than three thousand feet above the ground and directly overhead. They knew I was there and could see me and would tell me if anyone else was about. Also, that long runway made an excellent reference point for aerobatics.

At forty-five hundred feet, the air was cool. As long as I did not skid or slip the airplane, the tiny windscreen gave me some protection from the windblast. After a couple of clearing turns to check for other airplanes, I began a quarter of an hour of aerobatics. One maneuver flowed into another and gave me the impression of the world turning about the airplane. Sometimes, the air hummed mightily in the flying wires and then would fall to a whisper as the airspeed bled off in some vertical maneuver. I did not think of the physical requirements of flying anymore than a man who is in contemplation thinks of walking. The flat valley beneath me was only a backdrop to the dazzling colors of distant islands, seas, and the icy wastes of the north that crept out of my memory. I remembered the contentment of long and uneventful flights, the excitement of action or a difficult instrument approach, and the fear that sometimes diminished my skills to the instinctive responses learned years ago. Intruding in all of my reflections was the war, and it seemed somehow wrong that I should be so comfortable when our country had lost that war. Congress had abdicated its duty and handed its power to the president and the executive branch of the government upon the weak evidence of the Tonkin Gulf incident. Those who prosecuted the war ignored every military lesson learned in the long history of the conflict of nations. The country was confused and in disarray. We gave up the meager gains of seven years of conflict at the conference table in Paris. Many still living were lost in the darkness and their existence denied. No one has ever been held accountable for the endless hell that they were condemned to. Those men who lived by the Code of Conduct and believed in the honor of our country were now an embarrassment to its government. But in the history of nations, politicians have a sorry record of keeping promises, and those who made the decisions that committed so many to perdition now found it convenient to ignore the marker due and to deny that a debt existed.

It was not our finest hour.

Soon I would leave the Air Force. My flying days were coming to an end. I turned south and throttled back.

"Castle Tower, Pitts One Seven Delta Mike departing your area to the south."

"Roger Delta Mike, no reported traffic to the south."

Ten minutes later as I rolled out on final approach I thought, I have had some great flights. This was a great flight. It was my last great flight and the hell of was that I knew it.

APPENDIX ONE

♦♦♦♦♦♦♦♦♦♦♦♦♦♦♦♦♦♦♦♦♦♦♦♦

THE CODE OF CONDUCT

Executive Order 10631. Code of Conduct for members of the Armed Forces of the United States.

By virtue of the authority vested in me as President of the United States, and as Commander in Chief of the armed forces of the United States, I hereby prescribe the Code of Conduct for members of the Armed Forces of the United States which is attached to this order and hereby made a part thereof.

Every member of the armed forces of the United States is expected to measure up to the standards embodied in this Code of Conduct while he is in combat or in captivity. To ensure achievement of these standards, each member of the armed forces liable to capture shall be provided with specific training and instruction designed to better equip him to counter and withstand all enemy efforts against him, and shall be fully instructed as to the behavior and obligations expected of him during combat or captivity.

The Secretary of Defense (and the Secretary of the Treasury with respect to the Coast Guard except when it is serving as part of the Navy) shall take such action as deemed necessary to implement this order and to disseminate and make the said code known to all members of the armed forces of the United States.

Signed,

Dwight D. Eisenhower
The White House
August 17, 1955

I

I am an American fighting man. I serve in the forces which guard my country and our way of life. I am prepared to give my life in their defense.

II

I will never surrender of my own free will. If in command I will never surrender my men while they still have the means to resist.

III

If I am captured I will continue to resist by all means available. I will make every effort to escape and aid others to escape. I will accept neither parole nor special favors from the enemy.

IV

If I become a prisoner of war, I will keep faith with my fellow prisoners. I will give no information or take part in any action which might be harmful to my comrades. If I am senior, I will take command. If not, I will obey the lawful orders of those appointed over me and will back them up in every way.

V

When questioned, should I become a prisoner of war, I am **bound** to give **only** name, rank, service number, and date of birth. I will evade answering further questions to the utmost of my ability. I will make no oral or written statements disloyal to my country and its allies or harmful to their cause. (emphasis is mine)

VI

I will never forget that I am an American fighting man, responsible for my actions, and dedicated to the principles which made my country free. I will trust in my God and in the United States of America.

The Code of Conduct evolved from this original form over time. Articles one, two and six were changed slightly to make them non-gender specific, apparently in anticipation of women taking an active role in combat. In 1977 President Carter signed Executive Order 12017, changing article five to read: "When questioned, should I become a prisoner of war, I am required to give name, rank, service number, and date of birth. I will evade answering further questions to the utmost of my ability. I will make no oral or written statements disloyal to my country and its allies or harmful to their cause." By changing the word 'bound' to 'required' and deleting the word 'only' the article was significantly changed. Motivated by the routine and unbearable torture applied to American POWs during the Korean and Vietnam conflicts, the disgrace and legal implications of breaking under torture were removed by this change. The torture of POWs was denied by both the enemy and American peace activists and not brought to public attention until after the return of the POWs in 1973.

THE HONOR CODE

◆◆◆◆◆◆◆◆◆◆◆◆◆◆◆◆◆◆◆◆◆◆◆◆◆◆◆◆◆◆

Article 1. An Aviation Cadet will not knowingly make any false statements, written or verbal, while acting in any capacity, official or otherwise, in any situation reflecting on the Aviation Cadet Corps or the Air Force.

Article 2. An Aviation Cadet will not take or receive the property of another person, or persons, under any condition without specific authority of that person or persons.

Article 3. An Aviation Cadet will not impart or receive any unauthorized assistance, either outside or inside a classroom or place of instruction, which would tend to give any Aviation Cadet unfair advantage.

Article 4. An Aviation Cadet will not quibble, use evasive statements or technicalities in order to shield guilt or defeat the ends of justice.

Article 5. An Aviation Cadet will report any violation of honor by any other Aviation Cadet of which he is a witness or has unquestionable knowledge.

Article 6. An Aviation Cadet will not commit any act of intentional dishonesty which will reflect in any way on the Honor and Integrity of the Aviation Cadet Corps and the Air Force.

From the Officer Training Manual for Aviation Cadets. Text provided by the Aviation Cadet Museum. Inc. Eureka Springs, Ar. 72632

The Aviation Cadet Honor Code was typical of honor codes in use by U. S. officer training programs of the era, including the military academies. In the Aviation Cadet Program, the honor courts were convened by and consisted of the cadets themselves. The faculty and military staff were not involved, other than possibly charging a cadet with an honor violation.

A finding of guilty by an honor court resulted in immediate dismissal from Aviation Cadets. There was no appeal, and the Air Force did not intervene. Such a practice might seem draconian by today's easy standards of ethics, we are all familiar with the political intervention in past cheating scandals at the various military academies, but it welded a bond of trust that was a significant factor in the morale of airmen at a time when they were bitterly scorned by much of the American public. Of course, honor codes are in use today, but they are not enforced as rigidly. All too often, they have become political tools, and Article 4, the one that forbids quibbling, the use of technicalities or evasive statements has been suffocated to death.

APPENDIX TWO

◆◆◆◆◆◆◆◆◆◆◆◆◆◆◆◆◆◆◆◆◆◆◆◆◆◆

BOMBERS IN THE COLD WAR

During the early sixties the B-47 was the primary bomber. More than sixteen hundred were built, and its appetite for flight crews and maintenance people was voracious. The concept of the airplane was ahead of American engineering standards of the day. It was powered by six J47 axial flow jet engines which delivered a little over five thousand pounds of thrust each. A water-alcohol mix, injected into the engines during take-off, could raise that thrust to seventy two hundred pounds for approximately two minutes. In contrast, a single engine on the F-111 delivered over twenty five thousand pounds of thrust. Throughout the history of aviation aerodynamic engineering almost always was ahead of power plant design. Primitive solutions often lived on, in early B-47s the turbo-refrigeration unit was lubricated with whale oil. Later models used a synthetic lubricant. Most of the systems were electric powered, making the airplane an electrician's nightmare. The early bomb rack or U-2 clip, as it was called, was borrowed from the British. A safety pin was added to prevent the accidental release of the bomb. It consisted of a common pintel clip, available in any good hardware store, fitted into the U-2 clip with a long piece of parachute cord attached that led through the bomb bay tunnel to the copilots position. A notch was filed in the edge of the pressure doorframe to allow the cord to pass from the unpressurized area into the pressurized cabin. Should it be necessary for the bomb to be released, the copilot was to pull on this cord until the pin was brought into the cockpit.

The aerodynamics of high altitude and high speed flight in the United States were still in the explorative phase. There were several aerodynamic characteristics of the B-47 that could lead a thoughtful person to sleeplessness. At speeds in excess of 440 knots the ailerons became completely ineffective, leaving the airplane without roll control. Should the pilot find himself in a diving spiral, he would be unable to pull out. The pilot's handbook had an unnerving remark In the section on landing. It stated that abrupt application of rudder at near best flare speeds would cause the airplane to snap roll. B-47 pilots tended to be careful with the rudder pedals, especially during the landing phase. Much of navigation and bombing practice was conducted at altitudes as low as two hundred feet and at a speed of 425 knots. Should an aileron power control unit fail at high speed the airplane would abruptly pitch down. I suspect that at least some of the unexplained loses on the Oilburner or low level routes were caused by aileron power control unit failure.

It was the practice in those days to require every bomber crewmember to read and sign off on each accident report when it was completed. Every aspect of the crash, including autopsies, was examined in detail in this typically thick and thorough document. The accidents that I have covered in the chapters on the B-47 are only a few of the appalling number of crashes that occurred. They are dramatized from my notes and personal records. Several days after the crash, Larry Talovich related his escape from N. V. Meeks' aircraft to me. It is interesting to note that four decades later the official records of the bomb wings stationed at Lincoln during the early sixties are still classified.

THE TANKERS

For the first four decades of aviation history the fuel that kept an airplane aloft had to be on board that airplane at take-off. The idea of taking on fuel while in-flight was an accomplishment that seemed beyond reach, although some early aviators experimented with that possibility. Not until World War II did the problem of extending an airplane's range become critical.

The design and power of an airplane determines a maximum weight that it can lift. The airplane itself, the crew and their equipment comprise a large percentage of this maximum. What is left must be divided between fuel and payload. It is a finite amount, and to exceed it is to fly into an uncertain area that frequently leads to disaster. The further that one wishes to fly, the more fuel is required and the lighter the payload can be. Untold thousands of aircraft were lost in World War II because they simply ran out of fuel. Many aircraft that did make it back to base were found to have no measurable fuel on board. Few problems of flight are more discomforting to a pilot than empty fuel tanks, particularly if he is flying over hostile countryside or open ocean. The problem of escorting bombers over Europe, in that war, seemed insurmountable until the long range P 51 became available. Earlier fighter escorts could not fly far enough to protect the bombers for the full length of their long missions. Necessity breeds invention, and war seems to provide an abundance of necessity. The first practical aerial tankers were developed after World War II from the B 29 and B 50 bombers. The letter prefix K was chosen by the Air Force to indicate that in-flight refueling was the airplanes primary duty, so these aircraft became KB 29s and KB 50s.

The method of transfer was simple. A hose was trailed from the tanker with a basket on the end of it. The airplane to be refueled was equipped with a long probe that stuck out in front of the airplane. The receiver pilot flew up behind the basket and attempted to insert the probe into the open end of the basket, which guided the probe into a receptacle. Once that was accomplished fuel could be sent through the hose to the receiver aircraft. The tanker aircraft is passive during refueling. It maintains as steady a platform as possible and any necessary maneuvering is done by the receiver aircraft. This system works well for the transfer of smaller off-loads but is not satisfactory for the fuel loads required by large aircraft, which frequently exceed fifty tons in a single refueling.

To meet this requirement, the flying boom was developed by the Boeing Company. The flying boom consists of a rigid pipe attached by one end to a pod on the under-aft of the tanker fuselage. The boom is able to pivot about in the horizontal and vertical axis and is equipped with a set of wing-like devices that allows the operator to move or fly it from side to side and up and down. For in-flight refueling the boom is lowered to about forty forty five degree angle. In the end there is a section that the operator can telescope in and out. The receiver flies to a position behind and below the tanker. The boom operator then telescopes the boom outward and places the end of the boom in the receiver receptacle. Fuel is then be pumped to the receiver.

The first aircraft to utilize the flying boom on an operational basis was the KC 97, a cargo variant of the B 29, which also saw service in the airline industry as the Boeing Stratocruiser. The Strategic Air Command ran immediately into another problem. They now had the B-47, and the B- 52 was rapidly coming on line. The Cold War was growing more intense. In-flight refueling was the only practical way that bombers could be based in North America and have a global reach. The tankers were propeller driven, and the bombers were jet powered. Their speeds did not match. In order for a B-47 to refuel from a KC 97, the bomber had to descend from cruise altitude and slow to near stalling speed and the tanker had to operate its engines far beyond their rated continuous power settings. At night, the exhaust collector rings of the overheated tanker engines could be seen from the bomber cockpit. They appeared through their open cowl flaps as four white rings in the darkness.

SAC needed an all jet tanker. In 1954 Boeing rolled out the model 387-80. The ubiquitous Boeing 707 series of aircraft was born, and one of the siblings was the KC-135. SAC now had an all jet tanker and high altitude, high speed in-flight refueling became a routine operation. The KC-135, like its stablemate the B-52, is still operational in the first decade of the twenty first century. The airplanes themselves were born many years before most of their aircrew.

THE TACTICS

Strategic Air Command owned all of the tankers. Their designated mission was to support the Strategic Integrated Operations Plan or SIOP. A secondary role was to support the movement of bomber or fighter units to overseas stations. Much as the Navy looked upon submarines prior to Pearl Harbor, the tankers were fleet auxiliaries and were employed, most frequently, in giant fleets that moved across the sky in stately formations. Independent action was seldom employed. Early fighter aircraft, capable of in-flight refueling, were not equipped to accept the flying boom. To provide for these aircraft, a kit consisting of a length of hose and a basket was attached to the end of the boom. Unfortunately, the tanker could not refuel receptacle-equipped aircraft while that kit was installed.

The employment of tankers in the Southeast Asian conflict was three fold. They allowed B-52s to operate from Guam using large formations similar to the bombing tactics of World War II and the Korean conflict. They operated a pipeline ferrying smaller aircraft back and forth across the Pacific. And they provided support for Tactical Air Command aircraft that, along with the Navy, carried out the major portion of the bombing effort. The latter mission was called Young Tiger. For these missions tactical doctrine did not exist. The employment of large numbers of tankers in this type of conflict had not been anticipated, neither had the urgent need for air rescue of so many downed pilots been foreseen.

Two very fortunate conditions existed that allowed the development of tanker combat tactics. The first was non-interference by senior commanders. The tankers were support aircraft, and command assignment to them lacked glamour. Although the tanker crews were instructed not to enter hostile airspace, as well as other restricted areas, this was not enforced. Commanders at the squadron level were well aware of the flight crew's habit of ignoring such restrictions, and the flight crews maintained their commanders plausible deniability. On the several occasions that spectacular saves made it into the news, both commanders and crews seemed to hold their breath until the whole event blew over, then they went on about their business. For the most part these saves were day-to-day events that went unnoticed.

It takes years to train a combat pilot. This, added to the powerful sense of duty derived from the early training of American airmen, provided an enormous incentive to rescue a fellow airman. The KC-135 was equipped with a unique piece of equipment originally intended to aid in the rendezvous with a receiver aircraft but very well suited to locate a distress signal. It was a radio direction finder called the ARA 25 and designed to operate on the UHF band. This was the band used for military aircraft communication. It also was the same band used by the emergency locator beacons that all of our parachutes were equipped with. These emergency transmitters started operating as soon as the parachute opened and could be used on the ground to communicate with aircraft in the area. Tanker crews quickly took advantage of the ARA 25. By taking two or more bearings a navigator could fix the position of the distress signal, sometimes while the airman was still descending in his parachute. Those first minutes were often the most critical. The tanker crews utilized this time by calling in air support, directing them to the sight and remaining in the area to refuel the aircraft providing cover to the downed airmen. In the later years of the war this practice became highly organized and RESCAP became a planned activity for all strikes.

The second factor was the failure of the North Vietnamese to aggressively attack the tankers. They would loft a missile or a barrage of anti-aircraft fire at any tanker that wandered into range and on rare occasions a MIG would feint a pass, but they not did make a determined attempt to down one of these defenseless airplanes. If a tanker had been shot down over Laos while waiting to refuel post-strike aircraft, the tanker would have been lost and most likely the post-strike aircraft as well. This would have driven the tankers much further south and west, seriously reducing the effectiveness of the strike aircraft. The habit of the tankers of topping off the strike aircraft just short of their targets and waiting for them to return as close to the target area as they dared increased the fuel available to the fighter aircraft during his time over the target area. More fuel meant more speed and maneuverability, in effect acting as a force multiplier. It was one of the unexpected benefits of the KC-135 employment in Southeast Asia.

THE COVERT WAR

After January 1973 America officially stood aloof from Southeast Asia, but clandestine operations continued. This is well covered in chapter 28 of Stevenson's book "Kiss the Boys Goodbye". As time passes more information is declassified. Operations in Laos are alluded to in a National Security Council memorandum to Henry Kissinger dated July 15, 1975. The Cambodian conflict is discussed in a telegram from the ambassador to Cambodia, John Dean, to the State Department on February 6, 1975. A memorandum from Brent Scowcroft, a National Security Adviser, to President Gerald Ford, dated May 10, 1976, describes conditions in Cambodia.

Our hurried departure from the Southeast Asian conflict left many clandestine assets, as well as missing men, in the theater. It is here that I believe control by the U. S. Government became muddied. It is very easy for high level politicians or military commanders to say "this comes from the top" in order to get something done that he may believe needs to be done in the interest of national objectives, may be illegal or may simply be to protect that persons power. The man in the field has no choice but to believe his superior. I believe that Oliver North found himself in such a situation over the Iran-Contra affair. A remark that he made while being questioned seemed to reflect this. He said, that when given an order one salutes smartly and charges up the hill. The remark by itself reflects the basic duty of a soldier, however I suspect that he was saying more than the words purport. Lieutenant Colonels do not have the authority or power that Colonel North seemed to have. That degree of power is vested by people in the second level of government and their instructions to their underlings may or may not 'come from the top'. Such a situation can only exist if those who advise the president are telling him less than the truth. In the history of nations, many leaders have been misled by their advisers, almost always with disastrous results. What else, other than the interference of powerful men who could not withstand exposure, could explain the failure of our government to adequately pursue the many live sightings of Americans left behind in Southeast Asia. If these POWs returned and reported the activities in Laos and Cambodia, this shadow government would have been brought down and might very well have brought down the administration with it.

When the French surrendered to the Viet Minh at Dien Bien Phu on May 7, 1954, some French POWs were returned, others were not. Both live prisoners and remains were "banked" by the Viet Minh and, from time to time, ransomed back to the pragmatic French, thus providing a convenient cash source for the Vietnamese. Upon the American withdrawal, it would seem logical that the Vietnamese would try to work the same scam. Evidence suggests that this is exactly what happened, and that an aid package in excess of four billion dollars was being negotiated with the North Vietnamese in exchange for the return of U.S. POWs. While the Nixon administration pondered a face-saving method to bring home the missing Americans, the Watergate scandal broke and Nixon was forced to resign. The exchange deal died with the fall of that administration.

The single, live American returned after Mr. Kissinger had declared that no live POWs remained was a Marine, Bobby Garwood, captured on September 28, 1965. He managed to slip a note to a diplomat of a neutral country fourteen years later and was repatriated. His return was an enormous embarrassment to those who proclaimed that none were left alive. He was declared a deserter, court-marshaled, and convicted of informing on his comrades, serving as a guard for the VC, and simple assault against a fellow prisoner. One has to wonder why he would desert ten days before he was due to return home to Indiana, why he alone of returning POWs was prosecuted and why with such vitriol. Garwood's amazing story is covered in the Stevenson's book *Kiss the Boys Goodbye*, and Monika Jensen-Stevenson's more recent book, *Spite House*. Both books document covert operations after the end of the war in 1973.

RED MARKER FOUR

The forward aircontrollers in the Vietnam War were tasked with directing close air support. They flew a number of different aircraft, all noted for being slow and maneuverable, and were also able to operate close to the ground. The smallest of these airplanes was the Bird Dog, designated either O-1 or L-19, depending on which service was operating it. During an operational flight, the forward air controller, or FAC, would establish communications with ground forces and act as a go-between with those ground forces and the strike aircraft, referred to as "fast movers." He would usually mark the desired target with a smoke rocket and direct the fast movers in the manner of an air traffic controller.

I have reconstructed Don Hawley's death from interviews of several FACs of the same unit and one, Joe Granducci, who was on the scene and witnessed Del Fleener's attempt to rescue Don. There are some minor conflicts in their accounts, but considering the years that have passed and the emotions involved, this is understandable. If Del Fleener should read these words, his Red Marker friends would like to make contact with him. Del Fleener was awarded the Air Force Cross, a medal second only to the Medal of Honor for valor.

WHALER FIVE SEVEN

Whaler Five Seven was an F-111 lost on November 7, 1972. It was crewed by Robert Mack Brown and Robert David Morrissey and was the only U. S. aircraft lost on that date. Hanoi claimed to have shot down an F-111 on the same date. A joint field team visited the crash site on February 23, 1993. F-111 parts were found at the site and in the hands of local residents. Bob's wife Anne and their son David searched for decades for answers. None were provided.

Memos of John F. McCreary to the Vice Chairman of the Senate Select Committee on Prisoners of War and Missing in Action, dated April 27, 1992, reported the ordered destruction by Senator John Kerry of Massachusetts, the chairman of that Senate Select Committee, of the Staff Intelligence findings of April 9, 1992, and copies of statements made in meetings on April 15 and 16 to justify the destruction.

During a meeting on April 15,1992, Staff Chief Counsel J. William Codinha of Massachusetts was advised by members of the Staff of the possibility that they had committed a crime by participating in the destruction of the briefing text. Counsel asked who the injured party was and was told the 2,494 families of unaccounted-for U.S. servicemen. Counsel replied with the incredible question, "Who's gonna tell them? It's classified."

A message concerning a demarche (diplomatic maneuver) on the possible transfer of American POWs from Vietnam to Russia, which originated from the American Embassy, Moscow, discusses the Soviet MFA/USA and Canada Administration Deputy Director Lebedev's response to that question. He denies any knowledge of such movement of POWs, but states that the *KGB "worked behind steel doors,"* very separate from the rest of the embassy, and he could not rule out the possibility of the kinds of behavior alleged by KGB General Kalugin. Paragraph 7 of this message states, "Lebedev also passed on two non-papers on POW/MIA matters. The first responds to letters, apparently from family members, concerning the fate of Lt. Colonel R. Morrissey (phonetic from the Cyrillic), lost in 1972 over North Vietnam. According to the non-paper, the MOD and KGB have no information on this case".

A negotiation folder on Robert M. Brown and Robert D. Morrissey was passed during the 29 October to 1 November 1986 JCRC/VNOSMIA in Hanoi. Prior to his June 8, 1988 meeting with the Vietnamese Foreign Minister, Nguyen Co Thach, a U.S. MIA case folder was passed to the Vietnamese by General Vessey. As the result of an agreement between General Vessey and Foreign Minister Nguyen Co Thach, a case narrative pertaining to both Brown and Morrissey was passed on August 4, 1987 to the SRV embassy in Bangkok by the JCRC. These efforts failed to yield positive results.

Where did all these people go? One would be very naive to believe that nobody knows.

BIBLIOGRAPHY

◆◆◆◆◆◆◆◆◆◆◆◆◆◆◆◆◆◆◆◆◆◆◆◆◆◆◆

<u>Aircraft assigned Losses, 1965-1973, 8th Tactical Fighter Wing</u>, Web site of the 8th Tactical Fighter Wing. www.jsnet/~phantom/aircraftlosses.htm

"At Any Cost: U.S. Covert Operations." <u>National Radio Project</u>. Phillip Babich. Making Contact. January 27, 1999.

Bell, Garnett and Veith, George. "POWs and Politics: How Much Does Hanoi Really know." Center for the Study of the Vietnam Conflict Symposium, Texas Tech University. 19 April, 1996.

Boyne, Walter J. "Linebacker II". <u>Air Force Magazine</u> November 1997. <http://www.afa.org/magazine/1197lineback.html>

Boyne, Walter J. "Route Pack 6". <u>Air Force Magazine</u> November 1999. <http://www.afa.org/magazine/1199pack6html>

Boyne, Walter J. "The Young Tigers and Their Friends." <u>Air Force Magazine</u>, June, 1998: 74-79.

Brancato, Colonel John R. "USAF. Doctrinal Deficiencies in Prisoner of War Command." <u>Aerospace Power Journal</u>. Spring 1988. <www.airpower.maxwell.at.mil/airchronicles/apj/apj88/brancato.html>

Brush, Peter. "The Withdrawal From Khe Sanh." Vietnam Magazine.
    August,   1997.
    <http://www.thehistorynet.com/Vietnam/articles/1997/0897_text.htm>

Cawthorne, Nigel. The Bamboo Cage. Great Britain: Pen and Swords
    Ltd. 1991

Chinnery, Philip D. Full Throttle. New York: St. Martins. 1990.

Code of Conduct. National Archives and Records Administration,
    Eisenhower, President Dwight D. Executive Order 10631. Code of
    Federal Regulations, Title 3-The President, 1954-1958 compilation.

Covert Operations. Advocacy and Intelligence Index for Prisoners of
    War-Missing in Action/Senate Select Committee-XIX.
    <http://www.aiipowmia.com/ssc/ssc19.html>

Covert Operations. Advocacy and Intelligence Index for Prisoners of
    War-Missing in Action/Senate Select Committee-IX.
    <http://www.aiipowmia.com/ssc/ss9.html>

Coyne, Kevin. "F-111 Crew Module Escape and Survival". 1999-2001.
    <http://f-111.net/ejection.htm> March 2001.

Dean, Ambassador John. "Cable on the Cambodian Settlement,
    February 6, 1975." Gerald R. Ford Library.
    <http://www.ford.utexas.edu/library/exhibits/vietnam/750206a.htm>

Dorr, Robert F. Boeing KC-135, Stratotanker. Modern Combat Aircraft
    27. Motorbooks International. 1987.

Forward Air Controllers, the FACNET. Information concerning the
    shoot-down of Don Hawley and operations of the Red Markers was
    provided by members of the FACNET who were pilots assigned as
    Red Markers and involved in that particular incident. E-mail to the
    author. Jim Roper October 7, 2001. Charlie Pocock October 7,
    2001. Jim Meade October 8, 2001. Joe Granducci October 10,
    2001. Mike Morea October 11, 2001

Jeppesen, C. Home page. Invert Operations. September 11, 2000.
<http://home.att.net/~c.jeppeson/invert_ops.html>

Johnson, Thomas R. and David A. Hatch. "Full-Length Synopsis of the Cuban Missile Crisis." May, 1998. National Security Agency.
<http://www.nsa.gov/docs/cuba/synopsis.htm>

Kawell, Jo Ann. "Coke & the CIA: The Real Thing? Rev. of <u>Crack in America: Demon Drugs and Social Justice</u>. Ed. by Craig Reinarman and Harry G. Levine. University of California. <u>The Nation</u>. September 28, 1998, pg.25.

Lander, Mark. "McCain, in Vietnam, Finds the Past Isn't Really Past." The <u>New York Times</u> April 27, 2000.

McCoy, Alfred. "Drugs and Covert Ops: Brief History." <u>Convergence Magazine, Christic Institute</u>. October 12,1991. Topic 102.
<http://www.netti.fi/~makako/mind/drug_cow.txt>

McDaniel, Captain Eugene. <u>American Defense Institute</u>.
<http://www.ojc.org/adi/>

Middleton, Drew, ed. <u>Air War-Vietnam</u>. New York: Arno Press, 1978.

Military Analysis Network. "F-111." December 24, 1998.
<http://www.fas.org/man/dod-101/sys/ac/f-111.htm>

Newman, W. "Moscow Bound?-POW/MIA LCDR James Kelly Patterson, USN." February, 1998.
<http://members.home.net/winjr/patterson1.htm>

Patrick, Joe. "Testing the Rules of Engagement." Vietnam Magazine, December, 1997.
<http://www.historynet.com/Vietnam/articles/1997/12972_text.htm>

Peacock, Lindsay. <u>Boeing B-47 Stratojet</u>. Motorbooks International: 1987.

Scocroft, Brent. Memorandum for the President, May 10, 1976. "Life inside Cambodia." The Gerald R. Ford Library.
<http://www.ford.utexas.edu/library/exhibits/vietnam/760510a.htm>

Sherwood, John Darrell. Fast Movers. St. Martins: 2001.

Jensen-Stevenson, Monika. Spite House. W.W. Norton: 1997.

Jensen-Stevenson, Monika and William Stevenson. Kiss the Boys Goodbye. McClelland and Stewart. 1991.

Smyser, W. R. Memorandum to Secretary Kissinger July 15, 1975. "The Situation in Asia." Gerald R. Ford Library.
<http://www.ford.utexas.edu/library/exhibits/750715a.htm>

Testimony and Depositions, Senate Select Committee. Advocacy and Intelligence Index for Prisoners of War-Missing in Action/Donahe, Dr. Jeffery, transcript. Ibid.
<http://www.aiipowmia.com/ssc/dnhu.html>

Jensen-Stevenson, Monika. Transcript, November 7, 1971. Ibid.
<http://wwwaiipowmia.com/ssc/mjst.html>

Lundy, Albro III. Transcript, November 7, 1991. Ibid.
<http://www.aiipowmia.com/ssc/lundy.html>

McCreary, John F. Memo for Vice Chairman, Senate Select Committee on Prisoners of War and Missing in Action. Subject: Legal Misconduct and Possible Malpractice in the Select Committee. Ibid.
<http://www.aiipowmia.com/ssc/mccreary.html>

Turner, Norman M. Lt.Col. USAF, ret. Transcript. Ibid.
<http://www.aiipowmia.com/ssc/turnerssc.html>

Senate Select Committee on POW/MIA Affairs/Executive Summary.
<http://www.vwip.org/powssc-i.html>

Smith, Senator Bob (New Hampshire) Vice-Chairman, Senate Select Committee on POW/MIA Affairs./U. S. POW/MIAs Who May Have

Survived in Captivity. December 1, 1992.
<http://www.pownetwork.org/alive.htm>

USAF. Aviation Cadet Honor Code. Officer Training Manual for Aviation Cadets. circa 1957. Text provided courtesy of the Aviation Cadet Museum, Inc. Eureka Springs, Ar. 72632

USAF./Pilot's Abbreviated Flight Crew Checklist, OV-10A, www.ov-10bronco.net-normal.ctm>

USAF Museum. Cessna O-1G Bird Dog.
<http://www.wptab.at.mil/museum/air_power/ap46.htm>

Whaler Five Seven. Robert D. Morrissey, Lt. Col. USAF. Refno 1945-0-02. The Following Documents were obtained from the Library of Congress Photo Duplication Service Washington, D.C. 20540-4570 on October 10, 2001.

North Vietnam, pre-1975: Demarche on possible transfer of American POWs from Vietnam to USSR. Originator, American Embassy Moscow. Document # 051824ZNOV91. Reel 227, pgs. 313-316.

North Vietnam, pre-1975: Analysis of information and documentation from the Central Army Museum in Hanoi Concerning REFNO 1945 (Robert Morrissey-Robert Brown). Originator: JTFFA, Document # 021202ZMAR93, reel 227, pgs. 420-421.

Conversation with Major Harten, author of a paper titled "An Analysisof F-111 Combat Loses". Reel 227, pgs. 418-419.

North Vietnam, pre-1975: Correspondence between next of kin and the National League of Families. Reel 227, pgs. 284-286.

Correspondence between next of kin and the USAF. Type of document: letter. Subject: Killed. Reel 227, Pgs. 265-271.

Letter to wife regarding her husband's (Robert Morrissey) case. Originator: USAF. Reel 227, pgs. 275-277.

North Vietnam, pre-1975: Incident summary; Biographical data. Subjects: Aircraft downed; killed; Quang Ninh District; Le Thuy District; Luat Son; Quang Binh Province. Originator: Department of Defense, reel 227, pgs. 1-23.

North Vietnam, pre-1975: Missing persons supplementary report. Robert D. Morrissey. Subjects; Aircraft downed; missing; Luat Son. Originator: USAF. Reel 227, Pgs. 74-77.

North Vietnam, pre-1975: Evaluation of translation of Vietnamese Document. Subjects: Aircraft downed, Quang Binh Province. Originator: JTFFA. Reel 227, Pgs. 359-365.

North Vietnam, pre-1975: " The Bamboo Cage" (extract). Subjects, Aircraft downed, captured. Type of document, open source. Reel 227, pg. 287.

North Vietnam, pre 1975: Hanoi claims U.S. F-111, A-7 downed, over DRV, from Hanoi Domestic Service. Subjects: Aircraft downed, Nghe An Province. Reel 227, Pgs. 78-80.

GLOSSARY

◆◆◆◆◆◆◆◆◆◆◆◆◆◆◆◆◆

AC: Aircraft commander, used as an interphone call or as a nickname.

Article 15: The article of the Universal Code of Military Justice that administered punishment for offenses that did not warrant a court-marshal, analogous to the Captain's Mast in the Navy.

ATO: Sometimes called JATO or RATO, assisted take-off, either rocket or jet. In the B-47 this consisted of thirty rocket-bottles attached to the fuselage, which were dropped after take-off.

Authentication: A rapid means of verifying a radio message. If a challenge was issued, the receiving station would ask the sender to authenticate two letters. The sender would enter daily code tables and reply with a corresponding set of letters. Messages were often sent, especially in a general broadcast, with the authentication tacked onto the end of the message.

Base Operations or Base Ops: The location on the flight line of military flying fields where flight operations are conducted. It is here that flight plans are filed and transient aircraft check in and out. It is usually located in the area of the control tower and the weather office, and some kind of a snack bar is normally in the same building.

B-4 bag: A type of travel bag issued to flight crews. It is made of waterproof fabric, olive drab in color, and foldable. When opened out, it serves as a hanging bag for clothes and has side pockets for small articles. The owner's name and service number are stenciled on the outside.

CG: Short for center of gravity. This is a critical value on aircraft, especially when the aircraft carries heavy cargo or fuel loads; it must be constantly controlled as fuel or ordinance is consumed. To exceed the design limits, especially the aft limit, will cause loss of control and a crash.

Combat Ready: The term used to designate when a flight crew or other military persons have reached the level of training necessary to commit them to combat with some reasonable hope of their success.

Command Post: This differs from Base Operations, which deals with the air traffic component of military aircraft and may be by-passed during combat operations. The command post deals with military operations. Whenever possible military aircraft remain in radio contact with the command post. Large aircraft always are in contact even if only by shortwave (HF) radio (much more sophisticated means are available since satellites have come on line). Strike or other military orders would be issued by the command post.

DEFCON: acronym for defensive condition, a numerical designation of the military state of readiness. In SAC this ranged from four to zero during the Cold War. Four being SAC's normal state of readiness and zero indicating that the aircraft and missiles had been launched with a go code.

Flight orders: Written orders authorizing the flight. Flight orders always contained a full crew list. In the event of a substitution, the flight orders were amended prior to take-off, by radio, if necessary. Passengers were listed on separate manifest.

Hammerhead: A large paved area at the ends of a runway where airplanes may wait until their scheduled departure time. It is large enough to allow other aircraft to pass a waiting flight of large airplanes.

Head shed: Slang for headquarters.

Let Down Plates: Small area maps of the specific routes that an airplane must fly when approaching an airfield while operating under instrument flight rules.

Runway numbers: The number used to identify a runway. It corresponds to the magnetic heading of the runway and is painted in large white numbers at the approach end of the runway. A runway that is oriented northwest to southeast would be runway three zero if you were landing to the northwest and runway one two if landing to the southeast. The runway at a particular airport can actually change its number over time as the magnetic variation of the earth changes. Runway 30-12 at Castle in California is now 31-13

S-1 and S-2 speed: S-1 is the speed that a large airplane must reach in a given amount of time. This time is usually measured from the seventy-knot point in the take-off roll. Prior to this speed, the airplane has sufficient runway left to stop should an engine fail. After this speed there is enough runway left for the airplane to take off after the failure of one engine (assuming that the airplane has more than one engine to begin with). S-2 is the speed at which the pilot rotates the airplane to the take-off attitude. These terms correspond to V-1 and V-2 in airline operations.

Printed in the United States
1377800003B/193-213